THE MYTH OF THE STATE

The MYTH *of the* STATE

BY

ERNST CASSIRER

NEW HAVEN AND LONDON
YALE UNIVERSITY PRESS

Printed in the United States of America
by The Colonial Press Inc.
Clinton, Massachusetts.
ISBN: 0–300–00352–8 (cloth), 0–300–00036–7 (paper)

Published in Great Britain, Europe, and Africa by
Yale University Press, Ltd., London.
Distributed in Latin America by
Kaiman & Polon, Inc., New York City;
in Australasia and Southeast Asia by
John Wiley & Sons Australasia Pty. Ltd., Sydney;
in India by UBS Publishers' Distributors Pvt., Ltd., Delhi;
in Japan by John Weatherhill, Inc., Tokyo.

CONTENTS

FOREWORD

THIS was the last book written by Professor Ernst Cassirer. It had just been finished and copied from his manuscript a few days before his sudden and untimely death on April 13, 1945.

There is no need to introduce the author or his philosophy. The name and work of Professor Cassirer are already well known. The place he made for himself in American philosophy during the four years of his life in this country is to be witnessed in the present widespread demand for translations of his writings, which fortunately are appearing in fairly close succession.[1] There is promised also a memorial volume, to which many scholars have contributed and which is to be published in the Library of Living Philosophers (edited by Paul A. Schilpp, Northwestern University). An authorized biography, too, will come out in that same work. There will thus be rich opportunity elsewhere to learn more about the man himself and the significance of his extensive achievements in the world of learning.

But, though no introduction is necessary, a foreword is appropriate to this last book. All who know Locke's *Essay on the Human Understanding* will recall the livelier sense of personal interest they felt when they came to the passage where the author tells how his book came to be written, speaking particularly of those discussions with friends who had besought him to present to the world the thoughts that they had shared in conversation. There is a revealing detail of the same sort to be told about the present work.

Professor Cassirer came to this country from Göteborg, Sweden, in the spring of 1941, a scholar and philosopher of distinction, at the height of his career. He had published a masterly study of the problem of knowledge, ranging over nearly the whole of Western thought.[2] The qualification "nearly" is added because a fourth volume, treating of the subject "from the death of Hegel to the present"—the "present" being the year 1932—was still in manu-

---

1. The following translations have recently been published: *Rousseau, Kant, Goethe,* trans. by James Gutmann, Paul O. Kristeller, and John H. Randall, Jr. (Princeton University Press, 1945); *Myth and Language,* trans. by Susanne K. Langer (Harper & Brothers, 1946).

2. *Das Erkenntnisproblem* (Berlin, B. Cassirer, 1906, 1907, 1920). 3 vols.

script and actually left behind at his departure for America.[3] When we first welcomed him, as Visiting Professor at Yale University, we had no knowledge of that unpublished matter nor, indeed, of many other good things in store for us. What had been published seemed monumental achievement enough. We knew him as a great interpreter of the philosophy of Kant. His studies of the Renaissance [4] and of the eighteenth century [5] were indubitable evidence of historical genius. And since so much of what we knew had treated of the philosophy, science, and culture of periods in the past, we tended to admire him above all as a supremely fine historical scholar. There was another reason for this. We were on the lookout for that kind of scholarship, as something very much needed in philosophy today, and so we paid more attention to it than to those other high qualifications of mind and learning that were soon to be clearly revealed in the teaching and conversation of Professor Cassirer when he was actually working amongst us as a colleague.

Whenever Professor Cassirer treated of any subject he not only passed in review with fine understanding what the preceding philosophers had thought but he also brought together into an original, synoptic view whatever related to the subject from every aspect of human experience—art, literature, religion, science, history. In all that he undertook there was a constant demonstration of the relatedness of the different forms of human knowledge and culture. He possessed, therefore, the genius of philosophical synthesis as well as historical imagination and scholarship. These were the things his colleagues and many appreciative students came to cherish in those rare courses and seminars which he offered successively at Yale and Columbia University.

There had, of course, been some published evidence of the original and systematic thought which we expect of the true philosopher. Two scholars had taken the initiative years ago in producing an English translation of Professor Cassirer's *Substance and Function and Einstein's Theory of Relativity*.[6] That very same

3. This fourth volume on *The Problem of Knowledge* is being translated into English and will be published by the Yale University Press.

4. For instance, *Individuum und Kosmos in der Philosophie der Renaissance* (Teubner, Leipzig, Berlin, 1927).

5. *Die Philosophie der Aufklärung* (Tübingen, J. C. B. Mohr, 1932) and *Goethe und die Geschichtliche Welt* (Berlin, B. Cassirer, 1932).

6. William Curtis Swabey and Marie Collins Swabey (Chicago, Open Court Publishing Co., 1923).

year there had appeared in Germany the first of three volumes
on the subject of "symbolic forms." [7] This was his own adventure
of ideas. The philosophy of symbolic forms was, in a sense, the fulfilment of Professor Cassirer's ambition as a constructive thinker.
It was an elaborate study of the ways in which the world of human
experience is articulated through the various modes of symbolizing
activity that are characteristic of man. This view amplified the
Kantian insight into the role of certain forms of sensuous intuition
and logical categories in constituting our world of nature; other
forms, it was now argued, have a similar function in constituting
the world that man actually experiences and knows. Language,
myth, art, religion, history, science, all these forms of cultural expression alike enter into the knowledge man has both of himself
and of his total environment. Here was Professor Cassirer's own
philosophy of man and existence.

But that philosophy of symbolic forms was little known when
Professor Cassirer came over to do his work in American universi-
ties. The three volumes in the German were scarcely accessible to
the student of philosophy in this country. Besides, the demonstration of his theory involved a detailed examination of a vast
body of evidence concerning the diverse forms of culture, and not
many scholars had the experience of them or were so compre-
hensively informed as to be able to appreciate the argument. A
brief and simple version of that "philosophical anthropology," as
he called it, was thus very much needed in order to satisfy the
interest of an ever-widening circle of friends and students who
desired to know his philosophy. He liked his students, too, and his
many new associates, and he wanted, for his part, to be better
known to them all. So he very modestly, and almost without a word
about it, set to work to compose a short essay in English which
became his *Essay on Man*.[8]

But in writing that *Essay* the philosopher was also looking beyond the immediate circle of his friends and students. He discerned
a universal need of the time. In those wartime days the question
"What is man?" had a poignant force that no one could avoid. It
was plain to be seen that much more had to be attempted than
what Locke had undertaken or Kant or many another fine spirit

7. *Die Philosophie der Symbolischen Formen*, Berlin, B. Cassirer, 1923–29.
See also *Naturalistische und Humanistische Begründung der Kulturphilosophie*
(Göteborg, Flanders Boktryckerei Aktiebolag, 1939).
8. Yale University Press, 1944.

of that eighteenth century which Professor Cassirer loved so well. Other aspects had to be reckoned with besides the phenomena of the human understanding or reason. In that new *Essay on Man* Professor Cassirer recalled the still unexhausted imperative of wisdom uttered by Socrates: Know thyself. The argument of the book showed the course of that quest for self-knowledge through history and brought us to a better comprehension of the condition of man today. Thus the *Essay* served a large, general purpose as well as meeting the need of his friends. While it communicated to them the essentials of his philosophy of symbolic forms it also contributed to the wisdom of this day about man himself.

Still that was not the whole of Professor Cassirer's concern with the dark, troubled times in which we were living. Most people talked easily about the fact that we were going through a crisis of world history. It was natural to expect a confused welter of ideas in the public mind about the philosophy of history or about the nature of our own civilization. All sorts of quasi-philosophies were likely to spring up in such conditions, inspired by some ideology or the political interests of those who enunciated them. On this occasion, the friends of Professor Cassirer looked to him as the man who could speak with the wisest judgment, since he could interpret the situation of our time in the two great perspectives of history and philosophy. Some of those who were close to him ventured to ask: "Won't you tell the meaning of what is happening *today*, instead of writing about past history, science, and culture? You have so much knowledge and wisdom—we who are working with you know that so well—but you should give others, too, the benefit of it." He then set to work, in the winter of 1943–44, on a sketch of a book on the theme "the myth of the state." The magazine *Fortune* issued in June, 1944, an abbreviated version of what he had so far written. The present book, which was composed subsequently, during the years 1944–45, is the complete realization of this work of occasion begun originally in response to an appeal of his closest friends.

Professor Cassirer had asked me to serve as critic and editor of both the *Essay on Man* and this present book. My responsibility is now all the greater because this work appears posthumously. What I wish to make clear, in giving an accounting here of my friendly office, is that the book is presented practically as it was written by him. This is possible because it was one of his many remarkable powers that he could, unaided, write English clearly, fluently, and with a nice sense of the meanings of the language.

In the case of the previous work, the *Essay on Man*, it had been the practice of the author to submit a first draft of the book for criticism. He always wanted criticism of his philosophical argument as well as of his use of language. He received any suggested corrections or improvements gratefully. With delicate courtesy he would weigh and appreciate every observation and query. He took it as axiomatic that if a friendly critic could not see the matter clearly or logically as he had presented it, the fault must be his own, an assumption which links him with David Hume, who had the same respect for the mind of his reader. As it happened, indeed, by far the greater number of the suggestions made had to do merely with the need of abbreviation and succinctness. It was necessary, for instance, to limit the generous amplitude of his quotations, for he always wanted to let an author cited speak fully for himself, which not only increased the size of the volume unduly but also diminished proportionately what he himself had to say in it. Aside from such considerations there were merely minor points of criticism and alteration which he always accepted with good grace.

The present work has been prepared for publication in the same fashion as the *Essay on Man*. There is only this difference—that the author himself never saw Part III exactly as it is here presented. The changes that seemed necessary in the text of Parts I and II were practically all scrutinized by him, and most of them we had a chance actually to discuss in person. I hope that in editing the third and last part, without having the comforting assurance of his own final review of it, I have not altered anything that would have mattered to him. I am resting my faith in this respect upon the perfect understanding we had during our all-too-few years of association.

Before finishing the preparation of the text I was appointed, in July, 1945, to serve with the United States Army in England and to teach philosophy at an Army University. The editing of Chapter XVII on Hegel was not in quite satisfactory form at the time of my departure. I wish to acknowledge the kind services of my colleague, Professor Brand Blanshard of Yale University, who looked over the copy and made final corrections before it went to press.

Grateful acknowledgment must also be made for the faithful

and accurate work done by Dr. Friedrich W. Lenz, formerly of New Haven, who verified all the quotations and references and raised many questions about usage which had to be attended to and decided by an editor. Thanks to these services we can be sure that the work has a scholarly character in detail befitting a book issued under the name of Professor Ernst Cassirer.

It would be very much amiss on my part if I did not take this opportunity, on behalf of the friends and the family of Professor Cassirer, to tell of the generous personal interest shown by Mr. Eugene A. Davidson, Editor of the Yale University Press, whose relationship to this work is not merely a business one but much more that of fine, sympathetic appreciation. The author would have wanted this said, because that sort of interest was one of the things he was ever grateful for in his American experience.

CHARLES W. HENDEL

New Haven, Connecticut
April 13, 1946.

PART I

WHAT IS MYTH?

The Myth of the State

I

THE STRUCTURE OF MYTHICAL THOUGHT

IN THE last thirty years, in the period between the first and the second World Wars, we have not only passed through a severe crisis of our political and social life but have also been confronted with quite new theoretical problems. We experienced a radical change in the forms of political thought. New questions were raised and new answers were given. Problems that had been unknown to the political thinkers of the eighteenth and nineteenth centuries came suddenly to the fore. Perhaps the most important and the most alarming feature in this development of modern political thought is the appearance of a new power: the power of mythical thought. The preponderance of mythical thought over rational thought in some of our modern political systems is obvious. After a short and violent struggle mythical thought seemed to win a clear and definitive victory. How was this victory possible? How can we account for the new phenomenon that so suddenly appeared on our political horizon and in a sense seemed to reverse all our former ideas of the character of our intellectual and our social life?

If we look at the present state of our cultural life we feel at once that there is a deep chasm between two different fields. When it comes to political action man seems to follow rules quite different from those recognized in all his mere theoretical activities. No one would think of solving a problem of natural science or a technical problem by the methods that are recommended and put into action in the solution of political questions. In the first case we never aim to use anything but rational methods. Rational thought holds its ground here and seems constantly to enlarge its field. Scientific knowledge and technical mastery of nature daily win new and unprecedented victories. But in man's practical and social life the defeat of rational thought seems to be complete and irrevocable. In this domain modern man is supposed to forget everything he has learned in the development of his intellectual life. He is admonished to go back to the first rudimentary stages of human culture. Here rational and scientific thought openly confess their breakdown; they surrender to their most dangerous enemy.

In order to find the explanation of this phenomenon that at first sight seems to derange all our thoughts and defy all our logical standards we must begin with the beginning. Nobody can hope to understand the origin, the character, and influence of our modern political myths without first answering a preliminary question. We must know what myth *is* before we can explain how it *works*. Its special effects can only be accounted for if we have attained a clear insight into its general nature.

What does myth mean? And what is its function in man's cultural life? As soon as we raise this question we are plunged into a great battle between conflicting views. In this case the most disconcerting feature is not the lack but the abundance of our empirical material. The problem has been approached from every angle. Both the historical development of mythical thought and its psychological foundations have been carefully studied. Philosophers, ethnologists, anthropologists, psychologists, sociologists have their share in these studies. We seem now to be in possession of all the facts; we have a comparative mythology that extends over all the parts of the world and that leads us from the most elementary forms to highly developed and sophisticated conceptions. As regards our *data* the chain seems to be closed; no essential link is missing. But the *theory* of myth is still highly controversial. Every school gives us a different answer; and some of these answers are in flagrant contradiction of each other. A philosophical theory of myth must begin at this point.

Many anthropologists have asserted that myth is, after all, a very simple phenomenon—for which we hardly need a complicated psychological or philosophical explanation. It is simplicity itself; for it is nothing but the *sancta simplicitas* of the human race. It is not the outcome of reflection or thought, nor is it enough to describe it as a product of human imagination. Imagination alone cannot account for all its incongruities and its fantastic and bizarre elements. It is rather the *Urdummheit* of man that is responsible for these absurdities and contradictions. Without this "primeval stupidity" there would be no myth.

At first sight such an answer may seem to be very plausible; yet as soon as we begin to study the development of mythical thought in human history we are confronted with an important difficulty. Historically we find no great culture that is not dominated by and pervaded with mythical elements. Shall we say that all these cultures—Babylonian, Egyptian, Chinese, Indian, Greek—are nothing but so many masks and disguises for man's "primeval stupidity," that, at bottom, they lack any positive value and significance?

The historians of human civilization could never accept this view. They had to look for a better and more adequate explanation. But their answers were, in most cases, as divergent as their scientific interests. We can perhaps best illustrate their attitude by a simile. There is a scene in Goethe's *Faust* in which we see Faust in the witch's kitchen waiting for her drink by virtue of which he shall regain his youth. Standing before an enchanted glass he suddenly has a wonderful vision. In the glass appears the image of a woman of supernatural beauty. He is enraptured and spellbound; but Mephisto, standing at his side, scoffs at his enthusiasm. He knows better; he knows that what Faust has seen was not the form of a real woman; it was only a creature of his own mind.

We may remember this scene when studying the various theories that, in the nineteenth century, vied with each other in their explanations of the mystery of myth. The Romantic philosophers and poets were the first who had drunk from the magic cup of myth. They felt refreshed and rejuvenated. From now on they saw all things in a new and transformed shape. They could not return to the common world—to the world of the *profanum vulgus*. To the true romanticist there could be no sharp difference between myth and reality; just as little as there was any separation between poetry and truth. Poetry and truth, myth and reality interpenetrate each other and coincide with each other. "Poetry," said Novalis, "is what is absolutely and genuinely real. That is the kernel of my philosophy. The more poetic the more true." [1]

The consequences of this romantic philosophy were drawn by Schelling in his *System of Transcendental Idealism* and, later on, in his *Lectures on the Philosophy of Mythology and Revelation*. There can be no sharper contrast than that between the views

1. Novalis, Fr. 31, in "Schriften," ed. Jacob Minor (Jena, E. Diederichs, 1907), III, 11.

expressed in these lectures and the judgment of the philosophers of the Enlightenment. What we find here is a complete change of all former values. Myth that had occupied the lowest rank was suddenly elevated to the highest dignity. Schelling's system was a "system of identity." In such a system no clear-cut distinction could be made between the "subjective" and the "objective" world. The universe is a spiritual universe—and this spiritual universe forms a continuous unbroken organic whole. It is a false tendency of thought, a mere abstraction, that has led to the separation of the "ideal" from the "real." They are not opposed the one to the other; they coincide with each other. Starting from this presupposition Schelling developed in his lectures an entirely new conception of the role of myth. It was a synthesis of philosophy, history, myth, poetry, such as had never appeared before.

Later generations took a much more sober view of the character of myth. They were no longer interested in its metaphysics. They approached the problem from the empirical side and tried to solve it by empirical methods. But the old spell was never completely broken. Every scholar still found in myth those objects with which he was most familiar. At bottom the different schools saw in the magic mirror of myth only their own faces. The linguist found in it a world of words and names—the philosopher found a "primitive philosophy"—the psychiatrist a highly complicated and interesting neurotic phenomenon.

From the scientist's point of view there were two different ways to formulate the question. The mythical world could be explained according to the same principles as the theoretical world—the world of the scientist. Or the stress could be laid on the opposite side. Instead of seeking for any similarity between the two worlds, their incommensurability, their radical and irreconcilable difference could be insisted upon. To decide this struggle between the different schools by mere logical criteria was hardly possible. In an important chapter of his *Critique of Pure Reason* Kant deals with a fundamental opposition in the method of scientific interpretation. According to him there are two groups of scholars and scientists. The one is following the principle of "homogeneity"; the other the principle of "specification." The first endeavors to reduce the most disparate phenomena to a common denominator whereas the other refuses to accept this pretended unity or similarity. Instead of emphasizing the common features it is always looking for the differences. According to the principles of the Kantian philosophy itself both attitudes are not really in conflict with each other. For they do not express any fundamental *onto-logical* difference; a difference in the nature and essence of "things in themselves." They rather represent a twofold interest of human reason. Human knowledge can only attain its end by following both ways and by satisfying both interests. It must act according to two diverse "regulative principles"—the principles of similarity and dissimilarity, of homogeneity and heterogeneity. For the functioning of human reason both maxims are equally indispensable. The logical principle of genera which postulates identity is balanced by another principle, namely, that of species, which requires manifoldness and diversity in things and which prescribes to the understanding that it should pay no less attention to the one than to the other. "This distinction," says Kant,

shows itself in the different manner of thought among students of nature, some of them . . . being almost averse to heterogeneousness, and always intent on the unity of genera; while others . . . are constantly striving to divide nature into so much variety that one might lose almost all hope of being able to distribute its phenomena according to general principles.[2]

What Kant says here about the study of natural phenomena holds just as much for the study of cultural phenomena. If we trace the various interpretations of mythical thought given by the scholars of the nineteenth and twentieth centuries we find striking examples of both attitudes. There were always scholars of high authority who were apt to deny that there is any sharp difference between mythical and scientific thought. Of course the primitive mind is highly inferior to the scientific mind as regards the mere mass of known facts, the bulk of empirical evidence. But as to the interpretation of these facts it is in complete agreement with our own ways of thinking and reasoning. This view is, for instance, maintained in a work that more than any other is representative of the new science of empirical anthropology which began to develop in the second half of the nineteenth century.

2. Kant, *Critique of Pure Reason*. English trans. by F. Max Müller (London, Macmillan & Co., 1881), II, 561 f.

Sir James Frazer's *The Golden Bough* has become a mine of wealth for all sorts of anthropological research. In its fifteen volumes are contained amazing material taken from all parts of the world and from the most heterogeneous sources. But Frazer did not content himself with gathering the phenomena of mythical thought and placing them under general headings. He tried to understand them—and he was convinced that this task was impossible as long as myth was still regarded as an isolated province of human thought. We must, once for all, make an end to this isolation. Man's thought admits of no radical heterogeneity. From the beginning to the end, from the first rudimentary steps to the highest attainments, it remains always the same; it is homogeneous and uniform. Frazer applied this leading principle to the analysis of magic in the first two volumes of his book. According to his theory a man who performs a magic rite does not differ, in principle, from a scientist who in his laboratory makes a physical or chemical experiment. The sorcerer, the medical man of primitive tribes, and the modern scientist think and act upon the same principles. "Wherever sympathetic magic occurs in its pure and unadulterated form," says Frazer,

it assumes that in nature one event follows another necessarily and invariably without the intervention of any spiritual or personal agency. Thus its fundamental concept is identical with that of modern science; underlying the whole system is a faith, implicit but real and firm, in the order and uniformity of nature. The magician does not doubt that the same causes will always produce the same effects, that the performance of the proper ceremony accompanied by the appropriate spell, will inevitably be attended by the desired results. . . . Thus the analogy between the magical and the scientific conceptions of the world is close. In both of them the succession of events is perfectly regular and certain, being determined by immutable laws, the operation of which can be foreseen and calculated precisely, the elements of caprice, of chance, and of accident are banished from the course of nature. . . . The fatal flaw of magic lies not in its general assumption of a sequence of events determined by law, but in its total misconception of the nature of the particular laws which govern that sequence. . . . Magical rites are all mistaken applications of one or other of two great fundamental laws of thought, namely, the association of ideas by similarity and the association of ideas by contiguity in space and time. . . . The principles of association are excellent in themselves, and indeed absolutely essential to the working of the human mind. Legitimately applied they yield science; illegitimately applied they yield magic, the bastard-sister of science.[3]

Frazer was not alone in holding this view. He continued a tradition that goes back to the beginnings of a scientific anthropology in the nineteenth century. In 1871 Sir E. B. Tylor had published his book *Primitive Culture*. But although speaking of primitive culture he refused to accept the idea of a so-called "primitive mind." According to Tylor there is no essential difference between the savage's mind and the mind of the civilized man. The thoughts of the savage may, at first sight, appear to be bizarre; but they are by no means confused or contradictory. The logic of the savage is, in a sense, impeccable. What makes the great difference between the savage's interpretation of the world and our own conceptions are not the *forms* of thought, the rules of arguing and reasoning, but the *material*, the data to which these rules are applied. Once we have understood the character of these data we are in a position to put ourselves in the savage's place—to think his thoughts and to enter into his feelings.

According to Tylor the first requisite for a systematic study of the lower races is to lay down a rudimentary definition of religion. We cannot include in this definition the belief in a supreme deity, in a judgment after death, the adoration of idols or the practice of sacrifices. A closer study of the ethnological data convinces us that all these features are not necessary prerequisites. They give us only a special perspective, not a universal aspect of religious life.

Such narrow definition has the fault of identifying religion rather with particular developments than with the deeper motive which underlies them. It seems best to fall back at once on this essential source, and simply to claim, as a minimum definition of religion, the belief in Spiritual Beings.

The purpose of Tylor's book was to investigate, under the name of Animism, the deep-lying doctrine of Spiritual Beings, which embodies the very essence of Spiritualistic as opposed to Materialistic philosophy.[4]

3. Sir J. G. Frazer, *The Golden Bough: A Study in Magic and Religion*, Pt. I: *The Magic Art and the Evolution of Kings* (3d ed. New York, Macmillan Co., 1935), I, 220.

4. Sir Edward Burnett Tylor, *Primitive Culture* (London, 1871; 1st Am. ed. New York, Henry Holt & Co., 1874), chap. XI, pp. 417–502.

We need not enter here into the details of Tylor's well-known theory of animism; what interests us is not so much the results of Tylor's work as its method. Tylor pushed to extremes the methodological principle that in the *Critique of Pure Reason* had been termed the "principle of homogeneity." In his book the difference between the primitive mind and the mind of civilized man is almost obliterated. The primitive acts and thinks like a real philosopher. He combines the data of his sense-experience and tries to bring them into a coherent and systematic order. If we accept Tylor's description we must say that between the crudest forms of animism and the most advanced and sophisticated philosophical or theological systems there is only a difference of degree. They have a common starting point and move around the same center. The standing miracle and the standing terror for man—both for the savage and for the philosopher—was at all times the phenomenon of death. Animism and metaphysics are only different attempts to come to terms with the fact of death; to interpret it in a rational and understandable way. The methods of the interpretation are widely divergent; but the end aimed at is always the same.

In the first place, what is it that makes the difference between a living body and a dead one; what causes waking, sleep, trance, disease, death? In the second place, what are those human shapes which appear in dreams and visions? Looking at these two groups of phenomena, the ancient savage philosophers probably made their first step by the obvious inference that every man has two things belonging to him, namely, a life and a phantom. These two are evidently in close connexion with the body, the life as enabling it to feel and think and act, the phantom as being its image or second self; both, also, are perceived to be things separable from the body, the life as able to go away and leave it insensible or dead, the phantom as appearing to people at a distance from it. The second step would seem also easy for savages to make, seeing how extremely difficult civilized men have found it to unmake. It is merely to combine the life and the phantom. As both belong to the body, why should they not also belong to one another, and be manifestations of one and the same soul? Let them then be considered as united, and the result is that well-known conception which may be described as an apparitional-soul, a ghost-soul. . . . Far from these world-wide opinions being arbitrary or conventional products, it is seldom even justifiable to consider their uniformity among distant races as proving communication of any sort. They are doctrines answering in the most forcible way to the plain evidence of men's senses, as interpreted by a fairly consistent and rational primitive philosophy.[5]

We find the very reverse of this conception in Lévy-Bruhl's well-known description of "primitive mentality." According to Lévy-Bruhl the task that former theories had set themselves was impossible—a contradiction in terms. It is vain to seek for a common measure between primitive mentality and our own. They do not belong to the same genus; they are radically opposed the one to the other. The rules which to the civilized man seem to be unquestionable and inviolable are entirely unknown and constantly thwarted in primitive thought. The savage's mind is not capable of all those processes of arguing and reasoning that were ascribed to it in Frazer's or Tylor's theories. It is not a logical, but a "prelogical" or a mystic mind. Even the most elementary principles of our logic are openly defied by this mystic mind. The savage lives in a world of his own—in a world which is impermeable to experience and unaccessible to our forms of thought.[6]

How shall we decide this controversy? If Kant was right we must say that there is no strictly objective criterion to guide us in this decision. For the question is not an ontological or factual but a methodological one. Both the principle of "homogeneity" and the principle of "specification" only describe diverse tendencies of scientific thought and interests of human reason. "When purely regulative principles," said Kant,

are taken for constitutive, they may become contradictory, as objective principles. If, however, they are taken for *maxims* only, there is no real contradiction, but it is only the different interest of reason which causes different modes of thought. In reality, reason has one interest only, and the conflict of its maxims arises only from a difference and a mutual limitation of the methods, in which that interest is to be satisfied. In this manner one philosopher is influenced more by the interest of diversity (according to the principle of specification), another by the interest of *unity* (according to the principle of aggregation). Each believes that he has derived his judgment from his insight into the object, and yet founds it entirely on the greater or smaller attachment to one of the two principles, neither of which rests on objective grounds, but only on an interest of reason, and should therefore be called maxims

5. Tylor, *op. cit.*, I, 428 f.
6. See Lucien Lévy-Bruhl, *Les fonctions mentales dans les sociétés inférieures* (Paris, F. Alcan, 1910), Introduction. English trans., *How Natives Think* (London and New York, George Allen & Unwin, 1926).

rather than principles. . . . It is nothing but the twofold interest of reason, one party cherishing the one, another party the other. . . . But this difference of the two maxims of manifoldness or unity in nature may easily be adjusted, though as long as they are taken for objective knowledge they cause not only disputes, but actually create impediments which hinder the progress of truth, until a means is found of reconciling the contradictory interests, and thus giving satisfaction to reason.[7]

As a matter of fact it is impossible to come to a clear insight into the character of mythical thought without combining the two seemingly opposite tendencies of thought that are represented by Frazer and Tylor on the one hand and by Lévy-Bruhl on the other. In Tylor's work the savage was described as a "primitive philosopher" who develops a system of metaphysics or theology. Animism was declared to be the groundwork of the philosophy of religion from that of savages to that of civilized man. "Although it may at first sight seem to afford but a bare and meagre definition of a minimum of religion, it will be found practically sufficient; for where the root is, the branches will generally be produced. . . ." Animism is, indeed, a "world-wide philosophy of which belief is the theory and worship is the practice."[8] It is common to the "ancient savage philosophers" and to the most refined and sophisticated concepts of metaphysical thought.[8]

It is obvious that in this description mythical thought has lost one of its principal characteristics. It is thoroughly intellectualized. If we accept its premises we must accept all its conclusions; for these conclusions follow in a completely natural and, indeed, inevitable way from the original data. By virtue of this conception myth becomes, as it were, a chain of syllogisms which follow all the well known syllogistic rules. What is entirely lost out of sight in this theory is the "irrational" element in myth—the emotional background in which it originates and with which it stands or falls.

On the other hand it is easy to see that Lévy-Bruhl's theory fails in the opposite direction. If this theory were right, any analysis of mythical thought would become impossible. For what is such an analysis but an attempt to *understand* myth—that is to say, to reduce it to some other known psychological facts or logi-

7. Kant, *Kritik der reinen Vernunft,* "Werke," ed. E. Cassirer, III, 455. F. Max Müller trans. (see p. 7, n. 2), II, 571 f.
8. Tylor, *op. cit.,* pp. 426 f.

cal principles? If these facts or principles are missing; if there is no point of contact between our own mind and the prelogical or mystic mind, then we have to give up all hopes of finding an approach to the mythical world. This world would forever remain to us a sealed book. But was not Lévy-Bruhl's own theory an endeavor to read this book, to decipher the hieroglyphs of myth? We cannot expect, indeed, any one-to-one correspondence between our logical forms of thought and the forms of mythical thought. But if there were no connection at all, if they were moving on entirely different planes, every attempt to understand myth would be doomed to failure.

And there are still other reasons that convince us that the description of primitive mentality given in the works of Lévy-Bruhl [9] remains, in one essential point, inadequate and inconclusive. Lévy-Bruhl admits and emphasizes that there is a close relationship between myth and language. A special part of his work deals with linguistic problems, with the languages spoken by savage tribes. In these languages Lévy-Bruhl finds all those characteristics that he had ascribed to primitive mentality. They too are full of elements that are diametrically opposed to our own modes of thought. But this judgment is not in keeping with our linguistic experience. The best experts in this field, the men who have spent their lives in the investigation of the languages of savage tribes, have come to the opposite conclusion. In modern linguistics the very term and concept of a primitive language has become highly questionable. A. Meillet, who has written a book on the languages of the world, has told us that no known idiom can give us the slightest idea of what a primitive language may be. Language always shows us a definite and thorough-going logical structure, both in its sound system and in its morphological system. We have no evidence whatever for a "prelogical" language—the only one that, according to Lévy-Bruhl's theory, would correspond to the prelogical state of mind. Of course we must not understand the term "logic" in too narrow a sense. We cannot expect the Aristotelian categories of thought or the elements of our parts-of-speech system, the rules of our Greek and Latin syntax, in languages of aboriginal American tribes. These expectations are bound to fail; but this does not prove that these languages are in

9. See also *La mentalité primitive* (Paris, 1922), and *L'âme primitive* (Paris, 1928).

any sense "illogical" or even less logical than ours. If they are unable to express some differences that to us seem to be essential and necessary, on the other hand they often surprise us by the variety and subtlety of distinctions that we do not find in our own languages and that are by no means insignificant. Franz Boas, the great linguist and anthropologist, who died two years ago, in one of his last published essays, "Language and Culture," wittily remarked that we could read our newspapers with much greater satisfaction if our language, like the Indian idiom Kwakiutl, compelled us to say whether a report is based on self-experience, on inference, or on hearsay, or whether the reporter has dreamed it.[10]

What holds for "primitive" languages holds also for primitive thought. Its structure may seem to us to be strange and paradoxical; but it never lacks a definite logical structure. Even the uncivilized man cannot live in the world without a constant effort to understand that world. And for this purpose he has to develop and to use some general forms or categories of thought. To be sure we cannot accept Tylor's description of the "savage philosopher" who reaches his conclusions in a merely speculative way. The savage is no discursive thinker and no dialectician. Nevertheless we find in him, in an undeveloped and implicit state, the same capability of analysis and synthesis, of discernment and unification, that, according to Plato, constitute and characterize the dialectic art. When studying some very primitive forms of religious and mythical thought—for instance the religion of totemistic societies—we are surprised to find to what a high degree the primitive mind feels the desire and the need to discern and divide, to order and classify the elements of its environment. There is hardly anything that escapes its constant urge for classification. Not only is human society divided into diverse classes, tribes, clans which have different functions, different customs, different social duties. The same division appears everywhere in nature. The physical world is, in this respect, the exact duplicate and counterpart of the social world. Plants, animals, organic beings and objects of inorganic nature, substances and qualities are equally affected by this classification. The four points of the compass, the North, the East, the South, the West; the different col-

10. See Roman Jakobson, "Franz Boas' Approach to Language," *International Journal of American Linguistics*, Vol. X, No. 4 (October, 1944).

ors, the heavenly bodies—all of them belong to a special class. In some Australian tribes in which all men and women belong either to the Kangaroo clan or to the Snake clan, the clouds are said to belong to the first clan, whereas the sun belongs to the second. All this may seem to us to be entirely arbitrary and fantastic. But we must not forget that every division presupposes a *fundamentum divisionis.* This leading principle is not given us by the nature of things in themselves. It depends upon our theoretical and practical interests. Obviously these interests are not the same in these first primitive divisions of the world as in our scientific classifications. But that is not the point in question. What matters here is not the content, but the form of classification; and this form is entirely logical. What we find here is by no means a lack of order; it is rather a certain hypertrophy, a preponderance and exuberance of the "classifying instinct." [11] The results of these first attempts to analyze and systematize the world of sense-experience are far different from ours. But the processes themselves are very similar; they express the same desire of human nature to come to terms with reality, to live in an ordered universe, and to overcome the chaotic state in which things and thoughts have not yet assumed a definite shape and structure.

11. Concrete examples of these "primitive" methods of classification are given in my essay, *Die Begriffsform im mythischen Denken,* "Studien der Bibliothek Warburg" (Leipzig, 1922), I. See also Emile Durkheim et Marcel Mauss, "De quelques formes primitives de classification," *Année sociologique,* VI (Paris, 1901–2).

II

MYTH AND LANGUAGE

TYLOR'S *Primitive Culture* propounded an anthropological theory based upon general biological principles. He was one of the first to apply the principles of Darwin to the cultural world. The maxim *Natura non facit saltus* admits of no exception. It holds just as much for the world of human civilization as for the organic world. The civilized and the uncivilized man belong to the same species—to the species *homo sapiens.* The fundamental characteristics of this species are the same in every variant. If the theory of evolution is true we cannot admit any hiatus between the lower and higher stages of human civilization. We pass from the one to the others by very slow and almost imperceptible transitions, and we never find a break of continuity.

A different conception of the process of human civilization had been developed in an essay that was published in 1856—three years before the appearance of Darwin's book, *The Origin of Species.* In "Comparative Mythology" [1] F. Max Müller started from the principle that it is impossible to come to a true understanding of myth so long as we think of it as an isolated phenomenon. Yet, on the other hand, no natural phenomenon, no biological principle can guide us in our investigation. There is no real analogy between natural and cultural phenomena. Human culture must be studied according to specific methods and principles. And where could we find a better guide for this study than in human speech—the element in which man lives, moves and has his being? As a linguist and philologist Müller was convinced that the only scientific approach to a study of myth was a linguistic approach. But this end could not be attained until linguistics itself had found its own way and until grammar and etymology were founded upon a firm scientific basis. It was not until the first half of the nineteenth century that this great step was made.

1. First published in *Oxford Essays* (London, John W. Parker & Son, 1856), pp. 1–87. Reprinted in *Selected Essays on Language, Mythology and Religion* (London, Longmans, Green & Co., 1881), pp. 299–451.

Between language and myth there is not only a close relationship but a real solidarity. If we understand the nature of this solidarity we have found the key to the mythical world.

The discovery of the Sanskrit language and literature was a crucial event in the development of our historical consciousness, and in the evolution of all cultural sciences. In its importance and influence it may be compared to the great intellectual revolution brought about through the Copernican system in the field of natural science. The Copernican hypothesis reversed the conception of the cosmic order. The earth was no longer in the center of the universe; it became a "star among stars." The geocentric conception of the physical world was discarded. In the same sense the acquaintance with Sanskrit literature made an end to that conception of human culture which saw its real and only center in the world of classical antiquity. Henceforward the Greco-Roman world could only be regarded as a single province, a small sector of the universe of human culture. The philosophy of history had to be built upon a new and larger basis. Hegel called the discovery of the common origin of Greek and Sanskrit the discovery of a new world. The students of comparative grammar in the nineteenth century saw their work in the same light. They were convinced that they had found the magic word which alone could open the doors of understanding to the history of human civilization. Comparative philology, declared Max Müller, has brought the mythological and mythopoeic age of mankind that hitherto was veiled in darkness into the bright light of scientific research and within the pale of documentary history. It has placed in our hands a telescope of such power that, where formerly we could see but nebulous clouds, we now discover distinct forms and outlines; nay, it has given us what we may call contemporary evidence, exhibiting to us the state of thought, language, religion, and civilization at a period when Sanskrit was not yet Sanskrit, Greek not yet Greek, but when both, together with Latin, German and other Aryan dialects, existed as yet as one undivided language. The mist of mythology will gradually clear away, and enable us to discover, behind the floating clouds of the dawn of thought and language, that real nature which mythology has so long veiled and disguised.[2]

2. Müller, "Comparative Mythology," *op. cit.*, pp. 11, 33, 86. *Selected Essays,* I, 315, 358, 449 ff.

On the other hand the connection between language and myth, which promised a clear and definite solution of the old riddle, contained a great difficulty. To be sure language and myth have a common root, but they are by no means identical in their structure. Language shows us always a strictly logical character; myth seems to defy all logical rules; it is incoherent, capricious, irrational. How can we bring together these two incompatible elements?

To answer this question Max Müller and other writers belonging to the school of comparative mythology devised a very ingenious scheme. Myth, they declared, is, indeed, nothing but one aspect of language; but it is rather its negative than its positive aspect. Myth originates not in its virtues but in its vices. To be sure language is logical and rational, but on the other hand it is also a source of illusions and fallacies. The greatest achievement of language itself is a source of defect. Language consists of *general* names—but generality always means ambiguity. The polyonymy and synonymy of words are not an accidental feature of language; they follow from its very nature. As most objects have more than one attribute, and as, under different aspects, one or the other attribute might seem more appropriate to the act of denomination, it happened by necessity, that most objects, during the early period of human speech, had more than one name. The more ancient a language, the richer it is in synonyms. On the other hand these synonyms, if used constantly, must naturally give rise to a number of homonyms. If we may call the sun by fifty names expressive of different qualities, some of these names will be applicable to other objects also which happen to possess the same qualities. These different objects would then be called by the same name—they would become homonyms. That is the vulnerable point in language—and it is, at the same time, the historical origin of myth. How can we account, asks Max Müller, for that phase of the human mind which gave birth to the extraordinary stories of gods and heroes—of gorgons and chimaeras—of things that no human eye had ever seen, and that no human mind in a healthy state could ever have conceived? Unless this question can be answered our belief in a regular and consistent progress of the human intellect, through all ages and in all countries, must be given up as a false theory. Yet after the discovery of comparative linguistics we are in a position to avoid this skepticism and to remove this stumbling block. We see that the progress of language itself—one of the greatest facts in human civilization—inevitably led to another phenomenon, to the phenomenon of myth. Where two *names* existed for the same object, two *persons* could—quite naturally and, indeed, inevitably—spring up out of the two names, and as the same stories could be told of either, they would be represented as brothers and sisters, as parent and child.[3]

If we accept this theory the difficulty is removed. We can explain very well how the rational activity of human speech has led to the irrationalities and incomprehensibilities of myth. The mind of man always acts in a rational way. Even the primitive mind was a sound and normal mind; but on the other hand, it was an undeveloped and inexperienced mind. If this inexperienced mind was constantly exposed to a great temptation—to the fallacy and ambiguity of words—it is not to be wondered at that it succumbed. That is the true source of mythical thought. Language is not only a school of wisdom but also a school of folly. Myth reveals the latter aspect to us; it is nothing but the dark shadow cast by language on the world of human thought.

Mythology is thus represented as pathological both in its origin and in its essence. It is a disease that begins in the field of language and, by a dangerous infection, spreads over the whole body of human civilization. But though it be madness, there is method in it. In Greek mythology, as in many other mythologies, we find, for instance, the story of a great flood by which the human race was destroyed. Only one couple, Deucalion and his wife Pyrrha, were saved from the deluge sent by Zeus over Hellas. They landed on Mount Parnassus and here they were advised by an oracle to cast behind themselves the "bones of their mother." Deucalion found the true interpretation of the oracle; he picked up stones from the field and cast them behind his back. From these stones there arose the new race of men and women. What is more ridiculous, asks Max Müller, than this mythological account of the creation of the human race? And yet it becomes easily understandable with the key given us by the science of comparative etymology. The whole story turns out to be a mere pun—a confusion of two homonymous terms—of λαός and λᾶας.[4]

3. See Müller, *op. cit.*, pp. 44 f. *Selected Essays*, I, 378.
4. "Comparative Mythology," *op. cit.*, p. 8. *Selected Essays*, I, 310.

That, according to this view, is the entire secret of mythology.

If we analyze this theory we find that it is a strange mixture of rationalism and romanticism. The romantic element is obvious; and it seems to be preponderant. Max Müller speaks in a sense as a pupil of Novalis or Schleiermacher. He rejects the theory that the origin of religion is to be sought in animism or in the worship of the great natural powers. There is, indeed, a natural or physical religion—an adoration of the fire, the sun, the moon, the bright sky—but this physical religion is only a single aspect and a derivative phenomenon. It does not give us the whole and it does not lead us to the first and principal source. The real origin of religion is to be sought in a deeper stratum of thought and feeling. What first fascinated men were not the objects of his surroundings. Even the primitive mind was much more impressed by the great spectacle of nature taken as a whole. Nature was the unknown as distinguished from the known—the infinite as distinguished from the finite. It was this feeling that from the earliest times supplied the impulse to religious thought and language. The immediate *perception of the Infinite* has from the very beginning formed an ingredient and a necessary complement to all finite knowledge. The rudiments of later mythological, religious and philosophical expressions were already present in the early pressure of the Infinite upon our senses—and this pressure is the first source and the real origin of all our religious beliefs.[5] Why should we wonder at the ancients, asked Max Müller, with their language throbbing with life and reveling in color, if instead of the gray outlines of our modern thought, they threw out those living forms of nature, endowed with human powers, nay with powers more than human, inasmuch as the light of the sun was brighter than the light of a human eye, and the roaring of the storms louder than the shouts of a human voice?[6] That sounds very romantic; but we must not allow ourselves to be deceived by Max Müller's picturesque and romantic style. His theory, taken as a whole, is still strictly rationalistic and intellectualistic.

At bottom his conception of myth is not so very far from the

5. See F. Max Müller, *Natural Religion*, The Gifford Lectures, 1888 (London and New York, Longmans, Green & Co., 1889), Lect. v, "My Own Definition of Religion," pp. 103–140; *Physical Religion*, The Gifford Lectures, 1890 (Longmans, Green & Co., 1891), Lect. vi, "Physical Religion: The Natural and the Supernatural," pp. 119 ff.

6. "Comparative Mythology," *op. cit.*, p. 37. *Selected Essays*, I, 365.

eighteenth century, from the thinkers of the Enlightenment.[7] To be sure he sees no longer in myth and religion a mere arbitrary invention—a trickery of a cunning priesthood. But he agrees that myth, after all, is nothing but a great illusion—not a conscious but an unconscious deception, a deception brought about by the nature of the human mind, and, first and foremost, by the nature of human speech. Myth always remains a pathological case. But we are now in a position to understand the pathology of myth without taking recourse to the hypothesis of an inherent defect of the human mind itself. If language is recognized as the source of myth—then even the incongruities and contradictions of myth-ical thought are reduced to a universal and objective and thus to a thoroughly rational power.

It added very much to the influence of this doctrine that, with some critical reservations, it was accepted by the philosopher who first endeavored to create a "synthetic philosophy," a coher-ent and comprehensive survey of all activities of the human mind based on strictly empirical principles and on the general theory of evolution. Herbert Spencer found the first and principal source of all religion in ancestor-worship. The first cult, he declared, was not the cult of natural powers, but the cult of the dead.[8] Yet in order to understand the passage from ancestor-worship to the worship of personal gods, we must introduce a new hypothesis. According to Spencer it was the power and the perduring influ-ence of speech that made this step possible, and even necessary. Human speech is metaphorical in its very essence; it is filled with similes and analogies. The primitive mind is unable to under-stand these similes in a merely metaphorical sense. It takes them for realities and it thinks and acts according to this principle. It is this literal interpretation of metaphorical names that from the first elementary forms of ancestor-worship, from the worship of human beings, led to a worship of plants and animals, and finally of the great powers of nature. In primitive society it is a common and wide-spread habit to name a new-born child after plants, animals, stars or other natural objects. A boy is called "Tiger" or

7. It is a remarkable fact that the first elements of Max Müller's theory are to be found in the writings of one of the great rationalists. In his satire *Sur l'équivoque* Boileau had propounded the theory that the ambiguity of words is the real source of mythology.

8. See H. Spencer, *The Principles of Sociology* (1876), chap. xx (New York, D. Appleton & Co., 1901), I, 285 ff.

"Lion," "Raven" or "Wolf"; a girl is called "Moon" or "Star." In their origin all these names were nothing but *epitheta ornantia,* expressing some personal qualities that were attributed to human beings. According to the tendency of the primitive mind to understand all terms in a literal sense, the misinterpretation of these complementary names and metaphorical titles was inevitable. This is the true source of nature-worship. Once "Dawn" had been used as an actual name for a person; the traditions concerning one of such who became noted would, in the mind of the uncritical savage, lead to identification with the dawn; and the adventures would be interpreted in such a manner as the phenomena of the dawn made most feasible. Further, in regions where this name had been borne either by members of adjacent tribes, or by members of the same tribe living at different times, incongruous genealogies and conflicting adventures of the dawn would result.[9]

Here again the phenomenon of myth, the whole pantheon of polytheism is explained as a mere disease. The worship of conspicuous objects, conceived as persons, results from linguistic errors. The grave objections to which such a theory is liable are obvious. Myth is one of the oldest and greatest powers in human civilization. It is closely connected with all other human activities—it is inseparable from language, poetry, art and from early historical thought. Even science had to pass through a mythical age before it could reach its logical age: alchemy preceded chemistry, astrology preceded astronomy. If Max Müller's and Herbert Spencer's theories were right we should have to conclude that, after all, the history of human civilization was due to a simple misunderstanding, to a misinterpretation of words and terms. It is not a very satisfactory and plausible hypothesis to think of human culture as the product of a mere illusion—as a juggling with words and a childish play with names.

9. *Idem,* chaps. XXII–XXIV, I, 329–394.

III

MYTH AND THE PSYCHOLOGY OF EMOTIONS

NOTWITHSTANDING their many and important differences the theories of myth that we have so far considered have a common feature. The interpretations of Tylor and Frazer, of Max Müller and Herbert Spencer all start from the presupposition that myth is, first and foremost, a mass of "ideas," of representations, of theoretical beliefs and judgments. As these beliefs are in open contradiction to our sense-experience and as there exist no physical objects that correspond to the mythical representations it follows that myth is a mere phantasmagoria. The question necessarily arises why men cling so obstinately and forcibly to such phantasmagoria. Why do they not directly approach the reality of things and see it face to face; why do they prefer to live in a world of illusions, of hallucinations and dreams?

A new way to answer this question was indicated by the progress made in modern anthropology and psychology. We must study both aspects side by side; for they illustrate and supplement each other. Anthropological research has led to the result that, in order to come to an adequate understanding of myth, we must begin the investigation from a different point. Behind and below the mythical conceptions there has been discovered a deeper stratum that was formerly overlooked or at least not recognized in its full importance. Students of Greek literature and religion were always, more or less, influenced by the etymology of the Greek term μῦθος. They saw in myth a tale or a system of tales—of narratives relating the deeds of the gods or the adventures of heroic ancestors. This seemed to be sufficient as long as scholars were chiefly concerned with the study and interpretation of literary sources and as long as their interest was concentrated upon highly advanced stages of civilization—upon Babylonian, Indian, Egyptian or Greek religions. Later on it became necessary to enlarge this circle. There are many primitive tribes among whom we find no developed mythology, no narratives of the deeds of gods and no genealogy of gods. Nevertheless these peoples show all the well known characteristics of a form of life that is deeply penetrated with and wholly determined by mythical motives. But these motives find their expression not so much in definite thoughts or ideas as in actions. The active factor clearly predominates over the theoretical factor. The maxim that in order to understand myth we must begin with the study of rites seems now to have been generally accepted among ethnologists and anthropologists. In the light of this new method the savage appears no longer as a "primitive philosopher." When performing a religious ritual or ceremony man is not in a mere speculative or contemplative mood. He is not engrossed in a calm analysis of natural phenomena. He lives a life of emotions, not of thoughts. It has become clear that rite is a deeper and much more perdurable element in man's religious life than myth. "While creeds change," says the French scholar E. Doutté, "rite persists as the fossils of those extinct molluscs which serve to date geological epochs for us." [1]

The analysis of the higher religions confirmed this view. In his standard work, *The Religion of the Semites*,[2] W. Robertson-Smith made the most fertile use of the methodological principle that the right way to study religious *representations* is to begin with the study of religious *actions*. From this vantage ground even Greek religion appeared in a new and clearer light. "Greek religion," wrote Miss Jane Ellen Harrison in the introduction to her *Prolegomena to the Study of Greek Religion*,

as set forth in popular handbooks and even in more ambitious treatises, is an affair mainly of mythology, and moreover of mythology as seen through the medium of literature. . . . No serious attempt has been made to examine Greek ritual. Yet the facts of ritual are more easy definitely to ascertain, more permanent, and at least equally significant. What a people *does* in relation to its gods must always be one clue, and perhaps the safest, to what it *thinks*. The first preliminary to any scientific understanding of Greek religion is a minute examination of its ritual.[3]

The application of this principle met, however, with great obstacles. The emotional character of primitive religious rites is

1. E. Doutté, *Magie et religion dans l'Afrique du Nord* (Alger, Typographie Adolphe Jourdan, 1909), p. 602.
2. W. Robertson-Smith, *Lectures on the Religion of the Semites* (Edinburgh, A. and C. Black, 1889).
3. Jane Ellen Harrison, *Prolegomena to the Study of Greek Religion* (Cambridge, University Press, 1903), p. vii.

unmistakable. Yet it was very difficult to analyze and describe this character in a scientific way, as long as the psychology of the nineteenth century remained in its traditional state. From ancient times philosophers and psychologists had endeavored to give a general theory of emotions. But all these efforts were hampered and to a great extent made unfruitful by the fact that the only possible approach seemed to be purely intellectualistic. Affections, it was generally assumed, were to be defined in terms of "ideas." This seemed to be the only way to give a reasonable account of the very fact of emotions. The ethics of Stoicism were based upon the principle that passions are pathological facts. They were described as a sort of mental disease. The rationalistic psychology of the seventeenth century did not go so far. The passions were no longer regarded as "abnormal"; they were declared to be natural and necessary effects of the communion between body and soul. According to the theories of Descartes and Spinoza human affections have their origin in obscure and inadequate ideas. Even the psychology of the English empiricists did not change this general intellectualistic view. For even here the "ideas," understood as copies of sense-impressions, not as logical ideas, were still the center of psychological interest. In Germany Herbart and his school gave a mechanistic theory of the emotions according to which they were reduced to certain relations between perceptions, representations and ideas.

Thus matters remained until Th. Ribot developed a new theory which in contradistinction to the old *intellectualistic* thesis he described as the *physiological* thesis. In the preface to his work on the psychology of the emotions Ribot declared that, when compared to other parts of psychological research, the psychology of states of feeling was still confused and backward. The preference had always been given to other studies, such as those of perception, of memory, of images. According to Ribot the dominant prejudice which assimilates emotional states to intellectual states, considering them as analogous or even treating the former as dependent on the latter, can only lead to error. States of feeling are not merely secondary and derived; they are not merely the qualities, modes, or functions of cognitive states. They are, on the contrary, primitive, autonomous, not reducible to intelligence, and able to exist outside it and without it. This doctrine was based on general biological considerations. Ribot tried to connect all states of feelings with biological conditions and to regard them as the direct and immediate expression of the vegetative life.

From this standpoint feelings and emotions are no longer a superficial manifestation, a simple efflorescence; they plunge into the individual's depths; they have their roots in the needs and instincts, that is to say, in movements. . . . To wish to reduce emotional states to clear and definite ideas, or to imagine that by this process we can fix them, is to misunderstand them completely and to condemn ourselves beforehand to failure.[4]

The same view was upheld by W. James and the Danish psychologist, C. Lange.[5] Both of them, on the basis of independent considerations, had come to the same results. They insisted upon the prime importance of physiological factors in emotions. In order to understand the true character of the emotions and to appreciate their biological function and value, they declared, we must begin with a description of the physical symptoms. These symptoms consist in modifications of muscular innervation and in vaso-motor modifications. According to Lange the latter are the primary ones since the slightest circulatory variations profoundly modify the functions of the brain and spinal marrow. A disembodied emotion is a nonexistent one; it is a mere abstract entity. The organic and motor manifestations are not accessories; their investigation is part and parcel of the study of emotions. What do we find when analyzing an emotion like fear? We find, first and foremost, changes in the circulation; the blood vessels contract; the heart beats violently, the breathing becomes shallower and more rapid. The feeling of fear does not precede these bodily reactions; it succeeds them; it is the consciousness of these physiological states as they are occurring and after they have occurred. If, by a sort of mental experiment, we try to take away from the emotion of fear all the bodily symptoms, the beating of the pulse, the shivering of the skin, the trembling muscles—nothing remains of fear. As William James expressed it, there is no

4. Th. Ribot, *La psychologie des sentiments* (Paris, 1896). English trans., *The Psychology of the Emotions* (New York, Charles Scribner's Sons, 1912), Preface, pp. vii f.

5. C. Lange, *Über Gemütsbewegungen*. German trans. by H. Kurella (Leipzig, 1887). English trans., *The Emotions,* "Psychology Classics," Vol. I (Baltimore, Williams & Wilkins Co., 1922).

separate and independent "mind-stuff" out of which the emotion can be constituted. We must, therefore, reverse the order that hitherto was accepted both by common sense and scientific psychology.

Common-sense says, we lose our fortune, are sorry and weep; we meet a bear, are frightened and run; we are insulted by a rival, are angry and strike. The hypothesis here to be defended says that this order of sequence is incorrect, that the one mental state is not immediately induced by the other, that the bodily manifestations must first be interposed between, and that the more rational statement is that we feel sorry because we cry, angry because we strike, afraid because we tremble, and not that we cry, strike, or tremble, because we are sorry, angry, or fearful, as the case may be. Without the bodily states following on the perception, the latter would be purely cognitive in form, pale, colorless, destitute of emotional warmth. We might then see the bear, and judge it best to run, receive the insult and deem it right to strike, but we should not actually *feel* afraid or angry.[6]

It is, indeed, obvious that, biologically speaking, feeling is a much more general fact and belongs to an earlier and more elementary stratum than all the cognitive states of mind. To explain states of feeling in terms that belong to the latter sphere was, therefore, in a sense a *hysteron proteron*. In the case of feeling the motor states or impulses are primary; the affective manifestations are secondary. As Ribot points out, the basis, the root of the affective life, is to be sought in motor innervation and impulses not in the consciousness of pleasure and pain. "Pleasure and pain are only *effects* which must guide us in the search and determination of causes hidden in the region of instincts." It was a radical error to trust "in the evidence of consciousness" alone, to believe "that the conscious portion of an event is its principal portion," and therefore to assume "that the bodily phenomena which accompany all states of feeling are factors that are negligible and external, foreign to psychology, and without interest for it." [7]

By the development of this new approach a gap was filled that hitherto had existed between psychology and anthropology. In the traditional psychology which had placed the whole emphasis on the ideational aspect of the states of mind, anthropology could

6. James, *The Principles of Psychology* (New York, Henry Holt & Co., 1890), II, 449 f.

7. *Ribot, op. cit.*, p. 3.

find little help for its new interest in rites rather than in myths. Rites are, indeed, motor manifestations of psychic life. What they disclose are some fundamental tendencies, appetites, needs, desires; not mere "representations" or "ideas." And these tendencies are translated into movements—into rhythmical solemn movements or wild dances, into orderly and regular ritual actions, or violent orgiastic outbursts. Myth is the *epic* element in primitive religious life; rite is the *dramatic* element. We must begin with studying the latter in order to understand the former. Taken in themselves the mythical stories of gods or heroes cannot reveal to us the secret of religion, because they are nothing but the *interpretations* of rites. They try to give an account of what is present, what is immediately seen and done in these rites. They add the "theoretical" view to the active aspect of religious life. We can scarcely raise the question which of these two aspects is the "first" or the "second"; for they do not exist separately; they are correlative and interdependent; they support and explain each other.

A further step in this direction was made in the *psychoanalytic theory of myth.* When Sigmund Freud began to publish his articles on "Totem and Taboo" in 1913,[8] the problem of myth had reached a crucial point. Linguists, anthropologists, ethnologists had offered their several theories of myth. All these theories were useful to illuminate a certain sector of the problem; but they did not cover the whole field. Frazer saw in magic a sort of primitive science; Tylor described myth as a savage philosophy; Max Müller and Spencer saw in it a disease of language. All these conceptions were open to severe criticisms. Their adversaries had no difficulty in exposing the vulnerable points of these theories. No theoretical or empirical solution of the problem had yet been reached. But this state of affairs was changed by the appearance of the Freudian theory. Here was, after all, a new conception that opened a wide horizon and promised a better survey. Myth was no longer regarded as an isolated fact. It was connected with well-known phenomena which could be studied in a scientific way and which were capable of empirical verification. Thus myth became perfectly logical—almost too logical. It was no longer a chaos of the most bizarre and inconceivable things; it became a system. It could be reduced to a few very simple elements. To be sure, myth still remained a "pathological" phenomenon. But

8. First published in the periodical *Imago*, ed. by Sigmund Freud, Vol. I.

in the meantime psychopathology itself had made great progress. Pathologists no longer treated mental or neurotic diseases as if they were "a state within the state." They had learned to subsume them under the same general rules that hold for the processes of normal life. When passing from one field to the other the psychologist did not have to change his point of view. He could use the same methods of observation and argue upon the same scientific principles. There was no longer a deep chasm, no insurmountable gulf between "normal" and "abnormal" psychic life.

When applied to myth this principle was pregnant with important consequences and promises. Myth was no longer wrapped in mystery; it could be placed in the clear and sharp light of scientific research. Freud stood at the sickbed of myth with the same attitude and the same feelings as at the couch of an ordinary patient. What he found here was not at all surprising or disconcerting. He saw the same well-known symptoms with which he had become familiar by long observation. What strikes us most when we read those first essays of Freud is the clarity and simplicity with which he develops his views. Here we do not find those highly complicated theories which were introduced later on Freud's authority by his adherents and pupils. Nor do we find the dogmatic self-assuredness that is so characteristic of most of the later psychoanalytical writings. Freud makes no pretension of having solved the old long-standing riddle. He simply wants to draw a parallel between the psychic lives of savages and neurotics—a parallel that may be able to elucidate some facts which otherwise would remain dark and unintelligible. "The reader need not fear," he declares,

that psychoanalysis . . . will be tempted to derive anything so complicated as religion from a single source. If it necessarily seeks, as in duty bound, to gain recognition for one of the sources of this institution, it by no means claims exclusiveness for this source or even first rank among the concurring factors. Only a synthesis from various fields of research can decide what relative importance in the genesis of religion is to be assigned to the mechanism which we are to discuss; but such a task exceeds the means as well as the intentions of the psychoanalyst.[9]

9. Freud, *Totem und Tabu* (Vienna, 1920, first published in *Imago*, 1912–13), chap. IV, English trans. by A. A. A. Brill (New York, Moffat, Yard & Co., 1918; now Dodd, Mead & Co., New York), p. 165.

As a *psychologist* Freud was, in fact, in a better position to build up a coherent theory of myth than most of his predecessors. He was firmly convinced that the only clue to the mythical world must be sought in the *emotional* life of man. But on the other hand he developed a new and original theory of the emotions themselves. The former theories had favored the view of a "psychology without soul." What is essential in all emotions, said Ribot, are not the psychic states, but the motor manifestations— the tendencies and appetites translated into movements. For the explanation of these states we need no "obscure 'psyche' endowed with attractive or repulsive tendencies." We must purge our psychology of all anthropomorphic elements and establish it upon a strictly objective basis—upon chemical and physiological facts. The factor of the so-called "soul" must be eliminated; but after this elimination "there still remains the physiological tendency, that is to say, the motor element which, in some degree, from the lowest to the highest, is never quite wanting." [10]

Yet to eliminate all conceptions of the "soul" was by no means the ambition of Freud. He too defended a strictly mechanistic view—but he did not think it possible to reduce man's emotional life to merely chemical or physiological causes. We may and must, indeed, continue to speak of the mechanism of emotions as a "psychic" mechanism. But psychic life is not to be confused with conscious life. Consciousness is not the whole; it is only a small and vanishing fraction of psychic life; it cannot reveal, it rather masks and disguises its essence.

From the point of view of our problem this appeal to the "unconscious" was, to be sure, an important step. It called for a restatement of the whole question. In many of the former theories myth appeared, after all, as a very shallow thing. It was declared to be a simple *quid pro quo:* a wrong use made of the general laws of association, or a misinterpretation of terms and proper names. All these rather naïve assumptions were swept away by the Freudian theory. The problem was approached in a new way and seen in a new depth. Myth was deeply rooted in human nature; it was based upon a fundamental and irresistible instinct the nature and character of which remained to be determined. But this question was not open to a merely *empirical* answer. In his first analyses Freud spoke as a physician and empirical thinker.

10. See Ribot, *op. cit.,* pp. 5 f.

He seemed to be entirely absorbed in the study of very complex and highly interesting neurotic cases. But even in his first studies he was not satisfied with collecting facts. His method was deductive rather than inductive; he asked for a universal principle from which the facts could be derived. Freud was, indeed, an unusually keen observer. He discovered phenomena that hitherto had failed to arouse the physician's interest and at the same time he began to develop a new psychological technique for the interpretation of these phenomena. But even in these early studies of Freud there is much more than meets the eye. They were never meant as mere empirical generalizations. What Freud tried to reveal was the hidden *force* that lay behind the observable facts. For this purpose he suddenly had to change his whole method. While he continued to speak as a physician and psychopathologist, he thought as a determined metaphysician.

If we are to understand Freud's metaphysics we must trace it back to its historical origin. Freud lived in the atmosphere of German philosophy of the nineteenth century. What he found there were two conceptions of human nature and culture that were diametrically opposed to each other. The one was represented by Hegel; the other by Schopenhauer. Hegel had described the historical process as a fundamentally rational and conscious process. "The time must eventually come," says Hegel in the introduction to his *Lectures on the Philosophy of History*, "for understanding that rich product of active Reason, which the History of the World offers to us. . . . It must be observed at the outset, that the phenomenon we investigate—Universal History—belongs to the realm of *Spirit*. . . . On the stage on which we are observing it—Universal History—Spirit displays itself in its most concrete reality." [11] Schopenhauer defied and derided this Hegelian conception. To him such a rationalistic and optimistic view of human nature and human history seemed to be not only absurd but nefarious. The world is not a product of reason. It is irrational in its very essence and principle, being an offspring of a blind will. The intellect itself is nothing but one outcome of this blind will that has created it as an instrument to serve its own purposes. But where do we find the will in our empirical world, in the world of sense-experience? As a "thing-in-itself" it

11. Hegel, *Lectures on the Philosophy of History*. English trans. by J. Sibree (London, Henry G. Bohn, 1857), pp. 16 f.

is beyond the reach of human experience; it seems to be entirely inaccessible. There is, however, one phenomenon in which we become immediately aware of its nature. The power of the will —this true principle of the world—appears clearly and unmistakably in our *sexual instinct*. We need no other explanation. What we find here is easily and immediately understandable, because it is felt at every moment in its full and irresistible strength. It is ridiculous to speak of Reason, as Hegel did, as the "substantial power"—the "Sovereign of the World." The true sovereign— the center round which the life of nature and the life of man revolve—is the sexual instinct. As Schopenhauer said, this instinct is the Genius of the species which makes of the individual an instrument for the furtherance of its ends. All this had been developed in a famous chapter of Schopenhauer's *World as Will and Idea*,[12] which gives us the general metaphysical background, and in a sense, the nucleus of Freud's theory.

Here we are only concerned with the implications of this theory for the study of mythical thought. From a purely *empirical* point of view the transference of the psychoanalytical method to this field encountered great difficulties. Obviously the matter was not open to direct observation. All the arguments used by Freud remained highly hypothetical and speculative. The historical origin of the phenomena studied by him—of the taboo prescriptions and the totemistic system—was unknown. In order to fill this gap Freud had to go back to his general theory of emotions. He declared that the *only* source of the totemistic system was the savage's dread of incest. It was this motive that led to exogamy. Everybody descended from the same totem is consanguineous; that is, of one family, and in this family the most distant grades of relationship are recognized as an absolute obstacle to sexual union. But those anthropologists who had studied the problem most carefully had been led to quite different conclusions. Frazer, who had written a work of four volumes on the subject, declared that the two institutions of totemism and exogamy were really distinct and independent, though they were often conjoined.[13] Among the Arunta the whole religious and social life was deter-

12. "Über die Metaphysik der Geschlechtsliebe," *Die Welt als Wille und Vorstellung*, Ergänzungen zum vierten Buch, Kap. 44.
13. Frazer, *Totemism and Exogamy* (London, Macmillan & Co., 1910) I, xii. 4 vols.

mined by their totemistic system but this system had no effect on marriage and descent. The evidence of tradition seems even to point back to a time when a man always married a woman of his own totem.[14] The best that Frazer could say, after years of study, was that the ultimate origin of exogamy, and with it the law of incest, remains a problem nearly as dark as ever.[15]

In order to come to his conclusions Freud had to quash this cautious and critical attitude. What struck him most was the fact that the two commandments of totemism—not to kill the totem animal and not to use a woman belonging to the same totem for sexual purposes—agree in content with the two crimes of Oedipus who slew his father and took his mother to wife, and, on the other hand, with the child's two primal wishes whose insufficient repression or whose re-awakening form the nucleus of perhaps all neuroses.[16] Thus the Father-complex and the Oedipus-complex were declared to be the "Open Sesame" to the mythical world. This formula seemed to account for everything. According to the psychoanalytic principle of "displacement" all combinations became possible. Freud himself often expressed his surprise at the fertility of this principle. He tells us that the first wishes of the child appear, often in the most remarkable disguises and inversions, in the formation of almost all religions.[17]

The first question that we have to raise here is not a question of fact but of method. Let us assume that all the facts upon which the psychoanalytical theory depends are firmly established. Let us admit that there is not only a resemblance or analogy but a fundamental identity between the psychic lives of savages and neurotics, and that Freud has succeeded in proving his point, that all the motives of mythical thought are the same as we find in certain forms of neurosis—compulsion neurosis, *délire de toucher*, animal-phobia, obsessive prohibitions, and so on. Even in this case the problem would not be solved; it would only recur in a new shape. For it is not enough simply to know the *subject-matter* of myth in order to understand its character and nature.

The method of Freud seems at first sight to be entirely original. No one before him had looked upon the problem from this angle.

14. Sir Baldwin Spencer and F. J. Gillen, *The Native Tribes of Central Australia* (London and New York, Macmillan, 1899, reprinted 1938), p. 419.

15. Frazer, *op. cit.*, I, 165.

16. Freud, *op. cit.*, pp. 236 f.

17. Freud, *idem*, pp. 241 ff.

Nevertheless there is a common feature that connects Freud's conception of myth with that of his predecessors. Like most of them Freud was convinced that the surest, nay the only, way to understand the *meaning* of myth was to describe and list and to order and classify its *objects*. Yet even supposing we knew and understood all the things that myth is speaking about—would it help us very much to understand the *language* of myth? Like poetry and art, myth is a "symbolic form," and it is a common characteristic of all symbolic forms that they are applicable to any object whatsoever. There is nothing that is inaccessible or impermeable to them: the peculiar character of an object does not affect their activity. What would we think of a philosophy of language, a philosophy of art or science that began with enumerating all those things that are possible subjects of speech and of artistic representation and of scientific inquiry? Here we can never hope to find a definite limit; we cannot even seek it. Everything has a "name"; everything may become a theme for a work of art. It is the same with myth. It can make a likeness of anything "that is in heaven above, in the earth beneath, or in the water under the earth." Thus while the study of the subject-matter of myth may be highly interesting and may arouse our scientific curiosity, it cannot itself yield a definite answer. For what we wish to know is not the mere substance of myth; it is rather its function in man's social and cultural life.

In this regard most of the previous theories remained inadequate because they failed to see the real problem. They went in all directions but in a sense they were all following the same way. When comparing the older methods of comparative mythology with the recent methods of psychoanalysis we find a striking resemblance. Among the naturalistic theories of myth there was a solar mythology—introduced by Max Müller and later on renewed by Frobenius—a lunar mythology, represented by Ehrenreich or Winckler, a wind and weather mythology, represented by Adalbert Kuhn. Each school was eagerly and obstinately fighting for its special object. At first sight we do not feel inclined to find any resemblance or analogy between the Greek legends of Selene and Endymion, Eos and Tithonus, Cephalus and Procris, Daphne and Apollo. But, according to Max Müller, all of them mean the same thing. They are many variations of one identical mythical theme that is repeated over and over again. This theme is the rise and setting of the sun and the combat between light and darkness. Every new myth portrays the same phenomenon in a new and different perspective. Endymion, for instance, is not the Sun in the divine character of Phoebus, but a conception of the Sun in his daily course, as rising early from the womb of Dawn and, after a short and brilliant career, setting in the evening, never to return again to his mortal life. And what else is Daphne persecuted by Apollo than the dawn rushing and trembling through the sky, and fading away at the sudden approach of the bright sun? The same holds for the legend of the death of Heracles. The coat which Deianira sends to the solar hero is an expression for the clouds which rise from the waters and surround the sun like a dark raiment. Heracles tries to tear it off, but he cannot do it without tearing his own body to pieces, then at last his bright body is consumed in a general conflagration.[18]

It is a far cry from these old naturalistic interpretations, that have become completely obsolete, to our modern psychoanalytical theories. Nevertheless they do not disagree in their procedure but represent the same general tendency of thought. And I dare say that, after a few decades, the sex myths will share the fate of the solar or lunar myths. For they are open to the same objections. It is not a very satisfactory explanation of a fact that has put its indelible mark upon the whole life of mankind to reduce it to a special and single motive. Man's psychic and cultural life is not made of such simple and homogeneous stuff. Freud could not prove his point any more than Max Müller and all the other scholars of the Society for the Comparative Study of Myth. In both cases we find the same dogmatism. The students of comparative mythology spoke of the sun, the moon, the stars, the wind and the clouds as if they were the only subjects of mythical imagination. Freud has simply shifted the scene of the mythical tales. According to him they are not representations of the great drama of nature. What they tell us is rather the eternal story of man's sexual life. From prehistoric times to the present man was

18. See F. Max Müller, "Comparative Mythology," *Oxford Essays*, pp. 52 ff. (*Selected Essays*, I, 395 ff., 398 ff.), and *Lectures on the Science of Language* (London, Longmans, Green & Co., 1871), II, Lect. xi, "Myths of the Dawn," 506–571.

always haunted by the same two fundamental wishes. The wish to kill one's father and to marry one's mother appears in the child-hood of the human race just as it appears, in the strangest dis-guises and transformations, in the life of every individual child.

IV

THE FUNCTION OF MYTH IN MAN'S
SOCIAL LIFE

O F ALL things in the world myth seems to be the most incoherent and inconsistent. Taken at its face value it appears as a confused web woven out of the most incongruous threads. Can we hope to find any bond that connects the
most barbaric rites with the world of Homer—can we trace back
to one and the same source the orgiastic cults of savage tribes,
the magic practices of the shamans of Asia, the delirious whirl of
the dancing dervishes with the calmness and the speculative
depth of the religion of the Upanishads? To describe so widely
divergent and entirely incompatible phenomena by one name and
to subsume them under the same concept seems to be highly arbitrary.

The problem appears, however, in a different light when we
approach it from a different angle. The subjects of myth and the
ritual acts are of an infinite variety; they are incalculable and
unfathomable. But the motives of mythical thought and mythical
imagination are in a sense always the same. In all human activities and in all forms of human culture we find a "unity in the
manifold." Art gives us a unity of intuition; science gives us a
unity of thought; religion and myth give us a unity of feeling.
Art opens to us the universe of "living forms"; science shows us a
universe of laws and principles; religion and myth begin with
the awareness of the universality and fundamental identity of
life.

It is not necessary that this all-pervading life be conceived in a
personal form. There are religions that show us an "infra-personal"
or a "supra-personal" conception of the Divine. We find a "pre-
animistic" religion in which the sense of personality is still absent [1]
and we find, on the other hand, highly developed religions in
which the element of personality is overshadowed and at last
totally eclipsed by other motives. In the great religions of the

---

1. For the problem of Pre-Animism see R. R. Marett, "Pre-Animist Religion,"
The Threshold of Religion (London, Methuen & Co., 1909).

East—Brahmanism, Buddhism, and Confucianism—there appears this "drift toward the impersonal." [2] The identity conceived in the religion of the Upanishads is a metaphysical identity; it means the fundamental unity of the Ego and the Universe, of the "Atman" and the "Brahman." In primitive belief there is no room for such an abstract identity. What we find here is something quite different. It is a deep and ardent desire of the individuals to identify themselves with the life of the community and with the life of nature. This desire is satisfied by the religious rites. Here the individuals are melted into one shape—into an undistinguishable whole. If in a savage tribe the men are engaged in warfare or in any other dangerous enterprise and the women who have stayed at home try to help them by their ritual dances—this seems to be absurd and unintelligible when judged according to our standards of empirical thought and "causal laws." But it becomes perfectly clear and comprehensible as soon as we read and interpret this act in terms of our social rather than of our physical experience. In their war dances the women identify themselves with their husbands. They share their hopes and fears, their risks and dangers. This bond—a bond of "sympathy," not of "causality"—is not enfeebled by the distance that lies between them; on the contrary it is strengthened. The two sexes form one indivisible organism; what is going on in one part of this organism necessarily affects the other part. A great many positive and negative demands, of prescriptions and taboos, are nothing but the expression and application of this general rule. The rule holds not only for the two sexes, but for all the members of the tribes. When a Dayak village has turned out to hunt in the jungle, those who stay at home may not touch either oil or water with their hands; for if they did so the hunters would all be "butter-fingered" and the prey would slip through their hands.[3] This is not a causal but an emotional bond. What matters here are not the empirical relations between causes and effects, but the intensity and depth with which human relations are felt.

The same feature appears, therefore, in all the other forms of human kinship. In primitive thought blood relationship is not interpreted in a merely physiological way. The birth of man is

2. Cf. A. A. Bowman, *Studies in the Philosophy of Religion* (London, Macmillan & Co., 1938), I, 107.

3. *The Golden Bough*, Pt. I: *The Magic Art* (see above p. 9, n. 3), I, 120.

a mythical not a physical act. The laws of sexual procreation are unknown. Birth is, therefore, always regarded as a sort of reincarnation. The Arunta in Central Australia assume that the spirits of the dead who belonged to their totem wait for their rebirth in definite localities and penetrate into the bodies of the women who pass such a spot.[4] Even the relation between the child and his father is not regarded as a purely physical relation. Here too causality is replaced by real identity. In totemic systems the present generation not only descends from the animal ancestors; it *is* the embodiment of these ancestors. When the Arunta are celebrating their most important religious festival, when they perform their "Intichiuma" ceremonies, they not only represent or imitate the life, the deeds, and adventures of their forefathers. The forefathers reappear in these ceremonies; their presence, their beneficent influence is immediately seen and felt. Without this permanent influence nature and human life would come to a standstill. The rain would not fall, the soil would not bear its fruit; the whole country would be changed into a desert. By a first act of identification man asserts his fundamental unity with his human or animal ancestors—by a second act he identifies his own life with the life of nature. As a matter of fact there can be no sharp distinction between the two realms. They are on the same level; for to the primitive mind nature itself is not a physical thing governed by physical laws. One and the same society—the society of life—includes and embraces all animate and inanimate beings.[5] According to the Zuñis not only physical but even artificial things, not only the sun, the earth, the sea, but also the instruments made by men belong to one great system of life.[6]

If this life is to be preserved it must be constantly renewed. But this renovation is not conceived in mere biological terms. Even here the persistence of the human race depends upon social and not upon physiological acts. The clearest expression of this general conviction is to be found in the rites of initiation which are an important and indispensable element in all primitive societies. Up to a certain age, the attainment of puberty, the child

4. See Frazer, *Totemism and Exogamy,* IV, 59 ff., and Spencer and Gillen, *op. cit.,* chap. xv.

5. For further details see E. Cassirer, *An Essay on Man* (New Haven, Yale University Press, 1944), pp. 82 ff.

6. See Frank Hamilton Cushing, "Outlines of Zuñi," *13ᵗʰ Annual Report of the Bureau of American Ethnology* (Washington, 1891–92), p. 9.

is still regarded and treated as a merely "natural" being. It is in the care of its mother who takes charge of all its physical needs. But then comes a sudden reversal of this physical order. The child has to become an adult—a member of the society. That is a crucial point in man's life, an event which is marked by the strongest and most incisive religious and ritual ceremonies. If the new social being is to be born the physical being has, in a sense, to die. The young men that are to be initiated have, therefore, to pass the most severe trials. The neophyte has to leave his family; he lives for a time in perfect seclusion; he has to endure the greatest pains and cruelties. Sometimes he even has to assist in the ritual of his own burial. But when he has stood all these tests there comes the great moment in which he is admitted to the communion of men and the great mystery of society. This admission means a real regeneration, the beginning of a new and higher form of life.[7]

The same cycle of life that appears in human society and constitutes its very essence also appears in nature. The cycle of the seasons is not brought about by mere physical forces. It is indissolubly united with the life of man. The life and death of nature is part and parcel of the great drama of man's death and resurrection. In this regard the rites of vegetation that we find in almost all religions bear a close analogy to the rites of initiation. Even nature is in need of constant regeneration—it must die in order to live. The cults of Attis, Adonis, Osiris bear witness to this fundamental and ineradicable belief.[8]

Greek religion seems to be very far from all these primitive conceptions. In the Homeric poems we no longer find magical rites, ghosts and specters, fear of the dead. To this Homeric world we may apply the famous definition of Winckelmann, according to which the distinctive mark of the Greek genius is its "noble simplicity and quiet grandeur." But the modern history of religion has taught us that this "quiet grandeur" has never been undisturbed. "The Olympians of Homer," says Miss Jane Ellen Harrison in the introduction to her book mentioned above,[9] "are no

---

7. For more details see Spencer and Gillen, *op. cit.*, chap. vi, and A. van Gennep, *Les rites du passage* (Paris, E. Nourry, 1909).

8. See Frazer, *The Golden Bough*, Pt. IV, *Adonis, Attis, Osiris* (3d ed. New York, Macmillan, 1935) Vols. I and II.

9. See p. 24, n. 3.

more primitive than his hexameters. Beneath this splendid surface lies a stratum of religious conceptions, ideas of evil, of purification, of atonement, ignored or suppressed by Homer, but reappearing in later poets and notably in Aeschylus." And then came that deep crisis in Greek culture and Greek religious life in which all the Homeric conceptions were threatened with a complete breakdown. The simplicity and serenity of the Olympian gods seemed suddenly to fade away. Zeus, the god of the bright sky, Apollo, the god of the sun, had no power to resist and banish the demonic forces that appeared in the cult of Dionysus. In Homer Dionysus has no place among the Olympian gods. He came as a stranger and a latecomer into Greek religion—as an immigrant god from the North. His origin is to be sought in Thrace—and in all probability in Asian cults. We witness in Greek religion thereafter the continuous struggle between two opposite forces. The classical expression of this struggle is given in Euripides' *Bacchae*. If we read the verses of Euripides we need no other testimony as to the intensity, the violence, the irresistible power of the new religious feeling.

In the Dionysian cult we find scarcely any *specific* feature of the Greek genius. What appears here is a fundamental feeling of mankind, a feeling that is common to the most primitive rites and to the most sublime spiritualized mystic religions. It is the deep desire of the individual to be freed from the fetters of its individuality, to immerse itself in the stream of universal life, to lose its identity, to be absorbed in the whole of nature—the same desire as expressed in the verses of the Persian poet Mualānā Jalāl-uddīn Rūmī: "He that knows the power of the dance dwells in God." The power of the dance is to the mystic the true way to God. In the delirious whirl of the dance and of the orgiastic rites our own finite and limited Self disappears. The Self, the "dark despot" as it is called by Rūmī, dies; the God is born.

Yet Greek religion could not simply return to these primitive feelings. Though these sentiments had not lost their strength they had changed their character. The Greek mind is a perfectly logical mind; its demand of logic is universal. Even the most "irrational" elements of the Dionysian cult could not be accepted, therefore, without a sort of theoretical explanation and justification. This justification was given by the Orphic theologians. Orphism turned into a "system" what originally was a mere mass of the crudest and wildest primitive rites.[10] Orphic theology created the story of Dionysus Zagreus. He is described as the son of Zeus and Semele—loved and adopted by his father but persecuted by the hatred and jealousy of Hera. Hera urged the Titans to kill Dionysus in his infancy. He tried to escape them by repeated metamorphoses; but finally he was overcome, in the form of a bull. His body was torn to pieces which his foes thereupon devoured. As punishment for their crime the Titans were struck by Zeus's lightning flash and destroyed. From their ashes sprang the race of men, in whom, in conformity with their origin, the good derived from Dionysus Zagreus is mixed with the evil and demonic Titanic element.

This legend of Dionysus Zagreus is a typical example of the origin and meaning of mythical tales. What is related here is neither a physical nor a historical phenomenon. It is not a fact of nature nor is it a recollection of the deeds or sufferings of a heroic ancestor. Nevertheless the legend is not a mere fairy tale. It has a *fundamentum in re;* it refers to a certain "reality." But this reality is neither physical nor historical; it is *ritual.* What is *seen* in the Dionysic cult is *explained* in the myth. The Dionysic cults used to conclude with a "theophany." When the wild ecstasy of the Maenads has reached its highest pitch they call the god, they implore him to appear among his worshipers:

"O Dionysus, reveal thee!—appear as a bull to behold,
Or be thou seen as a dragon, a monster of heads manifold,
Or as a lion with splendours of flame round the limbs of him
    rolled." [11]

And the God listens to the prayer and grants the request. He makes his appearance and himself takes part in the cult. He shares the sacred frenzy of his adorers; he himself falls upon the beast selected as his victim; he seizes its bleeding flesh and devours it raw.

All this is wild, fantastic, extravagant, and unintelligible. But it was the function of myth to give a new turn to these orgiastic

10. As to this mission of Orphism in Greek religious and cultural life see Harrison, *op. cit.,* chaps. ix and x, and Erwin Rohde, *Psyche,* Pt. II, chap. x. English trans. by W. B. Hillis (New York, Harcourt, Brace & Co., 1925), pp. 335 ff. For the legend of Dionysus Zagreus see Rohde, *op. cit.,* pp. 340 f.

11. Euripides, *Bacchae,* vv. 1017 ff. English trans. Arthur S. Way (Loeb Classical Library, Cambridge, Mass., Harvard University Press, 1930), III, 89.

cults. In Orphic theology the ecstasis was no longer understood as mere madness; it became a "hieromania," a sacred madness in which the soul, leaving the body, winged its way to union with the god.[12] The One divine being has been dispersed by the powers of evil, by the rebellion of the Titans against Zeus, into the multiplicity of the things of this world and into the multiplicity of men. But it is not lost; it may be restored to its original state. This is only possible if man sacrifices his individuality; if he breaks down every barrier that lies between himself and the eternal unity of life.

Here we grasp one of the most essential elements of myth. Myth does not arise solely from intellectual processes; it sprouts forth from deep human emotions. Yet on the other hand all those theories that exclusively stress the emotional element fail to see an essential point. Myth cannot be described as bare emotion because it is the *expression* of emotion. The expression of a feeling is not the feeling itself—it is emotion turned into an image. This very fact implies a radical change. What hitherto was dimly and vaguely felt assumes a definite shape; what was a passive state becomes an active process.

To understand this transformation it is necessary to make a sharp distinction between two types of expression: between physical and symbolic expressions. Darwin has written a classical book about the expression of emotions in men and animals. We learn from this book that the *fact* of expression has a very broad biological basis. It is by no means a privilege of man; it extends over the whole animal world. If we ascend to the higher stages of animal life it constantly wins in strength and variety. R. M. Yerkes says that many, if not all, of the chief categories of human emotional expression are represented in chimpanzee behavior and that chimpanzee emotional expression is fascinating and at the same time baffling in its complexity and variability.[13] Also the emotions of lower animals, and their corresponding expressions, are of very wide range. Even such phenomena as have usually been ascribed to men alone, as for instance blushing and growing pale, can be ascertained in the animal world.[14] It is indeed clear

12. See Rohde, *op. cit.*, pp. 257 ff.

13. Robert M. Yerkes, *Chimpanzees. A Laboratory Colony* (New Haven, Yale University Press, 1943), p. 29.

14. Cf. Angelo Mosso, *Fear.* Authorized English trans. by E. Lough and F. Kiesow (London and New York, Longmans, Green & Co., 1896), pp. 10 ff.

that even the lowest organisms must have some means of distinguishing between certain stimuli and reacting differently to them.
They would not be able to survive if they could not discriminate,
in their behavior, between what is advantageous and disadvan-
tageous, beneficial or harmful. Every organism "seeks" certain
things and "avoids" certain things. An animal seeks its prey and
flees from its enemies. All this is regulated by a complicated network of instincts and motor impulses which do not require any
conscious activity. As Ribot points out, the first period in organic
life is that of protoplasmic, vital, preconscious sensibility. The
organism has its "memory"; it preserves certain impressions, certain normal or morbid modifications. "In the same way there exists an inferior unconscious form—organic sensibility—which is
the preparation and the outline of superior conscious emotional
life. Vital sensibility is to conscious feeling what organic memory
is to memory in the ordinary sense of the word." [15] If, in the
higher animals, consciousness intervenes and begins to play a
predominant role we cannot describe it in an anthropomorphic
way, in terms of perception or "ideas." The animal's behavior
seems rather to be determined by some "emotional qualities" that
awake in it the feeling of "familiarity" or "uncanniness," of attraction or repulsion. "Is it not an admissible hypothesis," asks
W. Köhler in a study on the Psychology of Chimpanzees,

that certain shapes and outlines of things have in themselves the quality of weirdness and frightfulness, not because any special mechanism
in us enables them to produce it, but because, granted our general
nature and psyche, some shapes inevitably have the character of the
terrible, others grace, or clumsiness, or energy, or decidedness? [16]

The awareness of these different emotional qualities neither presupposes an act of reflection nor can it be accounted for by the
individual experience of the animal. Small birds show, immediately after their birth, fear of the hawk or of snakes. This
fear is, however, still very undifferentiated. Young chickens crouch
with fear not merely in the presence of a bird of prey but also of
any other large object flying over them. These instinctive emo-

15. Ribot, *op. cit.*, pp. 3 f.
16. See W. Köhler, "Zur Psychologie der Schimpansen," *Psychologische Forschung*, I (1921), 39. English trans. by Ella Winter, *The Mentality of Apes* (London, Kegan Paul; New York, Harcourt, Brace & Co., 1925), App., p. 335.

tions have nothing specific; they bear no relation to a special class of objects of a dangerous character.

A new step is taken with the development of man. First of all the emotions become much more specified. They are no longer dim and vague feelings; they refer to special classes of *objects*. But there is still another feature that we find nowhere except in the human world, though there are, to be sure, still innumerable human reactions which do not differ in principle from animal reactions. If a man answers an insult by knitting his brows or clenching his fist, he acts precisely in the same way an animal does when it shows its teeth in the presence of an enemy. But, generally speaking, human *responses* belong to quite a different type. What distinguishes them from animal reactions is their *symbolic* character.[17] In the rise and growth of human culture we can follow step by step this fundamental change of meaning. Man has discovered a new mode of expression: symbolic expression. This is the common denominator in all his cultural activities: in myth and poetry, in language, in art, in religion, and in science.

These activities are widely different, but they fulfil one and the same task: the task of *objectification*. In language we objectify our sense-perceptions. In the very act of linguistic expression our perceptions assume a new form. They are no longer isolated data; they give up their individual character; they are brought under class-concepts which are designated by general "names." The act of "naming" does not simply add a mere conventional sign to a readymade thing—to an object known before. It is rather a prerequisite of the very conception of objects; of the idea of an objective empirical reality.[18]

Myth is not only far remote from this empirical reality; it is, in a sense, in flagrant contradiction to it. It seems to build up an entirely fantastic world. Nevertheless even myth has a certain "objective" aspect and a definite objective function. Linguistic symbolism leads to an objectification of sense-impressions; mythical symbolism leads to an objectification of feelings. In his magical rites, in his religious ceremonies, man acts under the pressure of deep individual desires and violent social impulses. He performs

17. For a detailed discussion of this problem see E. Cassirer, *An Essay on Man*, chap. iii, pp. 27 ff.

18. For more details see my article "Le langage et la construction du monde des objets," *Journal de psychologie normale et pathologique*, XXXᵉ Année (1933), 18–44.

these actions without knowing their motives; they are entirely unconscious. But if these rites are turned into myths a new element appears. Man is no longer satisfied with doing certain things—he raises the question of what these things "mean," he inquires into why and whither, he tries to understand where they have come from and to which end they tend. The answer he gives to all these questions may seem to be incongruous and absurd; but what matters here is not so much the answer as the question itself. As soon as man begins to wonder about his acts, he has taken a new decisive step; he has entered upon a new way which will in the end lead him far from his unconscious and instinctive life.

It is a well-known fact that every expression of an emotion has a soothing effect. A blow with the fist may assuage our wrath; an outburst of tears may relieve us from grief and sorrow. All this is easily understandable for physiological and psychological reasons. Physiologically it may be accounted for by a principle that was called by Herbert Spencer the "Law of Nervous Discharge." In a certain sense this "law of discharge" also holds for all *symbolic* expressions. But here we meet with an entirely new phenomenon. In our physical reactions a sudden explosion is followed by a state of rest. And once disappeared the emotion has come to its end without leaving any permanent trace. But if we express our emotions by *symbolic* acts the case is quite different. Such acts have, as it were, a double power: the power to bind and unbind. Even here the emotions are turned outward; but instead of being dispersed, they are, on the contrary, concentrated. In physical reactions the bodily movements that correspond to certain emotions become more and more extensive; they cover a wider area. According to Spencer this extension and diffusion follows a definite rule. At first the delicate muscles of the vocal organs and the small facial muscles are affected. When feeling is excessive the nervous discharge affects the vascular system.[19] But symbolic expression does not mean extenuation; it means intensification. What we find here is no mere exteriorization but condensation. In language, myth, art, religion our emotions are not simply turned into mere acts; they are turned into "works." These works do not fade away. They are persistent and durable. A physical reaction can only give us a quick and temporary relief;

19. For further details see H. Spencer, *Principles of Psychology*, (New York, D. Appleton & Co., 1873), Vol. II, §§ 495–502.

a symbolic expression may become a *momentum aere perennius.*
This power of objectification and solidification becomes particularly clear in poetry and art. Goethe regarded this gift as the essential feature of his poetry. "And thus began," he says in *Dichtung und Wahrheit,* speaking of his youth,

that tendency from which I could not deviate my whole life through: namely, the tendency to turn into an image, into a poem, everything that delighted or troubled me, or otherwise occupied me, and to come to some certain understanding with myself upon it, that I might both rectify my conceptions of external things, and set my mind at rest about them. The faculty of doing this was necessary to no one more than to me, for my natural disposition whirled me constantly from one extreme to the other. All my works therefore that have become known are only fragments of one great confession.[20]

In mythical thought and imagination we do not meet with *individual* confessions. Myth is an objectification of man's social experience, not of his individual experience. It is true that in later times we find myths made by individuals, as, for instance, the famous Platonic myths. But here one of the most essential features of the genuine myths is missing. Plato created them in an entirely free spirit; he was not under their power, he directed them according to his own purposes: the purposes of dialectical and ethical thought. Genuine myth does not possess this philosophical freedom; for the images in which it lives are not *known* as images. They are not regarded as symbols but as realities. This reality cannot be rejected or criticized; it has to be accepted in a passive way. But the first preliminary step on the new road that finally will lead to a new goal has been made. For even here emotions are not simply felt. They are "intuited"; they are "turned into images." These images are crude, grotesque, fantastic. But it is just for this reason that they are understandable to uncivilized man because they can give him an interpretation of the life of nature and of his own inner life.

Myth, and religion in general, have often been declared to be a mere product of fear. But what is most essential in man's religious life is not the *fact* of fear, but the *metamorphosis* of fear. Fear is a universal biological instinct. It can never be completely overcome or suppressed, but it can change its form. Myth is filled

20. Goethe, *Dichtung und Wahrheit,* Bk. VII. English trans. by John Oxenford (London, G. Bell & Sons, 1897), I, 240.

with the most violent emotions and the most frightful visions. But in myth man begins to learn a new and strange art: the art of expressing, and that means of organizing, his most deeply rooted instincts, his hopes and fears.

This power of organization appears in its greatest strength when man is confronted with the greatest problem—that of death. To ask for the causes of death was one of the first and most urgent questions of mankind. Myths of death are told everywhere—from the lowest to the highest forms of human civilization.[21]

Anthropologists have made great efforts to find what they called a "minimum definition of religion"—a definition that would comprise the fundamental and essential facts of religious life. The various schools did not agree as to the nature of these facts. Tylor saw in animism the groundwork of the philosophy of religion, from that of savages up to that of civilized man; later writers propounded the so-called "Taboo-manna formula" as the minimum definition of religion.[22] Both views were open to many objections. What seems, however, to be incontestable is the fact that religion, from its very beginning, was a question "of life and death." "What is the root of all the beliefs connected with the human soul," asks Malinowski,

with survival after death, with the spiritual elements in the Universe? I think that all the phenomena generally described by such terms as animism, ancestor-worship, or belief in spirits and ghosts, have their root in man's integral attitude towards death. Death . . . is a fact which will always baffle human understanding and fundamentally upset the emotional constitution of man. . . . And here religious revelation steps in and affirms life after death, the immortality of the spirit, the possibilities of communion between living and dead. This revelation gives sense to life, and solves the contradictions and conflicts connected with the transience of human existence on earth.[23]

Plato has given in his *Phaedo* a definition of the philosopher, according to which he is a man who has learned the greatest and

21. See, for instance, the myths of death among the natives of the Trobriand Islands reported by B. Malinowski, *Myth in Primitive Psychology* (London, Kegan Paul, 1926), pp. 80 ff.; (American ed. New York, W. W. Norton, 1926), pp. 60 ff.

22. See Marett, *The Threshold of Religion* (see p. 37, n. 1).

23. B. Malinowski, *The Foundations of Faith and Morals*, Riddell Memorial Lecture (London, Oxford University Press, 1936; pub. for the University of Durham), pp. 27 f.

most difficult art; who knows how to die. Modern thinkers have borrowed this thought from Plato. They declared that the only way to freedom that is left to man is to banish from his mind the fear of death. "He who has learnt to die has forgot what it is to be a slave. To know how to die delivers us from all subjection and constraint." [24] Myth could not give a rational answer to the problem of death. Yet it was myth which, long before philosophy, became the first teacher of mankind, the pedagogue who, in the childhood of the human race, was alone able to raise and solve the problem of death in a language that was understandable to the primitive mind. "Do not try and explain death to me," says Achilles to Odysseus in Hades.[25] But it was just this difficult task that myth had to perform in the history of mankind. Primitive man could not be reconciled with the fact of death; he could not be persuaded to accept the destruction of his personal existence as an inevitable natural phenomenon. But it was the very fact that was denied and "explained away" by myth. Death, it taught, means no extinction of man's life; it means only a change in the form of life. One form of existence is simply exchanged for another. There is no definite and clear-cut boundary between life and death; the border line that separates them is vague and indistinct. Even the two terms may be exchanged one for another. "Who knows," asks Euripides, "if life here be not really death, and death in turn be life?" In mythical thought the mystery of death is "turned into an image"—and by this transformation, death ceases being a hard unbearable physical fact; it becomes understandable and supportable.

24. Montaigne, *Essays*, I, 19, in "Works," trans. by W. Hazlitt, revised ed. by O. W. Wight (New York, H. W. Derby, 1861), I, 130. Montaigne, *Essais*, texte établi et présenté par Jean Plattard, Liv. I, chap. 20 (Paris, Fernand Roches, 1931), 117: "Qui a apris à mourir, il a desapris à servir. Le sçavoir mourir nous afranchit de toute subjection et contrainte."
25. Homer, *Odyssey*, Bk. XI, v. 488.

PART II

THE STRUGGLE AGAINST MYTH IN THE
HISTORY OF POLITICAL THEORY

V

"LOGOS" AND "MYTHOS" IN EARLY
GREEK PHILOSOPHY

A RATIONAL theory of the state came to light in Greek philosophy. Here, as in other fields, the Greeks were the
pioneers of rational thought. Thucydides was the first to
attack the mythical conception of history. The elimination of the
"fabulous" was one of his first and principal concerns.

The absence of romance in my history will, I fear, detract somewhat
from its interest; but if it be judged useful by those inquirers who
desire an exact knowledge of the past as an aid to the interpretation
of the future, which in the course of human things must resemble if it
does not reflect it, I shall be content. My history has been composed
to be a possession for all time, not the show-piece of an ephemeral
hour.[1]

But the Greek conception of history was not only based on new
facts and on a much deeper and more comprehensive psychological insight than had preceded it. The Greeks had also found
a new method that enabled them to see the problem in an entirely
new light. Before studying politics they had studied nature. In
this domain they had made their first great discoveries. Without
this preliminary step it would not have been possible for them
to challenge the power of mythical thought. The new conception
of nature became the common ground for a new conception of
man's individual and social life.

The victory could not be won at one blow. Here too we find
the same slow and methodical procedure that was one of the
most characteristic features of the Greek mind. It is as if the individual thinkers were following a preconceived strategic plan.
One position after another is conquered; the firmest fortifications
are laid low, till, at last, the stronghold of mythical thought is
shaken to its foundations. All the great thinkers and different
philosophical schools have their share in this common work. The

1. Thucydides, *The Peloponnesian War*, Bk. I, chap. xxii. English trans. by
Richard Crawley (Everyman's Library, New York, E. P. Dutton & Co., 1910),
p. 15.

first Greek thinkers, the thinkers of the Milesian school, are described by Aristotle as the "ancient physiologists." Nature (*physis*)
is the only object that attracts their attention. Their approach to
nature is the very opposite of the mythical interpretation of natural phenomena. It is true that, in early Greek thought, the boundaries between the two types of thought were not yet clearly determined but were vague and vacillating. Thales said that "all
things are full of gods," [2] and that the magnet is alive, because it
has the power of moving iron.[3] Empedocles describes nature as a
great struggle between two opposite forces—the forces of love
and strife. At one time all things unite in one through love, at another each is borne in different directions by the repulsion of
strife.[4] Undoubtedly these are mythical conceptions. As a matter
of fact a distinguished historian of Greek philosophy has written
a book in which he tries to show that Greek natural philosophy
was first conceived in a mystical rather than in a scientific spirit.[5]
But this view of the problem is misleading. It is true that the
mythical elements could not be overthrown at once; but they were
offset and counterbalanced by a new tendency of thought that
steadily developed and won an ever-increasing weight. The thinkers of the Milesian school—Thales, Anaximander, Anaximenes—
inquired into the beginning or "origin" of things. That is not a
new trend of thought; what was really new was their definition
of the very term "beginning" (*archē*). In all mythical cosmogo-
nies the origin means a primeval state that belongs to the remote
immemorial mythical past. It has faded away and vanished; it has
been replaced and superseded by other things. The first Greek
natural philosophers understand and define the beginning in quite
a different sense. What they are asking for is not an accidental
fact but a substantial cause. The beginning is not simply a com-
mencement in time but a "first principle"; it is logical rather than
chronological. According to Thales the world *was* not only water,
it *is* water: Water is the abiding and permanent element of all
things. From the element of water or air, from the "Apeiron" of
Anaximander, things have developed not in a haphazard way,

2. Aristotle, *De anima*, Bk. A. 5 411ᵃ 7.
3. *Idem*, Bk. A. 2 405ᵃ 19. See H. Diels, *Fragmente der Vorsokratiker* by W.
Kranz (5th ed. Berlin, Weidmannsche Buchhandlung, 1934), 11 A 22.
4. See Empedocles, Fr. 17, in Diels, *op. cit.*, I, 315.
5. See Karl Joël, *Der Ursprung der Naturphilosophie aus dem Geiste der Mystik*
(Basel, 1903).

according to the whims and caprices of supernatural agents, but in a regular order and according to general rules. The concept of such inalterable and inviolable rules is perfectly strange to mythical thought.

But nature is, after all, only the periphery of the mythical world; it is not its center. It was a much bolder enterprise and required a much greater intellectual courage to direct the attack against this center—against the mythical conceptions of the gods. The two opposite forces that built up Greek philosophy—the philosophy of "Being" and the philosophy of "Becoming"—were united in this attack. The same arguments were used by the Eleatic thinkers and by Heraclitus against the Homeric gods. Heraclitus did not shrink from saying that Homer should be turned out of the lists and whipped because of his misconstruction of the divine.[6] Behind the veils that the imagination of the poets and the myth makers had spun around the nature of divinity, the philosophers attempted to discover its true face. The poets and the myth makers yielded to the common temptation of men; they made their gods in their own image. The Ethiopians, says Xenophanes, make their gods black and snub-nosed, the Thracians give them blue eyes and red hair. And if oxen and horses or lions had hands and could paint with their hands, horses would paint the forms of gods like horses, and oxen like oxen.[7] Xenophanes rejected this mythical imagery for a double reason, speculative and religious. As a speculative thinker he insists that a plurality of gods is inconceivable and contradictory. In a passage of Aristotle's *Metaphysics* Xenophanes is styled "the first partisan of the One." [8] According to the fundamental dogma of the Eleatic school "Being" and "Unity" are convertible terms: *ens et unum convertuntur*. If God has true being, he must have a perfect unity. To speak of many gods who are struggling one against the other, who have their combats and feuds, is absurd from a speculative point of view and blasphemous from a religious and ethical point of view. Homer and Hesiod have ascribed to their gods all things that are a shame and disgrace among mortals: stealing and adultery and deception of one another. To these pseudo-gods Xenophanes opposes his own new and sublime reli-

---

6. Heraclitus, Fr. 42, in Diels, *op. cit.*, I, 160.
7. Xenophanes, Frs. 15, 16, in Diels, *op. cit.*, I, 132 f.
8. Aristotle, *Metaphysica*, Bk. A. 5 986[b] 21.

gious ideal: the conception of a deity that is free from all the limitations of mythical and anthropomorphic thought. There is One god, the greatest among gods and men, who is neither in form nor in thought like unto mortals. He sees all things, thinks of everything, and hears all things whatsoever; and without toil he swayeth all things by the thought of his mind.[9]

But the new conceptions of physical nature introduced by the Milesian school and of divine nature by Heraclitus and the Eleatic thinkers, were only the first and preliminary steps. The greatest and most difficult task still remained to be done. Greek thought had created a new "physiology" and a new "theology"; it had fundamentally changed the interpretation of nature and the conceptions of the deity. But all these victories of rational thought remained precarious and uncertain so long as myth was still in undisputed possession of its firmest stronghold. Myth was not really defeated so long as it had full sway over the human world and dominated man's thoughts and feelings about his own nature and destiny.

We meet with the same historical paradox here as in the criticism of the Homeric gods. The problem could only be solved by a combined and concentrated effort of thought that united two entirely different and diametrically opposed intellectual forces. Here, as in other fields, the unity of Greek thought proved to be a dialectic unity. To put it in the words of Heraclitus it was an attunement of opposite tensions ($\pi\alpha\lambda\acute{\iota}\nu\tau\rho\sigma\pi\sigma\varsigma$ $\dot{\alpha}\rho\mu\sigma\nu\acute{\iota}\eta$), like that of the bow and the lyre.[10] In the development of Greek intellectual culture there is perhaps no stronger tension, no deeper conflict than that between sophistic and Socratic thought. Yet in spite of this conflict the sophists and Socrates were in agreement upon one fundamental postulate. They were convinced that a rational theory of human nature was the first desideratum of any philosophic theory. All the other questions that had been treated in pre-Socratic thought were declared to be secondary and subordinate. From then on man was no longer regarded as a mere part of the universe; he became its center. Man, said Protagoras, is the measure of all things. This tenet holds, in a sense, both for the sophists and for Socrates. To "humanize" philosophy, to turn cosmogony and ontology into anthropology, was their common goal. Yet how-

9. Xenophanes, Frs. 11, 23–25, in Diels, *op. cit.*, I, 132, 135.
10. Heraclitus, Fr. 51, in Diels, *op. cit.*, I, 162.

ever agreeing in the end itself, they entirely disagreed in their means and methods. The very term "man" was understood and interpreted by them in two divergent and even opposite ways. To the sophists "man" meant the individual man. The so-called "universal" man—the man of the philosophers—was to them a mere fiction. They were fascinated by the ever-shifting scenes of human life, especially of public life. It was here that they had to play their roles and to display their talents. They were confronted with immediate, concrete, practical tasks. To all this a general speculative or ethical theory of man could be of no avail. The sophists regarded such theory as an obstacle rather than as a real help. They were not concerned about man's "nature"; they were absorbed in man's practical interests. The multiplicity and variety of man's cultural, social, and political life first aroused their scientific curiosity. They had to organize and control all these various and highly complicated activities, to lead them into definite channels of thought, and to find for them the right technical rules. What is most characteristic of the philosophy of the sophists and of their own minds is their astounding versatility. They felt equal to every task; and they approached all their problems with a new spirit, breaking through all barriers of traditional concepts, common prejudices, and social conventions.

The Socratic problem and the Socratic outlook was entirely different. In a passage of his dialogue *Theaetetus* Plato compares Greek philosophy to a battlefield on which two great armies meet and incessantly combat each other. On the one side we find the partisans of the "Many," on the other the partisans of the "One"; on the one side the "flowing ones," on the other those who try to fix all things and to stabilize all thoughts.[11] If this be true we cannot doubt the place of Socrates in the history of Greek thought and culture. His first and principal effort was one of stabilization. Like Xenophanes and the other Eleatic thinkers he was a resolute champion of the "One." But he is no mere logician or dialectician. He is not primarily interested in the unity of Being nor in the systematic unity of thought. What he is asking for is the unity of the will. In spite of all their talents and of all their multifarious interests—or perhaps because of these multifarious talents and interests—the sophists were unable to solve this problem. They were incessantly moving on the periphery;

11. *Theaetetus,* 181 A.

they never penetrated into the center of human nature and conduct. They did not even realize that there was such a center, and that it could be ascertained by philosophic thought. It is here that the Socratic question begins. According to Socrates the sophists only saw the *scattered remains* of human nature. As a matter of fact there was hardly anything that had not been treated in the writings of the famous sophists of the fifth century. Gorgias, Hippias, Prodicus, Antiphon had dealt with the most heterogeneous subjects. They had written treatises on mathematical and scientific problems, on history and economics, rhetoric and music, linguistics, grammar, and etymology. All this encyclopaedic knowledge is set aside and annulled by Socrates. As regards these different branches of knowledge he confesses his complete ignorance. He knows only *one* art: the art of forming a human soul, of approaching a man and convincing him that he does not understand what life is and means; letting him see the true end and helping him to attain it.

It is obvious that the Socratic ignorance is by no means a merely negative attitude. It represents, on the contrary, a very original and positive ideal of human knowledge and human conduct. What we may call the Socratic skepticism is only a mask, behind which Socrates, following his usual ironic way, hides his ideal. Socrates' skepticism is meant to destroy the many and multifarious ways of knowledge that obscure and make ineffective the only important thing: man's self-knowledge. In the theoretical as well as in the ethical field Socrates' effort was an effort not only of clarification but also of intensification and concentration. According to him it is a fundamental mistake to speak of "wisdom" or "virtue"—*sophia* or *aretē*—in the plural form. He emphatically denies that there is a plurality of knowledge or a plurality of virtues.

The sophists had declared that there are as many "virtues" as there are different classes of men. There is a virtue for men, another for women; a virtue for children, another for adults; a virtue for free men, another for slaves. All this is rejected by Socrates. If this thesis were true human nature would be at variance with itself; it would be diverse, incongruous, and disparate. How could such a disparate and discordant thing ever be brought to a real unity? Are there parts of virtue, asks Socrates in the Platonic dialogue *Protagoras,* in the same way in which there are parts of physical things—in which the mouth, nose, eyes, and ears are parts of a human face? Can man possess one virtue— courage, justice, temperance, holiness—without possessing the whole? [12] Wisdom and virtue have no parts. We destroy their very essence by breaking them into pieces; we must understand and define them as an indivisible whole.

The fundamental difference between Socrates and the sophists appears also in their attitude toward mythical thought. If we take things at their face value it seems that here, at last, we have found a bond linking Socratic to sophistic thought. However opposed the one to the other they were both fighting for a common cause; they had to criticize and purify the traditional conceptions of Greek popular religion. But in this combat, too, their strategy was widely different. The sophists invented a new method that promised a "rational" explanation of the mythical tales. In this field they proved once more the versatility and adaptability of their minds. They became the virtuosi of a new art of allegorical interpretation. By this art every myth, however strange and grotesque, could suddenly be turned into a "truth"—a physical or a moral truth.[13] But Socrates rejected and derided this subterfuge. His problem was different and much more serious. In the beginning of Plato's dialogue *Phaedrus* we are told how Socrates and Phaedrus during a walk are led to a lovely place on the river Ilissus. Phaedrus asks Socrates if that is not the place from which, according to the old legend, Boreas carried off Oreithyia, and he asks whether Socrates believes in the truth of this story. If I disbelieved, answers Socrates, as the wise men (the sophists) do, I would not be embarrassed. I might easily give a very clever explanation by saying that a blast of Boreas, the north wind, pushed Oreithyia off the rocks as she was playing with her playmates and that when she had died in this manner she was said to have been carried off by Boreas.

But I, Phaedrus, think such explanations are very pretty in general, but are the inventions of a very clever and laborious and not altogether enviable man, for no other reason than because after this he must explain the forms of the Centaurs and then that of the Chimaera, and there presses in upon him a whole crowd of such creatures, Gorgons and Pegas, and multitudes of strange, inconceivable, portentous na-

12. Plato, *Protagoras*, 329 D, E.
13. See above, Chapter I, p. 6.

tures. If anyone disbelieves in these, and with a rustic sort of wisdom, undertakes to explain each in accordance with probability, he will need a great deal of leisure. But I have no leisure for them at all; and the reason, my friend, is this: I am not yet able, as the Delphic inscription has it, to know myself; so it seems to me ridiculous, when I do not yet know that, to investigate irrelevant things. And so I dismiss these matters and accepting the customary belief about them, as I was saying just now, I investigate not these things, but myself, to know whether I am a monster more complicated and more furious than Typhon or a gentler and simpler creature, to whom a divine and quiet lot is given by nature.[14]

That was the true Socratic method, as it was understood and interpreted by his greatest disciple. We cannot hope to "rationalize" myth by an arbitrary transformation and re-interpretation of the old legends of the deeds of gods or heroes. All this remains vain and futile. In order to overcome the power of myth we must find and develop the new positive power of "self-knowledge." We must learn to see the whole of human nature in an ethical rather than in a mythical light. Myth may teach man many things; but it has no answer to the only question which, according to Socrates, is really relevant: to the question of good and evil. Only the Socratic "Logos," only the method of self-examination introduced by Socrates, can lead to a solution of this fundamental and essential problem.

14. Plato, *Phaedrus*, 229 C ff. English trans. by H. N. Fowler (Loeb Classical Library, Harvard University Press, Cambridge, Mass., 1933), I, 421.

VI

PLATO'S REPUBLIC

ALL THE great intellectual tendencies that formed Greek culture were preserved in the doctrine of Plato—none of them in its original shape, however. They were molded into a new form by Plato's genius. In his theory of Being, Plato followed the Eleatic thinkers. He always spoke of "Father Parmenides" with the greatest awe and admiration. But that did not prevent him from criticizing, in the sharpest and most penetrating manner, the fundamental principles of Eleatic logic. In his theory of the human soul, moreover, Plato went back to the conceptions of the Pythagoreans and the Orphics. But here, too, we cannot agree with Erwin Rohde that Plato was simply "following in the track of the theologians of earlier times" and that he had in fact borrowed his doctrine of immortality from those sources.[1] When he advanced his own theory based upon his doctrine of ideas, he had to correct the Pythagorean definition of the soul.[2] The same independence of mind appears also in Plato's attitude toward Socrates. He was the most faithful and devoted pupil of Socrates and accepted both his method and his fundamental ethical ideas. Yet even in his first period, in the so-called "Socratic Dialogues," there is one element alien to the thought of Socrates. He had convinced Plato that philosophy had to begin with the problem of man. But according to Plato we cannot answer this Socratic question without enlarging the field of philosophical investigation. We cannot find an adequate definition of man so long as we confine ourselves within the limits of man's individual life. Human nature does not reveal itself in this narrow compass. What is written in "small characters" in the individual soul, and is therefore almost illegible, becomes clear and understandable only if we read it in the larger letters of man's political and social life. This principle is the starting point of Plato's *Republic*.[3] From now on the whole problem of man was changed: politics was declared to be the

1. See Erwin Rohde, *Psyche* (see p. 42, n. 10), pp. 468 ff.
2. See Plato, *Phaedo*, 85 E ff.
3. See *Republic*, 368.

clue to psychology. This was the last and decisive step necessary to the development of Greek thought which had begun with an attempt to conquer nature and continued by asking for rational norms and standards of ethical life. It culminated in a new postulate of a rational theory of the state.

Plato's own intellectual development mirrors all these various stages. In recent literature widely divergent views have been held about the true character of Plato's philosophy. There is one group of scholars who are convinced that Plato was, first and foremost, a metaphysician and a dialectician. They see in Plato's Logic the central part, the core of the Platonic system. Others have stressed the opposite view; they tell us that Plato's interest in politics and education was, from the very beginning, the mainspring and the great formative power of his philosophy.[4] In his *Paideia* Werner Jaeger severely criticizes the former view. According to Jaeger not logic nor theory of knowledge but *politeia* and *paideia* are to be regarded as the two foci of Plato's work. Paideia, says Jaeger, is not a mere external link that keeps the work together; it constitutes its true inner unity. In this regard Rousseau had a much truer conception of Plato's *Republic* than the positivism of the nineteenth century when he said that this work was not a political system, as might be thought from its title, but the first treatise on education ever written.[5]

We need not go here into the details of this much discussed question. In order to find the right answer, we should distinguish between Plato's personal and his philosophical interests. Plato belonged to an aristocratic family that had played a considerable role in Athens' political life. In his youth he may still have cherished the hope of becoming one of the leaders of the Athenian state. But he gave up this hope when he first met Socrates. He then became a student of dialectic and was so much absorbed by his new task that there was a time in which he seemed to have forgotten all political problems and to have resigned all his ambitions. Yet it was dialectic itself that led him back to politics. Plato began to realize that the Socratic demand for self-knowledge

4. As to the first view I refer to Paul Natorp, *Platos Ideenlehre* (Leipzig, 1903; 2d ed. increased by an important appendix, Leipzig, Felix Meiner, 1921); as to the second see Julius Stenzel, *Platon der Erzieher* (Leipzig, Felix Meiner, 1928), and Werner Jaeger, *Paideia* (New York, Oxford University Press, 1943), Vol. II.

5. Jaeger, *op. cit.*, II, 200, 400 f.

could not be fulfilled so long as man was still blind with regard to the principal question and lacked a real insight into the character and the scope of political life. The soul of the individual is bound up with the social nature; we cannot separate the one from the other. Private and public life are interdependent. If the latter is wicked and corrupt, the former cannot develop and cannot reach its end. Plato has inserted in his *Republic* a most impressive description of all the dangers to which an individual is exposed in an unjust and corrupt state. *"Corruptio optimi pessima"*—the best and noblest souls are particularly liable to these dangers.

We know it to be true of any seed or growing thing, whether plant or animal, that if it fails to find its proper nourishment or climate or soil, then the more vigorous it is, the more it will lack the qualities it should possess. Evil is a worse enemy to the good than to the indifferent; so it is natural that bad conditions of nurture should be peculiarly uncongenial to the finest nature and that it should come off worse under them than natures of an insignificant order. . . . So is it, then, with this temperament we have postulated for the philosopher: given the right instruction, it must grow to the full flower of excellence; but if the plant is sown and reared in the wrong soil, it will develop every contrary defect, unless saved by some miracle.[6]

That was the fundamental insight by which Plato, from his first studies in dialectic, was led back to his study of politics. We cannot hope to reform philosophy if we do not begin by reforming the state. That is the only way if we wish to change the ethical life of men. To find the right political order is the first and most urgent problem.

I cannot accept, however, the thesis of Jaeger that Plato regarded the Republic as the "true home of the philosopher." [7] If the Republic means the "earthly state," this judgment is contradicted by Plato himself. To him as well as to St. Augustine the home of the philosopher was the *civitas divina,* not the *civitas terrena.* But Plato did not allow this religious tendency to influence his political judgment. He became a political thinker and a statesman not by inclination but from duty. And he inculcated this duty in the minds of his philosophers. If they would follow their

6. *Republic,* 491. English trans. by F. M. Cornford (Oxford, Clarendon Press, 1941), p. 194.
7. Jaeger, *op. cit.,* pp. 258 ff.

own way they would prefer by far a speculative life to political life. But they must be summoned back to earth, and, if necessary, compelled to participate in the life of the state. The philosopher, the man who constantly holds converse with the divine order, will not easily condescend to return to the political arena.

A man whose thoughts are fixed on true reality has no leisure to look downwards on the affairs of men, to take part in their quarrels, and to catch the infection of their jealousies and hates. He contemplates a world of unchanging and harmonious order, where reason governs and nothing can do or suffer wrong. . . . So the philosopher, in constant companionship with the divine order of the world, will reproduce that order in his soul and, so far as man may, become godlike. . . . Suppose, then, he should find himself compelled to mould other characters besides his own and to shape the pattern of public and private life into conformity with his vision of the ideal, he will not lack the skill to produce such counterparts of temperance, justice, and all the virtues as can exist in the ordinary man.[8]

The conflict between the two tendencies in Plato's thought, the one tending to surpass all limits of the empirical world, the other leading him back to this world in order to organize it and to bring it into rational rules, is never resolved. We find no period in his life in which one of these two forces gained the definitive victory over the other. They are always there, complementing each other and struggling the one with the other. Even after having written his *Republic*, after having become a political reformer, Plato, as a metaphysician and as an ethical thinker, never feels completely at home in his earthly state. He sees all the necessary evils and the inherent defects of this human order. It is impossible, says Plato in the *Theaetetus*, that evil should be done away with, for there must always be something opposed to the good. On the other hand, evil cannot have its place among the gods, but must inevitably hover about mortal nature and this earth. "Therefore we ought to try to escape from here to the dwelling of the gods as quickly as we can; and to escape is to become like God, so far as this is possible; and to become like God is to become righteous and holy and wise." [9] But in spite of his deep yearning for the *unio mystica*, for a complete union be-

8. *Republic*, 500. Cornford trans., p. 204.
9. *Theaetetus*, 176 A. Trans. by H. N. Fowler (Loeb Classical Library [see above, p. 60, n. 14]), II, 128 f.

tween the human soul and God, Plato never could become a mystic in the sense of Plotinus and the other thinkers of the Neo-Platonic school. There is always another power in him to counterbalance the power of mystical thought and feeling.[10] Plato admits no mystical ecstasy by which the human soul can reach an immediate union with God. The highest aim, the knowledge of the idea of the Good, cannot be attained in this way. It needs a careful preparation and a slow methodical ascent. The end cannot be reached by one leap. The idea of the Good in its perfect beauty cannot be seen in a sudden rapture of the human mind. In order to see and understand it the philosopher must choose "the longer way," [11] the way that leads him from arithmetic to geometry, from geometry to astronomy, from mathematics to dialectic.[12] None of these intermediate steps can be left out. The mystical mind in Plato was checked both by his logical and by his political mind. His logic prescribed to him a definite order— a regular ascent and descent. His ethics and politics commanded him always to look back from the "heavenly state" to the human and earthly state and to fulfil its demands and to care for its needs.

It is this "categorical imperative," this demand for order and measure, that determines Plato's attitude toward mythical thought. The clearest expression of this fundamental tendency is to be found in his dialogue *Gorgias*. As Plato points out, the triad of Logos, Nomos, Taxis—Reason, Lawfulness, Order—is the first principle both of the physical and the ethical world. It is this triad that constitutes beauty, truth, morality. It appears in art, in politics, in science, and in philosophy. If regularity and order are found in a house it will be a good and beautiful one; if it appears in a human body we call it health or strength; if it appears in the soul we call it temperance (*sōphrosynē*) or justice. The virtue of each thing, whether of an implement or of a body, or again of a soul or any live creature, does not arrive by accident but by an order of rightness or art that is apportioned to each. "And wise men tell us that heaven and earth and gods and men

10. For the relation between Platonism and Mysticism see Ernst Hoffmann, "Platonismus und Mystik im Altertum," *Sitzungsberichte der Heidelberger Akademie der Wissenschaften, Philosophisch-historische Klasse,* 1934–35, 2. Abhandlung (Heidelberg, Carl Winters Universitätsbuchhandlung, 1935).
11. *Republic,* 504 B.
12. *Idem,* 525 ff.

are held together by communion and friendship, by orderliness, temperance, and justice; and that is the reason why they call the whole of this world by the name of order (kosmos), not of disorder or dissoluteness." The principle of this universal order appears, in a clear and striking way, in geometry. Here it is expressed by the concept of "geometrical equality," of the right proportion between the elements that constitute a geometrical body.[13] We need only transfer this principle from geometry to politics to discover the true constitution of the state. Plato never thought of political life as a detached province, as an isolated part of Being; he finds in it the same fundamental principle that governs the Whole. The political cosmos is only a symbol, and the most characteristic one, of the universal cosmos.

That leads us immediately to the very center of Plato's criticism of mythical thought. It may appear, at first sight, that Plato in his views on popular Greek religion is not very original. All he says had been repeated over and over again since the first beginning of Greek philosophy. He simply resumes the arguments of Xenophanes by saying that the fundamental character of divine nature is its goodness and unity.[14] But he adds a new and very specific feature. He insists that without having found a true and more adequate conception of his gods man cannot hope to order and rule his own human world. As long as we think of the gods, in the traditional way, as fighting or deceiving each other, cities will never cease from ill. For what man sees in the gods is only a projection of his own life—and vice versa. We read the nature of the human soul in the nature of the state—we form our political ideals according to our conceptions of the gods. One thing implies and conditions the other. To the philosopher, to the ruler of the state, it is therefore of vital importance to begin his work at this point. The first step to be taken is to replace the mythical gods by what is described by Plato as the highest knowledge: the "Idea of the Good."

That accounts for one of the most paradoxical features of Plato's *Republic*. Plato's attack on poetry always proves a stumbling block to his critics and commentators. Not only the fact and the manner but also the place of this attack is strange and un-

13. *Gorgias*, 506 E ff. Translated by W. R. M. Lamb (Loeb Classical Library [see above, p. 60, n. 14]), pp. 467 ff.
14. See above, p. 55 f.

usual. No modern writer would ever think of inserting his objections to poetry and art into a work dealing with politics. We see no connection between the two problems. This connection becomes evident, however, if we bear in mind the connecting link: the problem of myth. Obviously we cannot think of Plato as an enemy of poetry. He is the greatest poet in the history of philosophy. In their artistic value many of his dialogues—*Phaedo, Symposium, Gorgias, Phaedrus*—are not inferior to the great Greek works of art. Even in the *Republic* itself Plato could not forbear professing his love and deep admiration for the Homeric poems. But here he was no longer speaking as an individual, and he does not allow himself to be influenced by personal inclinations. He speaks and thinks as a lawgiver who estimates and judges the social and the educational values of art. "You and I," says Socrates addressing Adeimantus, "are not, for the moment, poets, but founders of a commonwealth. As such, it is not our business to invent stories ourselves, but only to be clear as to the main outlines to be followed by the poets in making their stories, and the limits beyond which they must not be allowed to go." [15] What are these limits that no poet, neither the epic nor the lyric and tragic poet, is allowed to transgress? What is combated and rejected by Plato is not poetry in itself, but the myth-making function. To him and to every other Greek both things were inseparable. From time immemorial the poets had been the real myth makers. As Herodotus said, Homer and Hesiod had made the generations of the gods; they had portrayed their shapes and distinguished their offices and powers. [16] Here was the real danger for the Platonic *Republic*. To admit poetry meant to admit myth, but myth could not be admitted without frustrating all philosophic efforts and undermining the very foundations of Plato's state. Only by expelling the poets from the ideal state could the philosopher's state be protected against the intrusion of subversive hostile forces. Plato did not entirely forbid mythical tales; he even admitted that, in the education of a young child, they are indispensable. But they must be brought under a strict discipline. From now on they are to be measured by a higher standard, by that of the "Idea of the Good." If this idea is the essence and the very core of divine nature the conception that God is the

15. *Republic*, 379 A. Cornford trans., p. 69.
16. Herodotus, *History*, II, 53.

author of evil becomes absurd. Such a conception is no longer to be said or sung or heard, neither in verse nor in prose. It is declared to be impious, self-contradictory, and disastrous to the commonwealth.[17]

But all this gives only the negative aspect of Plato's thesis. What compensation was possible for the highest and noblest force that hitherto had determined the form of Greek life and Greek culture? What could he substitute for the work of Homer, Hesiod, Pindar, and Aeschylus? The loss seemed, indeed, to be irreparable. To compete with the *Iliad* and the *Odyssey* and with the great Greek tragedies seemed to be an attempt that was doomed to failure. Yet Plato did not recoil from this attempt. For he was in possession of a new conception that he thought to be far superior to all the previous Greek ideals.

Long before Plato there had appeared Greek thinkers and statesmen who were inspired by the will to reform the state and who were endowed with deep political wisdom. In this sense Solon may be styled the "Creator of Athenian political culture." [18] What distinguished Plato from these first pioneers of political thought was not so much the answer given by him as the question itself. As to the answer we may criticize it very severely. Many features of the Platonic doctrine that he himself thought to be eternal and universal may now easily be recognized as accidental. They depend upon special conditions of Greek social life. Plato's tripartite division of the human soul, and the corresponding division of the social classes, his views about the community of property or the community of wives and children—all this is open to grave objection. But all these objections cannot detract from the fundamental value and merit of his political work. Its greatness depends on the new *postulate* introduced by Plato. This postulate was unforgettable. It stamped the whole future development of political thought.

Plato began his study of the social order with a definition and an analysis of the concept of justice. The state has no other and no higher aim than to be the administrator of justice. But in Plato's language the term justice does not mean the same as in common speech. It has a much deeper and more comprehensive

17. See *Republic*, 380. Cornford trans., p. 70.
18. See the chapter on "Solon" in Jaeger's *Paideia* (see above, p. 62, n. 4) (1939), I, 134–147.

meaning. Justice is not on the same level with other virtues of man. It is not, like courage or temperance, a special quality or property. It is a general principle of order, regularity, unity, and lawfulness. Within the individual life this lawfulness appears in the harmony of all the different powers of the human soul; within the state it appears in the "geometrical proportion" between the different classes, according to which each part of the social body receives its due and coöperates in maintaining the general order. With this conception Plato became the founder and the first defender of the Idea of the Legal State.

Plato was the first to introduce a "theory" of the state, not as a knowledge of many and multifarious facts, but as a coherent system of thought. Political problems in the fifth century were in the center of the intellectual interest. More and more "wisdom" (*sophia*) tended to become political wisdom. All the famous sophists regarded their doctrine as the best, and indeed, as an indispensable introduction into political life. "Who will listen to me," says Protagoras in the Platonic dialogue which bears his name, "will learn to order his own house and he will be best able to speak and act in the affairs of the state." [19] Long before Plato the question of the "best state" had been often and eagerly discussed. But Plato is not concerned with this question. What he is asking for is not the best but the "ideal" state. That makes a fundamental difference. It is one of the first principles of Plato's theory of knowledge to insist upon the radical distinction between empirical and ideal truth. What experience gives is, at best, a right opinion about things; it is not real knowledge. The difference between these two types, between *doxa* and *episteme*, is ineffaceable. Facts are variable and accidental; truth is necessary and immutable. A man may be a statesman in the sense that he has formed a right opinion about political things and that he has a natural talent which, in Plato's language, is described as a gift of the gods (θεία μοῖρα). Yet that does not enable him to give a firm judgment, because he has no "understanding of the cause." [20]

According to this principle Plato had to reject all mere practical attempts to reform the state. His was quite a different task: he had to *understand* the state. What he demanded and what he was looking for was not a mere accumulation or an experimental study of

19. Plato, *Protagoras*, 318 E.
20. *Meno*, 97 A ff., 99 E.

segregated and haphazard facts of man's political and social life but an idea that could comprehend these facts and bring them to a systematic unity. He was convinced that without such a unifying principle of thought all our practical attempts are doomed to failure. There must be a "theory" of politics, not a mere routine work of empirical prescriptions.[21] All mere experience, without a dialectic, a conceptual foundation, is declared by Plato to be vain and futile.[22] When a man does not know his own first principle, and his results are constructed out of he knows not what, how can he think that such a fabric of convention can ever become science? [23] As Plato says in his *Gorgias,* true politics is distinguished from ordinary political practice and routine as cookery is distinguished from medicine. Cookery goes to work in an utterly untheoretical way ($\dot{\alpha}\tau\acute{\epsilon}\chi\nu\omega\varsigma$), whereas medicine has investigated the nature of the person whom it treats and the cause of its proceedings, and can give an account of each of these things.[24]

This urge for "causes" (*aitiai*) and "first principles" was the radical innovation of Plato. Personally and practically we cannot speak of him as a radical. We may describe him as a conservative; we may even charge him with being a reactionary. But that is not the decisive question. His was an intellectual not a political revolution. He did not begin with a criticism of a special political constitution. In his *Republic* he gives us a systematic survey of all the different forms of government and of the mental attitudes of the "souls" which correspond to these forms. There is the ambitious nature, the oligarchic, the democratic, and the tyrannical nature. And each of them answers to a particular constitution—to timocracy, to plutocracy, ochlocracy, tyranny.[25] All this is determined by definite rules: each constitution has its virtue and its vice, its merits and its disadvantages, its constructive principle and its inherent defect that leads to deterioration and decay. In this theory of the rise and decline of constitutions Plato speaks as a keen observer of political phenomena. His description is a very "realistic" one. He does not conceal his personal predilections or antipathies; but all this does not influence or obscure his judgment. There is

21. See the distinction between *empeiria* (experience) and *technē* (knowledge, theory), *Republic,* 409 B; *Gorgias,* 465 A ff., 501 A.
22. *Symposium,* 203 A; *Republic,* 496 A, 522 B f.
23. *Republic,* 533 B.
24. *Gorgias,* 501 A.
25. Cf. *Republic,* 543 ff.

only one thing that he absolutely rejects and condemns: the tyrannic soul and the tyrannic state. They are to him the worst corruption and degeneracy. As to the others he gives of them a very careful and penetrant analysis that shows an entirely open mind. He insists upon all the defects of Athenian democracy; but, on the other hand, he does not accept the Lacedaemonian state as a real model. The model he is looking for is far beyond the empirical and historical world. No historical phenomenon is adequate to the ideal pattern of the state, for, as he says in his *Phaedo,* the phenomena "aim at being" but fall short and are unable to be like their archetypes.[26] Not for a moment could Plato think of putting on the same level a given empirical fact and his Idea of the Legal State—the state of justice. That would have meant the denial of the fundamental principle of Platonism. In a passage of his *Laws* Plato declares that the poems of Tyrtaeus which praise the Spartan ideal of courage should be rewritten and that the glorification of military courage should be replaced by that of higher and nobler things.[27] "In spite of all Plato's respect for Sparta, and all he borrows from it," says Jaeger, "his educational state is really not the pinnacle of admiration for Sparta's ideal, but the severest blow that ideal ever suffered. It is a prophetic anticipation of its weakness."[28]

All this becomes understandable if we bear in mind that Plato had to solve a problem very different from that of any other political reformer. He could not simply replace one political system or form of government by another and better one. He had to introduce a new method and a new postulate into political thought. In order to create the rational theory of the state, he had to lay the ax to the tree: he had to break the power of myth. But here Plato encountered the greatest difficulties. He could not solve the problem without, in a certain sense, surpassing himself and going beyond his own limits. Plato felt the whole charm of myth. He was endowed with a most powerful imagination that enabled him to become one of the greatest myth makers in human history. For we cannot think of Platonic philosophy without thinking of the Platonic myths. In these myths—in the myths of the "supercelestial place," of the prisoners in the cave, of the soul's choice of its future

26. *Phaedo,* 74 D.
27. *Laws,* 665, 666.
28. Jaeger, *op. cit.,* II, 329 f.

destiny, of the judgment after death, Plato expressed his most profound metaphysical thoughts and intuitions. And at the end he
gave his natural philosophy in an entirely mythical form: he introduced, in *Timaeus*, the conceptions of the demiurge, of the good
and the evil world soul, of the twofold creation of the world.

How is it to be accounted for that the same thinker who admitted mythical concepts and mythical language so readily into
his metaphysics and his natural philosophy spoke in an entirely
different vein when developing his political theories? For in this
field Plato became the professed enemy of myth. If we tolerate
myth in our political systems, he declared, all our hopes for a
reconstruction and reformation of our political and social life are
lost. There is only one alternative: we have to make our choice
between an ethical and a mythical conception of the state. In the
Legal State, the state of justice, there is no room left for the
conceptions of mythology, for the gods of Homer and Hesiod.
"Shall we simply allow our children to listen to any stories that
anyone happens to make up, and so to receive into their minds
ideas often the very opposite of those we shall think they ought
to have when they are grown up? No, certainly not. It seems, then,
our first business will be to supervise the making of fables and
legends, rejecting all which are unsatisfactory; and we shall in-
duce nurses and mothers to tell their children only those which
we have approved, and to think more of molding their souls with
these stories than they now do of rubbing their limbs to make
them strong and shapely." If we continue to speak of the wars
in heaven, of the plots and fightings of the gods against one another, of the battles of the giants and all the innumerable other
quarrels of gods and heroes with their friends and relatives, we
shall never find order, harmony, unity in our own human world.[29]

This conception entails another important consequence. If we
abandon the mythical gods we suddenly seem to lose our ground.
We no longer live in the atmosphere which appears to be the
vital element of social life, the atmosphere of tradition. In all
primitive societies tradition is the supreme and inviolable law.
Mythical thought does not acknowledge any other or any higher
authority.[30] What is held here in the highest esteem is, to put it
in the words of Schiller's Wallenstein, the "eternal yesterday":

29. See *Republic*, 377 f. Cornford trans., pp. 67 f.
30. See above, Chapter IV, p. 37 f.

"Whatever was, and ever more returns
Sterling to-morrow, for to-day 'twas sterling." [31]

To break the power of the "eternal yesterday" became one of
the first and principal tasks of Plato's political theory. Yet here
he had to overcome the strongest resistance. Even in modern
philosophy and even by the great champions of rationalism we
are often told that custom and habit are the very constituents,
the indispensable conditions of political life. "The striving for a
morality of one's own," said Hegel in his treatise concerning the
scientific methods of treating natural right, "is futile and by its
very nature impossible of attainment. In regard to morality the
saying of the wisest men of antiquity is the only true one—to be
moral is to live in accordance with the moral traditions of one's
country." [32] If this were true, we could not reckon Plato among
the wisest men of antiquity. For he constantly rejected and attacked this view. He declared that to build our moral and political life upon tradition meant to build on shifting sands. Whoever
trusts in the mere power of tradition, whoever proceeds only by
practice and routine, says Plato in his *Phaedrus*, acts like a blind
man who has to grope his way. Yet surely he who pursues any
study in the method of science (*technē*) ought not to be comparable to a blind or a deaf man. He must have a lodestar—a
guiding principle of his thought and of his actions. [33] Tradition
cannot play this role—for it is blind itself. It is following rules
that it can neither understand nor justify. Implicit faith in tradition can never be the standard of a true moral life. In his *Phaedo*
Plato speaks with disdain and irony of certain types of men who
think themselves righteous and just simply by accepting all the
conventional rules of morality and by following meticulously all
written statutes. These are mild and harmless creatures, he says,
but from the point of view of a higher and of a really conscious
morality, they are of little worth. If we accept the Orphic and
Pythagorean doctrine of a transmigration of souls, and if we think
that, after the death of man, his soul will be emprisoned in creatures which correspond to the practices of his former life, then
we must say that those who have chosen injustice and tyranny

31. Schiller, *Wallensteins Tod,* Act I, Sc. 4. Coleridge trans.
32. See Hegel, "Werke," ed. Ph. Marheinecke (2d ed.), I, 389. For a detailed
discussion of Hegel's theory see Chapter XVI.
33. *Phaedrus,* 270 D, E.

and robbery pass into the bodies of wolves and hawks and kites. But those who have obeyed the rules of conventional morality, who, by nature and habit, have practiced the social and civil virtues, they will pass again into some such social and gentle species as that of bees or wasps or ants.[34]

There was, however, still another barrier that had to be removed, and another adversary overcome, before Plato could establish his own theory of the Legal State. He had to struggle not only with the power of tradition but also with the very opposite power—a theory that repudiated all conventional and traditional standards and tried to build up the political and social world upon an entirely new basis. The conception of the Power State had become prevalent in all the sophistical theories. It was not always openly admitted and defended, but there was a general feeling and a tacit consent that this conception was the only one that could make an end to all vain and superfluous discussions about the "best state." The thesis that "might is right" was the simplest, the most plausible and radical formula. It appealed not only to the "wise men" or sophists but also to the practical men, the leaders of Athenian politics. To attack and destroy this dictum was the principal concern of Plato's theory.

The first attack was made in the *Gorgias,* in the dialogue between Socrates and Callicles, the second was made in the first book of the *Republic* in the duel between Socrates and Thrasymachus. Plato never made any attempt to enfeeble the thesis of his opponents; on the contrary he gave it its greatest strength and its full persuasive power. But it is precisely by this culmination and climax that the thesis finally refutes itself. Plato's method may be said to be a sort of psychological *reductio ad absurdum.* What is the nature and the aim of every desire and passion? he asks. Obviously we do not wish for the sake of wishing—we aim at a certain end and we try to attain this end. But the lust of power does not admit of any possible attainment. It is the very character and essence of the will to power that it is inexhaustible. It can never come to a rest; it is a thirst that is unquenchable. Those who spend their lives in this passion are comparable to the Danaïdes: they strive to pour water into a leaking butt. The appetite for power is the clearest example of that fundamental vice that, in Plato's language, is described as "pleonexia"—as the "hunger

34. *Phaedo,* 82 A, B.

for more and more." This craving for more and more exceeds all measure and destroys all measure—and since measure, right proportion, "geometrical equality" had been declared by Plato to be the standard of the health of private and public life, it follows that the will to power, if it prevails over all other impulses, necessarily leads to corruption and destruction. "Justice" and the "will to power" are the opposite poles of Plato's ethical and political philosophy. Justice is the cardinal virtue that includes all the other great and noble qualities of the soul; the greed for power entails all fundamental defects. Power can never be an end in itself; for that only can be called a good that leads to a definitive satisfaction, to a concord and harmony. No other thinker had such a clear insight into what the Power State really is and means, and no other writer has given such a clear, impressive, and penetrating description of its true nature and character as Plato did in his *Gorgias*.[35]

Plato's philosophy comes from two different sources but these two sources flow together to form one mighty stream of thought. He began as a disciple of Socrates. He accepted the Socratic thesis that "happiness" is the highest aim of every human soul. On the other hand he insisted, with Socrates, that the "pursuit of happiness" is not the pursuit of pleasure. The two things are diametrically opposed the one to the other. The Greek term for happiness is "eudaimonia"—and eudaimonia means to possess a "good demon." To this Socratic definition Plato added a new feature. At the end of his *Republic* he gives his famous description of the soul's choice of its future life. Here too a mythical motive is turned into its very contrary. In mythical thought man is possessed by a good or evil demon; in Plato's theory man *chooses* his demon. This choice determines his life and his future destiny. Man ceases being under the iron grip of a superhuman, divine, or demonic force. He is a free agent who has to take full responsibility. "The blame is his who chooses; Heaven is blameless." [36] To Plato happiness, eudaimonia, means inner freedom—a freedom that does not depend upon accidental and external circumstances. It depends upon the harmony, the "right proportion" in man's own being. "Reason" (*phronēsis*) is the condition of temperance and moderation (*sōphrosynē*)—and this moderation

35. *Gorgias*, 466 B ff.
36. *Republic*, 617. Cornford trans., p. 346.

alone can give the right temper to man's personality and to all his actions.[37]

All this is strictly Socratic but at the same time it goes far beyond all the ethical conceptions of Socrates. The Socratic ideal was transferred by Plato to a new sphere, that of political life. According to the parallel drawn by Plato between the individual soul and the soul of the state it is clear that the state too is under the same obligation. Instead of accepting its fate, it has to create it. To rule others it must first learn to rule itself. But this is an ethical end which cannot be attained by a display of sheer physical force. It was the radical error of the leaders of Athenian politics that they completely failed to see this point. They identified the well-being of the state with its physical welfare. Even the greatest and noblest souls, men like Miltiades or Pericles, were liable to this error. They were not equal to the real task of statecraft and political leadership; they missed the mark because they never succeeded in "making the souls of the citizens better." [38] Not only the individual man but also the state has to choose its demon. That is the great and revolutionary principle of Plato's *Republic.* Only by choosing a "good demon" can a state secure its eudaimonia, its real happiness. We cannot leave the attainment of this highest goal to mere chance, nor can we hope to find it by a stroke of luck. In social life as well as in individual life rational thought (*phronēsis*) must take the leading part. It must show us the way and illuminate the way from the first to the last step. The welfare of a state is not its increase in physical power. The desire to have "more and more" is just as disastrous in the life of a state as in individual life. If the state yields to this desire, that is the beginning of its end. The enlargement of its territory, the superiority over its neighbors, the advance in its military or economic power, all this cannot avert the ruin of the state but rather hastens it. The self-preservation of the state cannot be secured by its material prosperity nor can it be guaranteed by the maintenance of certain constitutional laws. Written constitutions or legal charters have no real binding force, if they are not the expression of a constitution that is written in the citizens' minds. Without this moral support the very strength of a state becomes its inherent danger.

37. *Gorgias,* 506 C ff.
38. *Idem,* 503 B ff.

All this shows us once more the unbroken unity of Plato's thought. In his philosophical doctrine we do not find that specialization which was introduced by later thinkers. His whole work was from the same mold. Dialectic, theory of knowledge, psychology, ethics, politics, all this was fused together in one coherent and inseparable whole. It bears the stamp of Plato's philosophical genius and of his personality. This holds also for Plato's attitude toward mythical thought. His struggle against myth followed from his conception and his very definition of dialectic. In the dialogue *Philebus* Plato points out that all things whatever are composed of two different and opposed elements: of "limit" (*peras*) and the "unlimited" or "undeterminate" (*apeiria*). It is for dialectic to bridge the gulf between these two opposite poles: to determine the undeterminate, to reduce the infinite to fixed measures, to set bounds to the boundless.[39] If we accept this definition of philosophy and dialectic it becomes clear why Plato had to exclude myth from his *Republic,* that is to say, from his system of education. Of all things in the world myth is the most unbridled and immoderate. It exceeds and defies all limits; it is extravagant and exorbitant in its very nature and essence. To banish this dissolute power from the human and political world was one of the principal aims of the *Republic.* Plato's logic and dialectic teach us how to classify and systematize our concepts and thought; how to make the right divisions and subdivisions. Dialectic, says Plato, is the art of dividing things by classes, according to their natural joints, and not trying to break any part after the manner of a bad carver.[40] Ethics shows us how to rule over emotions; how to moderate them by virtue of reason and temperance. Politics is the art of unifying and organizing human actions and directing them to a common end. Thus the Platonic parallel between the individual soul and the soul of the state is by no means a mere figure of speech or a simple analogy. It is the expression of Plato's fundamental tendency: the tendency to unify the manifold, to bring the chaos of our minds, of our desires and passions, of our political and social life into a cosmos, into order and harmony.

39. *Philebus,* 16 D ff.
40. *Phaedrus,* 265 E.

VII

THE RELIGIOUS AND METAPHYSICAL
BACKGROUND OF THE MEDIEVAL
THEORY OF THE STATE

Plato's theory of the Legal State became an everlasting possession of human culture. It could exert a deep and permanent influence, for it was not bound to special historical conditions or to a particular cultural background. It survived the breakdown of Greek life and politics. Seven centuries later St. Augustine could take up the problem in the same shape in which it had been left by Plato. The very title of his work is borrowed. "There is a pattern set up in the heavens," said Plato in the *Republic*, "for one who desires to see it and, seeing it, to found one in himself. But whether it exists anywhere or ever will exist is no matter; for this is the only commonwealth in whose politics he can ever take part." [1]

Medieval culture was, however, not the immediate result of Greek thought. With the rise of Christianity there had appeared a stronger power which henceforth absorbed all human theoretical and practical interests. Plato's ideal state was beyond space of time; it had no "here" and "now." It was a *paradeigma*: a standard and pattern for human actions, but it had no definite ontological status, no place in reality. St. Augustine could not accept this solution. In Christian thought the "ideal" and the "real" world do not bear the same relation to each other as in Greek speculation. The world of sense-experience, of fleeting and changing phenomena, not only expresses or imitates the intelligible world but it is a result and outgrowth of this intelligible world. In the Christian religion the Platonic category of "participation" (*methexis*) had been changed into the dogma of creation and incarnation. In the doctrine of Augustine the Platonic ideas have become the thoughts of God. In accordance with this transformation all concepts of ancient philosophy had to undergo a radical change. "You see what we should strive towards as through a

1. Plato, *Republic*, 592. Cornford trans., pp. 312 f.

veil," says Augustine in the *City of God* addressing the Neo-Platonic philosophers.

The incarnation of the unchangeable Son of God, whereby we are saved and are enabled to reach the things we believe, . . . this is what you refuse to recognize. You see in a fashion, . . . although with filmy eye, the country in which we should abide; but the way to it you know not. . . . But in order to your acquiescence in this truth, it is lowliness that is requisite, and to this it is extremely difficult to bend you. . . . This is the vice of the proud. It is a degradation for learned men to pass from the school of Plato to the discipleship of Christ who by His Spirit taught a fisherman to think and to say "In the beginning was the Word, and the Word was with God, and the Word was God." [2]

That was the great metamorphosis brought about by Christian thought: the transition from the Greek to the Christian "Logos." Augustine is longing for another world—far beyond the world of Greek intellectual culture. Even in the ideal state, as described by Plato, Augustine could not find a fixed pole, a point in which to rest. The state, even the most perfect state, cannot satisfy our desires. The only real repose for man is the repose in God. "Fecisti nos ad te domine," says Augustine in the beginning of his *Confessions*, "et inquietum est cor nostrum, donec requiescat in te"— "Thou hast formed us unto Thyself, and our hearts are restless till they find rest in Thee." Unhappy is the man who knows all terrestrian and celestial things, but knows Thee not, but happy is he who knows Thee though these he may not know. [3] In Plato's theory man had to choose the "longer way" to attain the idea of the good and to understand its nature: the way that leads from arithmetic to geometry, from geometry to astronomy, harmonics, and dialectic. [4] Augustine rejects this longer and circuitous way The revelation of Christ has taught him a better and surer access. "The good," he says, "that must be sought for the soul is not one above which it is to fly by judging, but to which it is to cleave by loving; and what can this be except God? Not a good mind, or a good angel, or the good heaven, but the good good." [5] There are

2. St. Augustine, *City of God*, Bk. X, chap. xxix. English trans. by M. Dods, "The Works of Augustine" (Edinburgh, T. and T. Clark, 1871 ff.), I, 423–426.
3. *Confessions*, Bk. V, chap. iv, 7.
4. *Republic*, 521 C–531 C.
5. *De trinitate*, Bk. VIII, chap. iii. Dods trans., VII, 205.

not many sciences or many wisdoms; there is only one wisdom in which are untold and infinite treasures of things intellectual wherein are all invisible and unchangeable reasons of things visible and changeable which were created by it.[6]

What separated Augustine from Plato was, therefore, not a philosophical conception but his view of life. As a philosopher he felt the highest admiration for Plato's work. "Among the disciples of Socrates," he said, "Plato was the one who shone with a glory which far excelled that of the others, and who not unjustly eclipsed them all." [7] Nevertheless Augustine could never become a "Platonist." His knowledge of Plato's works was scanty; he knew no Greek and could not read the dialogues in the original text. He saw the Platonic doctrine only in a sort of refractor: through the medium of Cicero and Neo-Platonic writers.[8] Yet even if Augustine had known the whole work of Plato and had made a profound study of it, he would not have changed his judgment. He declared all learning and philosophical speculation to be null and void in so far as it does not lead us to the principal goal, the knowledge of God. "God and the soul," he said, "that is what I desire to know. Nothing else? Absolutely nothing." [9]

These words are in a sense the clue to the whole philosophy of the Middle Ages. Philosophy is the love of wisdom. But in the medieval system there was no room for two different loves: the love of wisdom and the love of God. The one was dependent on the other. "The fear of the Lord is the beginning of Wisdom." When Plato tried to define and determine his ideal of justice, he spoke of it in terms of geometry; he described it as "geometrical equality." And geometry means to him something *eternal and immutable.* Geometrical truth has not been "made" by anyone: it simply "is." Geometry is a knowledge of what eternally exists, not of anything that comes to be this or that at some time and ceases to be.[10] If this analogy between ethics and geometry holds, we cannot speak of an "origin" of ethical laws. They have no origin; they have always been what they are, and they will al-

6. *City of God,* Bk. XI, chap. x, 3. Dods trans., I, 450.

7. *Idem,* Bk. VIII, chap. iv. Dods trans., I, 310.

8. See Ernst Hoffmann, "Platonism in Augustine's Philosophy of History," *Philosophy and History, Essays Presented to Ernst Cassirer* (Oxford, Clarendon Press, 1936), pp. 173–190.

9. *Soliloquia,* Lib. I, cap. i, 7.

10. *Republic,* 527. Cornford trans., p. 238.

ways remain the same. In this point Plato is in complete harmony with the general trend of Greek thought and culture. He expresses, in his philosophical language, the same conviction as the great Greek tragic poets Aeschylus and Sophocles. The "unwritten laws," the laws of justice, have no beginning in time; they have not been created by any human or divine power:

> "Not of to-day nor yesterday, the same
> Throughout all time they live; and whence they came
> None knoweth." [11]

This Greek conception of an eternal and impersonal law was unacceptable and incomprehensible to the Christian thinkers of the Middle Ages. They were not primarily concerned with the solution of speculative problems. In a theoretical sense they were and remained simply the heirs of Greek thought and it was not here that they could find their real inspiration. The deepest and preëminent source of their philosophical conceptions and religious ideals was Jewish monotheism. Between the *philosophic* monotheism of the Greek thinkers and the *religious* monotheism of the Jewish prophets we may find many points of contact. Christian thinkers have often insisted upon their perfect harmony. Marsilius Ficinus used to speak of Plato as the "Attic Moses."

Nevertheless it is impossible to put the Mosaic and the Platonic conception of the law on the same level. They are not only widely divergent but incompatible. The Mosaic law presupposes a *lawgiver*. Without this lawgiver who reveals the law and guarantees its truth, its validity, and its authority, the law becomes meaningless. This idea is far removed from what we find in Greek philosophy. The ethical systems developed by the Greek thinkers, Socrates and Democritus, Plato and Aristotle, Stoics and Epicureans, have a common feature. They are all expressions of one and the same fundamental *intellectualism* of Greek thought. It is by rational thought that we are to find the standards of moral conduct, and it is reason, and reason alone, that can give them their authority. In contrast with this Greek *intellectualism* prophetic religion is characterized by its deep and resolute *voluntarism*.

11. Sophocles, *Antigone*, vv. 456 ff. Gilbert Murray trans. (London, George Allen & Unwin, 1941), p. 38.

God is a person—and that means a will. No mere logical methods of arguing and reasoning can make us understand this will. God must reveal himself, he must speak to us, he must make known his commandments. The prophets reject all other kinds of communion with the deity. Man cannot get in touch with the divine by the performance of physical acts, by rituals or ceremonies. The only way of knowing God is by the fulfilment of his demands; the only way of communicating with him is not by prayers or sacrifices but by obedience to his will. "This shall be the covenant that I will make with the house of Israel," says Jeremiah: "I will put my law in their inward parts and write it in their hearts." [12] "He has shewed thee, O man," says Micah, "what is good; and what does the Lord require of thee, but to do justly, and to love mercy, and to walk humbly with thy God." [13] Here God is not, as in Greek thought, described as the summit of the intellectual world, as the highest object of knowledge, the knowledge of the Good. It is from God himself, from the revelation of his will, not from dialectic, that man has to learn good and evil.

The conflict between these two tendencies pervades the whole scholastic philosophy and determines its course throughout the centuries from St. Augustine to Thomas Aquinas. The perpetual struggles between "theologians" and "dialecticians" become clear and understandable if we trace them back to their historical origin in the tension between the speculative elements that had to be borrowed from Greek thought and the purport, the ethical and religious meaning, of Jewish and Christian revelation. Theoretically speaking Christian thought cannot claim any real originality. None of the Fathers of the Church spoke as a philosopher; nor did any of them intend to introduce a new philosophical principle. But the very formula of the Christian dogma and the commentaries given by the Fathers of the Church show the profound imprint of Greek thought.[14] Hellenism always remained one of the strongest elements of medieval philosophy. Yet, in spite of this perduring influence of Hellenism, medieval culture is radically different from Greek culture. Even those elements that seem to be preserved had to undergo a profound change of meaning before they could be fitted into the medieval system. This change

12. Jeremiah 31.33.
13. Micah 6.8.
14. See E. Gilson, *La philosophie au moyen âge* (Paris, Payot, 1922), pp. 5 ff.

appears not only in the field of religious and ethical life; it is no less evident in all theoretical conceptions. The scholastic thinkers did not develop a separate and independent theory of knowledge. In this respect they had to rely upon the Greek tradition entirely. Their thoughts about this subject seem to be nothing but a sort of eclecticism—a mixture of Platonic, Aristotelian, and Stoic conceptions. Even here we cannot speak of a simple imitation or reproduction. No entirely new feature is added but everything has assumed a new shape because it is seen in a new perspective and referred to a new center: the religious life.

Augustine is the first and the classical witness of this process of thought. His theory of knowledge is impregnated with Platonic elements. Plato's theory of reminiscence (anamnēsis) has put its stamp upon Augustine's doctrine. He likes to quote the example of the young slave in Plato's *Meno* who, by his own efforts and by a purely rational process of thought, succeeds in discovering some fundamental geometrical truths. To learn means to remember: "nec aliud quidquam esse id quod dicitur discere quam reminisci et recordari." [15] It is impossible that the human soul can learn anything from outward objects: all it knows and learns it knows by itself and from sources within. Self-knowledge is the first and indispensable step. It is not only the prerequisite to all knowledge of an external reality but also to all knowledge of God. "Noli foras ire, in te ipsum redi; in interiore homine habitat veritas," says Augustine. ("Do not go out of thyself, return to thyself, it is in the interior essence of man that the truth resides.") [16] This is entirely in the spirit of the Greek classical tradition and of Socrates, Plato and Stoicism. But after this there follow the words that mark the sharp difference. The truth resides in the interior of man; but what man finds here is only a mutable and inconstant truth. In order to find an unchangeable, an absolute truth man has to go beyond the limit of his own consciousness and his own existence. He has to surpass himself. "Si tuam naturam mutabilem inveneris, transcende et te ipsum . . . illuc tende, unde ipsum lumen rationis accenditur." [17] By this transcendence the whole method of dialectic, the Socratic and Pla-

---

15. Augustine, *De quantitate animae*, cap. xx, 34.
16. Augustine, *De vera religione*, cap. xxxix, 72.
17. *Ibid.* "Transcend thyself . . . turn thither from which the light of reason itself is kindled."

tonic method, is completely changed. Reason gives up its independence and autonomy. It has no longer a light of its own; it shines only in a borrowed and reflected light. If this light fails, human reason becomes ineffective and impotent.

The clearest expression of this fundamental metamorphosis of Greek classical thought is to be found in Augustine's treatise *De magistro*.[18] Here Augustine objects to the very ideal of a purely human wisdom and the concept of a human teacher. From the Christian point of view the only master, not only the master of human conduct but also the master of human thoughts, is God. In him, and in him alone, we find the true *magisterium*. All knowledge whatever, the knowledge of the sensible world as well as mathematical or dialectic knowledge, is based upon an illumination by this eternal source of light. Every rational process of thinking or arguing is such an illumination and, therefore, an act of divine grace. God is "pater veritatis, pater sapientiae, . . . pater intelligibilis lucis," "pater evigilationis atque illuminationis nostrae": the father of the intelligible light and the father of our enlightenment.[19]

It is impossible to account for this radical change in the theory of knowledge in a mere logical way. Logically speaking the Augustinian theory of illumination always remained a great paradox. Most of the scholastic thinkers were perfectly aware of this paradoxical character of the doctrine. They tried to modify the principle of Augustinianism; and in the end these principles were overthrown and replaced by that new conception of human knowledge which was introduced by Thomas Aquinas on the authority of Aristotle. Augustine's theory becomes, however, very clear and transparent if, instead of asking for its mere logical or speculative reasons, we approach it by way of its historical origin. Augustine could accept all the presuppositions of the Platonic doctrine of the ideal world. As he points out in his *Retractationes*, Plato was right in his fundamental conception of the truth and reality of an intelligible world. What is objectionable is not the Platonic conception as such but the *terms* in which Plato expressed his thought; for these terms are not appropriate to Christian or

18. "Patrologia Latina," ed. Jacob Migne, Tom. 32, col. 1193–1220.

19. See Augustine, *Soliloquia*, Lib. I, cap. I, 2; cf. *De civitate Dei*, Lib. X, cap. II: ". . . animam rationalem vel intellectualem . . . sibi lumen esse non posse, sed alterius veri luminis participatione lucere."

ecclesiastical language.[20] If Augustine speaks of logic or geometry, if he speaks of ideas as the eternal archetypes of things, if he compares the highest spiritual good to the light of the sun which illuminates the physical world, if he praises the power of number and of form, in which all things partake and from which they derive their beauty,[21] we often believe we hear Plato himself. There remains, however, a great and ineffaceable difference. All the terms of Augustine must be read and interpreted in the sense of his religious experience. It is this that gives all his concepts a new tinge, if not an entirely new meaning.

The *itinerarium mentis in Deum*,[22] the itinerary of the human soul to God, as it is described by the medieval speculative thinkers, is widely different from the Platonic description of the ascent of the soul to the intelligible world. Plato begins with the first elements of human knowledge. His path leads, in a continuous progress, from arithmetic to geometry, from here to stereometry and astronomy, from mathematics and astronomy to dialectic—and, at the end, to the highest knowledge, the knowledge of the good. Only the philosopher, the dialectician is able to traverse the whole road that leads from the sensible to the intellectual world. And even to him the idea of the good does not reveal its whole nature and full meaning. When Socrates in the *Republic* begins to speak about the good, he speaks tentatively and hesitatingly. He cannot promise to define its essence; he can only show its effects. "We should be quite content with an account of the Good," says Glaucon, "like the one you gave us of justice and temperance and the other virtues." "So should I be," replies Socrates,

much more than content. But I am afraid, it is beyond my powers; with the best will in the world I should only disgrace myself and be laughed at. No, for the moment let us leave the question of the real meaning of good; to arrive at what I at any rate believe it to be would call for an effort too ambitious for an inquiry like ours. However, I will tell you . . . what I picture to myself as the offspring of the Good and the thing most nearly resembling it.[23]

20. Augustine, *Retractationes*, Lib. I, cap. iii.
21. Cf. Augustine, *De libero arbitrio*, Lib. II, cap. xvi, 42; *De vera religione*, cap. xxx, 56.
22. See Bonaventura, *Itinerarium mentis in Deum* (1259).
23. *Republic*, 506. Cornford trans., p. 212.

According to Plato's description the essential form or absolute Good, is the last thing to be perceived and only with great difficulty.[24] All these hesitations and reservations have completely vanished in the mind and in the work of Augustine. His theory of illumination has shown him a new way. The Platonic good is identified with God, and this God, the God of the prophets and Christian revelation, is not remote from us or inaccessible to us. He is the beginning and the end; in him we live and move and have our being.

This view pervades the whole philosophy of Augustine and gives it its specific character. Augustine became the founder of medieval philosophy by making his personal religious experience the center of the whole intellectual world. The prophets had spoken of the *ethical* law; they had declared this law to be meaningless and incomprehensible without a personal lawgiver. Augustine transfers this conception from the ethical sphere to the entire theoretical sphere. God is the whole of wisdom: through him we know everything, without him we do not know anything. "Deus sapientia, in quo et a quo et per quem sapiunt quae sapiunt omnia. . . . Deus intelligibilis lux, in quo et a quo et per quem intelligibiliter lucent, quae intelligibiliter lucent omnia." [25] "Behold and see, if thou canst (O soul)," says Augustine, "God is truth. . . . Ask not what *is* truth; for immediately the darkness of corporeal images and the clouds of phantasms will put themselves in the way and will disturb that calm which at the first twinkling shone forth to thee, when I said truth. See that thou remainest, if thou canst, in that first twinkling with which thou art dazzled, as it were, by a flash, when it is said to thee: Truth." [26]

That is the gospel, the "glad tidings," that Augustine and his disciples and followers opposed to the worldly wisdom of the philosophers. All the efforts of the philosophic systems ended in discord and doubt. As Augustine points out in his treatise *Contra academicos*, it was the Platonic theory of knowledge that led to the skepticism of the New Academy. No one, before the revelation by Christ, was able to find the Archimedean point to move the world of truth. The wisest of the wise men, Socrates, had to avow his ignorance. From the new religious point of view this

24. *Idem*, 517. Cornford trans., p. 226 (μόγις ὀφθεῖσα).
25. *Soliloquia*, Lib. I, cap. I, 3.
26. *De trinitate*, Bk. VIII, chap. II. Dods trans., VII, 204.

objection was not unfounded. By his Christian admirers Socrates was always held in the highest esteem. They even thought it impossible that he could have found his fundamental ethical principles without a special revelation. The Renaissance, too, spoke of Socrates as a real saint: "St. Socrates, pray for us," said Erasmus. But Socrates himself never spoke as an inspired teacher. He was started in his work of self-examination and of the examination of others by the Delphic oracle but he did not regard himself as the spokesman of Apollo or any other deity. He was convinced that there is no divine or human teacher of truth, that every individual had to find his way himself; and that, only by the dialectic process of questioning and answering, can the truth be attained. The Greek conception of dialectic is in flagrant contradiction to any kind of revealed truth. A truth that is not found by ourselves is no truth at all. According to Plato the process which we call "learning" does not mean that we acquire an entirely new truth: we only regain what we had previously possessed; we recover a knowledge which is our own.[27] Augustine accepts all the premises of Greek philosophy; but he rejects the conclusion. According to him the only sound and valid conclusion is that it is vain to look for a *human* teacher of wisdom. From the authority of Socrates or Plato Augustine addresses himself to the higher authority of the divine Word: "Call no man your father upon the earth: for one is your Father which is in heaven. Neither be ye called masters: for one is your Master, even Christ." [28] "Ille autem qui consulitur docet, . . . id est incommutabilis Dei virtus atque sempiterna Sapientia." [29]

Medieval culture has often, and justly, been admired for its deep unity and homogeneity. It seems to lack all those conflicts, all those contradictions and dissonances that are the stigma of our modern civilization. In the Middle Ages all forms of human life—science, religion, moral and political life—were pervaded and saturated with the same spirit. Yet all this cannot make us forget that medieval life was the outgrowth of two conflicting intellectual and moral forces. It needed the heroic effort of all the great scholastic thinkers to bridge this gulf and bind together the opposing elements of thought and feeling. The problem

27. *Phaedo*, 75 E, 76 D, E.
28. Matthew 23.9, 10; see Augustine, *De magistro*, XIV, 45, 46.
29. *De magistro*, XI, 38.

seemed, at last, to be solved in the system of Thomas Aquinas.
Yet the God of Thomas Aquinas, the God of the Bible and of
Christian revelation, is by no means the same as the God of Plato
or Aristotle. The scholastic thinkers were prone to forget this fundamental difference, because they did not read the classical texts
in our modern way. They did not care for historical truth. They
only knew and acknowledged a symbolic truth. They had no
critical or philological standards of interpretation; they used the
medieval method of allegorical and spiritual interpretation. In
virtue of these methods they tried to find out the *sensus moralis,*
the *sensus anagogicus,* the *sensus mysticus* of the classical authors.

Throughout the Middle Ages the dialogue *Timaeus* was the
principal, if not the only, source of Platonism. And Plato's thought
and style in the *Timaeus* proved to be very pliable to this kind
of symbolic interpretation. It was easy to find here all the elements of Christian revelation. Had not Plato, in the beginning
of the *Timaeus,* declared that the world, being visible and tangi-
ble and having a body, has been created, and that which is created must of necessity have a cause? Had he not said that it is
extremely difficult to find out the "father and maker" of this universe—and that even if we found him, it would be impossible to
tell of him to all men? [30] Was not all this a prophecy of a higher
and better revelation, of the incarnation of Christ?

That the medieval thinkers read and interpreted the Platonic
text in this way, is understandable and it was, indeed, unavoidable. It is, however, rather surprising that the same view has still
been maintained and defended by modern scholars who have a
thorough knowledge of the whole work of Plato and are in possession of all the modern methods of critical and historical interpretation. They too have tried to convince us that, at the bottom,
there is a complete harmony, if not an identity, between the
Platonic "demiurge" and the personal God of the Old Testament.
But this thesis is untenable. First of all it is clear that Plato, in his
Timaeus, never meant to develop a coherent "theology." In order
to learn his real conceptions of the deity we must study his other
works, most of which were unknown to the medieval thinkers.
What he gave in the *Timaeus* was no philosophical or theological
system. He himself constantly warns us against such a view; he

30. *Timaeus,* 28 C, 37 C.

tells us that he can only offer "probable opinions." "As being is to becoming," says Plato,

so is truth to belief. If then, amid the many opinions about the gods and the generation of the universe, we are not able to give notions which are altogether and in every respect exact and consistent with one another, do not be surprised. Enough, if we adduce probabilities as likely as any others; for we must remember that I who am the speaker, and you who are the judges, are only mortal men, and we ought to accept the tale which is probable and enquire no further.[31]

That does not sound as if Plato were speaking here as the prophet of a new religion. He even goes so far as to say that his tale of the creation claims to be no more than a work of recreation, "a wise and moderate pastime." [32] If a thinker intends to reveal a fundamental religious truth he does not speak of it as a pastime. Plato's demiurge is a cosmological concept not an ethical or religious concept. To speak of a worship of the demiurge would be an absurdity.

And there are other more important reasons that do not allow us to draw any parallel between Plato's myth of the demiurge and the monotheism of the Old Testament. Plato's demiurge is no creator, he is an "artificer." He does not create the world out of nothing; he only imbues a formless matter with form; he introduces regularity and order. His power is not infinite; it is restricted by a "necessity" which is opposed to and which thwarts his creative action. "The creation is mixed, being made up of necessity and mind. Mind, the ruling power, persuaded necessity to bring the greater part of created things to perfection, and thus . . . when the influence of reason got the better of necessity, the universe was created." [33]

In order to understand Plato's religion in its true sense we cannot content ourselves with the description given in the *Timaeus*. What we find here is only a by-product; it shows us the periphery, not the center, of Plato's religious thought. The center is to be found in the sixth book of the *Republic* in Plato's description of the Idea of the Good. In both ancient and modern times the Idea

31. *Timaeus*, 29 B f.; cf. 48 D–E. Jowett trans., III, 449, 468.
32. *Idem*, 59 C–D, *loc. cit.*, p. 480.
33. *Idem*, 47 E f., *loc. cit.*, p. 467.

of the Good has often been identified with the Platonic demiurge.[34] Yet a closer analysis of Plato's text and thought shows that
such an identification is impossible. Neither logically nor metaphysically is the Idea of the Good on the same level as the demiurge. The demiurge is a mythical, whereas the Idea of the Good
is a dialectical conception. The former belongs to the realm of
"probable opinions," the latter to the realm of truth. The former
is described as a personal agent; he is a "craftsman" or "artificer."
The Idea of the Good can never be conceived in this way. Like
all the other ideas it has an objective meaning and truth. It is the
archetype, the pattern according to which the divine craftsman
shapes his work. Looking at the Idea of the Good he makes the
world and he is anxious that his work come as nearly as possible
to the perfection of the eternal paragon. The Platonic demiurge
is good, but he is by no means "the Good." He is not the Good
itself, but only its agent and administrator. In the Platonic system
this means a fundamental difference that is very clearly expressed
in the *Timaeus* itself. "If the world be indeed fair and the artificer
good, it is manifest that he must have looked to that which is
eternal; but if what cannot be said without blasphemy is true,
then to the created pattern. Every one will see that he must have
looked to the eternal; for the world is the fairest of creations and
he is the best of causes." [35] The Idea of the Good cannot be described as such a "cause." It is a formal or final, not an efficient
cause. It belongs to the realm of being, not of becoming. Between
these two realms there is a sharp separation, a real gulf. We cannot pass from one to the other. The Idea of the Good may and
must, indeed, be described as the "reason" of all things. But this
reason is not a personal or individual *will*. To ascribe personality
to an idea would be a contradiction in terms; for an idea is a universal, not an individual. In the famous simile in the *Republic*
Plato tells us that the Idea of the Good has the same place in the
intellectual world as the sun in the sensible world. The sun stands
in the same relation to vision and visible things as that which the
Good itself bears in the intelligible world to intelligence and to
intelligible objects. The sun not only makes the things we see

34. Among the modern scholars who have maintained this view is Theodor
Gomperz; see his book, *Griechische Denker*, Bk. V, chap. xix. English trans. by
G. G. Berry (London, John Murray, 1905), III, 211 f.
35. *Timaeus*, 29 A, *loc. cit.*, p. 449.

visible but also brings them into existence and gives them growth. And so with the objects of knowledge: these derive from the Good not only their power of being known, but their very being and reality.[36] But in Plato's language reality, true being, never means empirical reality. The Good is, in Plato's system, the *ratio essendi* as well as the *ratio cognoscendi;* but it is not the *ratio fiendi;* for no idea can produce or engender a finite empirical thing. If we speak of such generation we can only mean it in a metaphorical and not in an ontological sense.

Aristotle's view seems to be quite different. He denies the Platonic severance between the phenomenal and the intelligible world. In his system God is both the efficient and the final cause. He is the first mover, being unmoved himself. It was much easier to draw a parallel between this Aristotelian God and the Christian God. Thomas Aquinas found, indeed, no difficulty in accepting the whole of Aristotle's theology and metaphysics. But he could only do so by interpreting Aristotle's doctrine in his own sense and lending to its author all his personal religious feelings. When studying the work of Aristotle himself we find quite a different picture. Aristotle's God is the best and classical example of Greek intellectualism. It is true that in Aristotle's *Physics* and *Metaphysics* the love of God is described as the first moving principle. God moves the world not by a mechanical impulse but by a spiritual attraction—in the same sense as a beloved object moves the lover. The final cause produces motion by being loved; and by that which it moves, it moves all other things. The first mover, then, of necessity exists; and in so far as it is necessary, it is good, and in this sense a first principle. But this prime mover is unmoved, not only in a physical but also in an ethical sense. He is inaccessible to human wishes, and he cannot yield to human desires. All this is far below him. God is *actus purus*—pure actuality. But his activity is an intellectual not an ethical activity. He is absorbed by his thought and has no other object than his thought. Hence Aristotle could ascribe life to God; but this life, the life of thought, is not a personal life. It is purely theoretical and contemplative.

On such a principle, then, depend the heavens and the world of nature. And it is a life such as the best which we enjoy, and enjoy for but a short time (for it is ever in this state, which we cannot be) . . .

36. *Republic,* 507, 508. Cornford trans., pp. 214 f.

thought thinks on itself because it shares the nature of the object of thought; for it becomes an object of thought in coming into contact with and thinking its objects, so that thought and object of thought are the same. . . . But it is *active* when it *possesses* this object. Therefore the possession rather than the receptivity is the divine element which thought seems to contain, and the act of contemplation is what is most pleasant and best. . . . And life also belongs to God; for the actuality of thought is life, and God is that actuality; and God's self-dependent actuality is life most good and eternal.[37]

This eternal life of God as described by Aristotle is not the same type of life that we find in prophetic religion. To the prophets God is not a thought which has itself for its object. He is a personal lawgiver, the source of the moral law. That is his highest, and in a sense it is his *only* attribute. We cannot describe him by any objective quality borrowed from the nature of things. If a name means the designation of such a quality, then he has no name. In Exodus we are told how Moses asks God for his name. "Behold, when I come unto the children of Israel, and shall say unto them: The God of your fathers hath sent me unto you, and they shall say to me: What is his name?—what shall I say unto them? And God said unto Moses: I Am That I Am: and he said, Thus shalt thou say unto the children of Israel, I Am has sent me unto you." [38] These words mark, as it were, the watershed between Greek and Jewish thought, between the God of Plato and Aristotle and the God of Jewish monotheism. God is not comparable to any object of thought nor can his essence be described by the act of pure thought. His essence is his *will;* his only revelation is the manifestation of his personal will. Such a personal revelation which is an ethical and not a logical act is quite alien to the Greek mind. The ethical law is not "given" or proclaimed by a superhuman being; we have to find and to prove it ourselves by rational and dialectic thought. That is the real difference between Greek and Jewish religious thought—and this difference is insurmountable and ineffaceable. "Greek thought," says E. Gilson in his lectures on the spirit of medieval philosophy, "did not attain to that essential truth which is struck out at one blow, and with-

37. Aristotle, *Metaphysica*, Bk. XII, 1072^b. English trans. by W. D. Ross, "The Works of Aristotle" (2d ed. Oxford, Clarendon Press, 1928), Vol. VIII.
38. Exodus 3.13, 14.

out a shadow of proof, by the great words of the Bible: Audi
Israel, Dominus Deus noster, Dominus unus est." [39] No scholastic
thinker, not even Thomas Aquinas, could accept without reservation the Greek solution of the problem. All of them—St. Augustine, St. Jerome, St. Bernard, Bonaventura, Duns Scotus—have
quoted the text of Exodus, the words: "ego sum qui sum," "I am
that I am." [40] "Persona," says Thomas Aquinas, "significat id quod
est perfectissimum in tota natura, scilicet subsistens in rationali
natura. Unde . . . conveniens est ut hoc nomen › persona ‹ de
Deo dicatur; non tamen eodem modo quo dicitur de creaturis, sed
excellentiori modo." [41]

We must bear in mind this twofold historical origin of medieval
thought in Greek speculation and Jewish prophetic religion in
order to understand its systematic development. In the whole
course of scholastic philosophy we always meet with the same
struggle between "faith" and "reason" or between the "theologians" and the "dialecticians." Between these two extremes no
understanding or reconciliation seemed to be possible. There were
always the fanatics of faith who demanded the complete abdica-
tion of reason. They rejected and denounced all rational activities. In the eleventh century Petrus Damiani was one of these
hotspurs of theology. Perhaps no other medieval thinker spoke of
reason in such a contemptuous way. And reason meant to him
not only philosophy but the whole field of the liberal arts and
secular knowledge. He spoke of an "inflation" of science.[42] Not
only dialectic but also grammar was declared to be one of the
most dangerous enemies of true religion. According to Petrus
Damiani the devil was the inventor of grammar and the first
grammarian. The first lesson of grammar was, at the same time,
a lesson in polytheism; for the grammarians were the first to
speak of "gods" in the plural form.[43] If reason is to be admitted
at all, it has to obey blindly; it has to submit to the commands of

39. E. Gilson, *L'esprit de la philosophie médiévale*, Gifford Lectures, 1931–32
(Paris, Vrin, 1932), p. 49. English trans. (New York, Charles Scribner's Sons),
p. 46. The passage referred to by Gilson is Deuteronomy 6.4.

40. For the evidence see Gilson, *op. cit.*, chaps. III, V, X.

41. Thomas Aquinas, *Summa theologica*, Pars Prima, Quaest. XXIX, art. 3.

42. Petrus Damiani, *De sancta simplicitate scientiae inflanti anteponenda*, "Patrologia Latina," Tom. 145, col. 695–704. Cf. J. A. Endres. *Petrus Damiani und
die weltliche Wissenschaft*, "Beiträge zur Geschichte der Philosophie des Mittel-
alters," herausg. von Cl. Baeumker (Münster, Aschendorff, 1910), VIII. 3.

43. *De sancta simplicitate*, cap. 1, col. 695 B.

faith.[44] For even if our logic were complete and faultless it would apply only to human, not to divine things. We cannot attain a knowledge of God by syllogisms; and God is not bound to the petty rules of our human logic. It is only the saintly simplicity, the simplicity of faith, that can save us from the snares and fallacies of reason: "In Deo igitur, qui vera est sapientia, quaerendi et intelligendi finem constitue." One does not kindle a candle, says Petrus Damiani, in order to see the sun.[45]

The mystics of the Middle Ages speak in a milder tone but they are no less categorical and uncompromising in their condemnation of reason. Bernard of Clairvaux launched a powerful attack against the dialecticians of his time and attained his end when he achieved the condemnation of Abélard.[46] He too saw in dialectic one of the gravest obstacles to a true Christian life. All heresies have their source in the same fundamental vice, the presumption and arrogance of human reason. Reason can never be the judge and master; for it stands in the way of the principal aim, the mystical union of the human soul with God. Bernard of Clairvaux complained that philosophers and dialecticians had given the example of indulging in complicated and sophisticated speculative problems and of deriding the faith of the simple-minded.[47]

The pioneers of dialectic in the eleventh century, the "rationalistic" thinkers, men like Anselm of Canterbury and Abélard, took up the challenge. Their theological adversaries had charged them with enfeebling the authority of Christian revelation and undermining the foundations of faith. They turned this accusation on their aggressors and opponents. To deny or minimize the value of rational thought, they declared, means to deprive faith of one of its firmest and principal supports. Far from being a danger or obstacle, reason is one of the most powerful weapons and one of the indispensable elements of true religion. Anselm of Canterbury did not content himself with giving his famous ontological proof

44. Damiani, *De divina omnipotentia,* cap. 5, "Patrologia Latina," Tom. 145, col. 603 C: "Quae tamen artis humanae peritia, si quando tractandis sacris eloquiis adhibetur, non debet jus magisterii sibimet arroganter arripere; sed velut ancilla dominae quodam famulatus obsequio subservire, ne, si praecedit, oberret, et, dum exteriorum verborum sequitur consequentias, intimae virtutis lumen et rectum veritatis tramitem perdat."

45. *De sancta simplicitate,* cap. viii, *op. cit.,* Tom. 145, col. 702 A.

46. Cf. Endres, *op. cit.,* p. 14.

47. See Gilson, *La théologie mystique de Saint Bernard* (Paris, Vrin, 1934).

of the existence of God. He was bold enough to extend the same method to the whole realm of Christian dogmatics. In his theory of satisfaction [48] he tried to demonstrate that the incarnation of Christ is not only an accidental historical fact but a necessary truth. In the same way he treated the doctrine of the three persons in God. The Christian dogma in his work became, as it were, permeable to reason; the mystery seemed to fade away.

Nevertheless there remained one point in which there was no real dissension among the extremists of the two parties. To speak of a medieval "rationalism" is to speak in a very inaccurate and inadequate way. In the medieval system there was no room for our modern rationalism, the tendency of thought that we find in Descartes, Spinoza, Leibniz, or in the "philosophers" of the eighteenth century. No scholastic thinker ever seriously doubted the absolute superiority of the *revealed* truth. In this regard the dialecticians and theologians were unanimous. "Nolo sic esse philosophus," wrote Abélard in one of his letters to Héloise, "ut recalcitrem Paulo; non sic esse Aristoteles, ut secludat a Christo." [49] The "autonomy" of reason was a principle quite alien to medieval thought. Reason cannot be its own light; in order to perform its work it needs a higher source of illumination. In this respect the Augustinian theory of the *magisterium Dei* never lost its authority upon the minds of the medieval thinkers. Here too we can trace medieval thought to its historical origin in prophetic religion. Augustine had quoted the saying of Isaiah: "Nisi credideritis, non intelligetis"—"if you do not believe you will not understand." [50] This word became the cornerstone of the medieval theory of knowledge. Reason left to itself is blind and impotent, but when guided and illuminated by faith it proves its whole strength. If we begin with the act of faith we can confide in the power of reason, for reason has been given to us not for any independent use of its own but for an understanding or interpretation of what is taught by faith. The authority of faith must always precede the use of reason—"naturae quidem ordo ita se habet, ut cum aliquid discimus rationem praecedat auctoritas." But this authority once acknowledged and firmly established the way is open. The two

48. See Anselm's treatise *Cur Deus homo,* "Patrologia Latina," Tom. 158, col. 359–432.

49. Abélard, *Epistolae,* "Patrologia Latina," Tom. 178, col. 375 C: Epistola XVII.

50. Isaiah 7.9.

powers can complete and confirm each other—"ergo intellige ut credas, crede ut intelligas."[51]

This principle is adopted by all scholastic thinkers. It found its classical expression in the work of Anselm of Canterbury. Notwithstanding his "rationalism" Anselm begins with emphasizing that we have to accept the fundamental truths of Christian religion without any demonstration. By mere dialectic we can never hope to attain these truths, and we cannot add anything to their firmness by rational methods. The dogma as such remains uncontested, unshakeable and irrefutable.[52] But although religious truth cannot be *established* by reason it is not opposed or reluctant to reason. There is a real harmony between the two realms. It is true that a special act of divine grace is needed for man to grasp this harmony. Anselm begins his investigation with a prayer in which he asks God to assist him in his endeavor to comprehend what he firmly believes.[53] That is the only true way: "As the right order prescribes that we first believe the deep mysteries of Christian faith, before we presume to discuss them, so it seems to me to be a neglect, if, after having been established in faith, we do not endeavor to understand what we believe." [54]

This was no real escape from the dilemma. It was a deep longing for the solution of the problem rather than the solution itself. The old conflict between reason and faith broke out time and again. But the formula *Fides quaerens intellectum* presented at least a common platform, a basis for all further discussions. All the representatives of scholastic thought from Anselm to Thomas could accept this formula. The system of Thomas Aquinas seemed to promise a definitive solution. By Thomas Aquinas' device, *ratio confortata fide*, reason was reinstated to all its rights and dignities; it had full sway over the natural and the human world.

51. For more details see the texts quoted by Gilson, *Introduction à l'étude de Saint Augustin* (3d ed. Paris, Vrin, 1931), chap. i.
52. Anselm, *Cur Deus homo*, Lib. I, cap. 2, *op. cit.*, Tom. 158, col. 362 C: "ut etiam si nulla ratione quod credo possim comprehendere, nihil tamen sit quod me ab ejus firmitate valeat evellere."
53. See Anselm, *Proslogion*, "Patrologia Latina," Tom. 158, col. 227 C, cap. 2: "Domine, qui das fidei intellectum, da mihi, ut, quantum scis expedire, intelligam, quia es, sicut credimus; et hoc es, quod credimus."
54. *Cur Deus homo*, Lib. I, cap. 2.

VIII

THE THEORY OF THE LEGAL STATE IN MEDIEVAL PHILOSOPHY

Even by its greatest admirers Plato's *Republic* had always been described as a political utopia. It was regarded as the classical paragon of political thought but it seemed to have little, if anything, to do with actual political life. Yet if we look at medieval public and social life we must correct this judgment. Here the Platonic idea of the Legal State proved to be a real and active power: a great energy that not only influenced the thoughts of men but became a powerful impulse of human actions. The thesis that the first and principal task of the state is the maintenance of justice became the very focus of medieval political theory. It was accepted by all the medieval thinkers, and it found its way into all forms of medieval civilization. The first Fathers of the Church, the theologians and philosophers, the Roman lawyers and the political writers, the students of civil and canon law, were unanimous in this respect.[1] In a passage of his *Republic*, quoted by Augustine, Cicero had said that justice is the foundation of law and of organized society: where there is no justice, there is no commonwealth, no real *res publica*.[2]

Yet although in this point there is a complete agreement between the medieval theory and that of classical antiquity, there remains, nevertheless, a difference that has not only a theoretical interest but entails the most important practical consequences. According to its fundamental principles, the Middle Ages could not conceive of any abstract, impersonal justice. In monotheistic religion the law must always be traced back to a personal source. Without a lawgiver there can be no law. And if justice was not to be regarded as an accidental thing, as a mere matter of convention, this lawgiver had to be above all human forces. It is a superhuman will that manifests itself in justice. Now Plato's Idea

1. For this question see the rich evidence in the work of R. W. and A. J. Carlyle, *A History of Medieval Political Theory in the West* (3d ed. Edinburgh and London, W. Blackwood & Sons, 1930). 6 vols.
2. See Augustine, *City of God*, Bk. II, chap. xxi. Dods trans., I, 77.

of the Good was not in need of such a superhuman authority. In Plato's thought and language every idea is αὐτὸ καθ' αὑτό, is an *ens per se*. It exists and subsists by itself; it has an objective, absolute validity. Augustine could not accept this principle. In order to give to the Platonic ideas a place in his own doctrine he had to re-define them; he had to turn them into the thoughts of God. That was no mere metaphysical or ontological distinction; it meant much more. The Good could no longer maintain and guarantee itself. By dialectic methods alone we cannot hope to attain the Good; and we cannot grasp its real meaning. Here too the human intellect must submit to a higher power. We may continue to speak of a "natural" law in contradistinction to the divine law. But in Christian thought even nature has no separate, independent existence. It is the work and creation of God. In the same sense all ethical laws are created things; they are the revelation of a personal will. From the beginning the Fathers of the Church had urged this view. In his treatise *Against Celsus* Origen admits that law is king of all things. But he adds that, to all true Christians, this law is not something separate or independent; it coincides with the will of God.[3]

There was, however, still another and even more important feature in which the medieval theory of natural law deviated from Plato and Aristotle. Plato had defined justice as "geometrical equality." Every individual has a share in the life of the commonwealth; but these shares are by no means the same. Justice is not the same as equality of rights. The Platonic state gives to everyone and to all the social classes their allotted work in the common work; but their rights and duties are widely different. That follows not only from the character of Plato's ethics, but, first and foremost, from the character of his psychology. Plato's metaphysical psychology is based upon his division of the human soul. The character of man is determined by the proportion between these three elements. "Do we gain knowledge," asks Plato,

with one part, feel anger with another, and with yet a third desire the pleasures of food, sex, and so on? . . . It is clear that the same thing cannot act in two opposite ways or be in two opposite states at the same time. . . . So if we find such contradictory actions or states among the elements concerned, we shall know that more than one must have been involved.[4]

3. Origen, *Contra Celsum*, V, 40; Carlyle, *op. cit.*, I, 103 f.
4. Plato, *Republic*, 436 A f. Cornford trans., p. 129.

We may call that part of the soul whereby it reflects, rational; the other with which it feels hunger or thirst or any other sensual desire, appetitive.

But between the two there is still another element that in Plato's language is described as the θυμοειδές—the "irascible" or "spirited" element. The same distinction appears in the soul of the state.[5] The different classes into which the Platonic state is divided have as many different souls—they represent different types of human characters. These types are fixed and unchangeable. Every attempt to change them, i.e., to efface or diminish the differences between the rulers, the guardians, and the ordinary men, would be disastrous. It would mean a revolt against the unchangeable laws of human nature to which the social order has to conform. Since the philosophic or the "spirited" *soul* is not the same as that of a tradesman or craftsman, since each of them has a certain unalterable structure, we cannot ascribe to the different classes the same functions; we cannot put them on the same level. "And so, after a stormy passage," concludes Plato,

we have reached the land. We are fairly agreed that the same three elements exist alike in the state and in the individual soul. . . . Our principle that the born shoemaker or carpenter had better stick to his trade turns out to have been an adumbration of justice. . . . The just man does not allow the several elements in his soul to usurp one another's functions; he is indeed one who sets his house in order, by self-mastery and discipline coming to be at peace with himself, and bringing into tune those three parts, like the terms in the proportion of a musical scale.[6]

Aristotle proceeds in a different way; but in the end he is led to the same result. His is not a metaphysical or deductive but an empirical method. What he tries to give in his *Politics* is a descriptive analysis of the various forms of constitutions. Yet, precisely as an empirical observer, he finds it impossible to deny the fundamental inequality in men. Men are unequal both in natural gifts and character. From this there follows the necessity of slavery. Slavery is not a mere convention, it is rooted in nature. Plato spoke of "born carpenters or shoemakers"; Aristotle speaks of born slaves. There are a great many men who are incapable of ruling themselves. They cannot be members of the state. They have no rights or responsibilities of their own and must be com-

5. *Idem,* 434 D ff. Cornford trans., p. 127 ff.
6. *Idem,* 441 C ff. Cornford trans., p. 136 ff.

manded by their superiors. According to Aristotle the abolition of slavery is no political or ethical ideal; it is a mere illusion. The same holds for the relations of Greeks and barbarians. Plato had pointed out in his *Republic* that the rules of conduct which hold for the mutual intercourse between Greek states are not applicable to barbarians. Even in times of war Greeks should always be treated as friends, at least as potential friends, whereas barbarians are natural enemies. "We shall speak of war when Greeks fight with foreigners whom we may call their natural enemies. But Greeks are by nature friends of Greeks, and when they fight, it means that Hellas is afflicted by dissension which ought to be called civil strife. . . . They should remember that the war will not last for ever; some day they must make friends again." [7] Aristotle went still farther. He seems to extend his judgment that some men are born slaves to all barbarian nations. He has no doubts that the Greek is the born ruler of the barbarians:

"Right it is that Hellenes rule barbarians, not that alien yoke
    Rest on Hellenes. . . . They be bondmen, we be freeborn folk,"

he says, quoting Euripides.[8]

Yet all these discriminations between free men and slaves, between Greeks and barbarians, were called into question and finally swept away by the development of Greek ethical thought. In the system of Stoicism there arose a new intellectual and moral force. From a merely theoretical point of view Stoicism has little claim to originality. In their physics, logic, and dialectic the Stoics borrowed much of their theories from other sources. Their philosophy seems to be a mere eclecticism. They select doctrines from Heraclitus, Plato, and Aristotle. But in their general conception of man and his place in the universe the Stoic philosophers did open a new way. They introduced a principle that proved to be a turning point in the history of ethical, political, and religious thought. To the Platonic and Aristotelian ideal of justice there was added an entirely new conception: the conception of the *fundamental equality of men.*[9]

7. *Idem*, p. 470. Cornford trans., p. 169.

8. Aristotle, *Politica*, Bk. A. 2 1252^b 8. See Euripides, *Iphigenia in Aulis*, v. 1400. English trans. by A. S. Way (Loeb Classical Library, 1930), I, 131.

9. Historically we can trace this conception to some sophists of the fifth century; but its real purport and its radical consequences did not appear until Stoic philosophy.

The principal ethical demand of the Stoics was "to live in accordance with nature (ὁμολογουμένως τῇ φύσει ζῆν). But the "law of nature" to which they appeal is a moral not a physical law. Of course the Stoics never denied that, in a physical sense, there are innumerable differences between men; differences of birth, rank, temperament, intellectual talents. But from an ethical point of view all these differences are declared to be of no account. They are a matter of indifference because they do not affect the *form* of human life. What matters alone, what determines a man's personality, are not the things themselves but his *judgment* about things. These judgments are not bound to any conventional standards. They depend upon a free act which creates a world of its own. The Stoics draw a sharp line between what is necessary and what is accidental in human nature. Only those things are necessary that regard the "essence," that is to say, the moral value of man. Whatever depends on external circumstances, on conditions that are not in our own power, is to be left out; it does not count.

To obliterate or minimize the most important differences between men seems, at first sight, to be only an utopian thought, a philosopher's dream. But we must not forget that such thoughts were expressed by Marcus Aurelius, who was not only a philosophical thinker but also one of the great statesmen of antiquity and ruler of the Roman Empire. That there ever was a time in which such a connection was possible is one of the most remarkable facts in the history of human civilization.

Stoicism could not have fulfilled its historical mission without that clear alliance between philosophic and political thought. The conquest of Roman public life by the Stoic doctrines began very early. We can trace it back to the flowering season of the Roman Republic. Many of the great political leaders were then imbued with Stoic thoughts. The younger Scipio was a disciple of Panaetius, the Stoic philosopher. He was a great admirer of Greek culture; but he never forgot or denied the old Roman conceptions of political life. He and his friends were fighting for the greatness and military glory of the Roman Republic; but at the same time they began to form and to cultivate a new ideal that was not only a national but also a cosmopolitan ideal. If we study the classical works of Greek ethics, for instance Aristotle's *Nicomachean Ethics,* we find there a clear and systematic analysis of the different virtues, of magnanimity, temperance, justice, courage, and liberality, we do *not* find the general virtue called "humanity" (*humanitas*). Even the term seems to be missing from the Greek language and literature. The ideal of humanitas was first formed in Rome; and it was especially the aristocratic circle of the younger Scipio that gave it its firm place in Roman culture. Humanitas was no vague concept. It had a definite meaning, and it became a formative power in private and public life in Rome. It meant not only a moral but also an esthetic ideal; it was the demand for a certain type of life that had to prove its influence in the whole of man's life, in his moral conduct as well as in his language, his literary style, and his taste. Through later writers such as Cicero and Seneca this ideal of humanitas became firmly established in Roman philosophy and Latin literature.[10]

This coalescence of political and philosophic thought was a fact of paramount importance. It was calculated to change the whole conception of social life. In its beginning, Stoicism was not especially concerned with social problems. Most of the Stoic thinkers were determined individualists. If the wise man has to free himself from all outward bonds, he must begin with emancipating himself from all social conventions and obligations. How could the Stoic philosopher maintain his independence of mind, his self-reliance, his firm and imperturbable judgment in the turmoil of political passions and in the arena of political struggles? But that was not the manner in which the Roman writers, men like Cicero, Seneca, or Marcus Aurelius, understood and interpreted the Stoic ideal. They admitted no cleft between the individual and the political sphere. For they were convinced that reality taken as a whole, physical reality as well as moral life, was one great "republic." This republic is the same for all nations, the same for gods and men. All rational beings are members of the same commonwealth. "Universus hic mundus," said Cicero, "una civitas communis deorum atque hominum existimanda est."[11] He who lives in harmony with himself, with his

10. The development of the idea and of the term "humanitas" in Greek and Roman life has been studied in a paper of Richard Reitzenstein, *Werden und Wesen der Humanität im Altertum* (Strassburg, Trübner, 1907). In addition see Richard Harder, "Die Einbürgerung der Philosophie in Rom," *Die Antike,* V (1929), 300 ff., and "Nachträgliches zu Humanitas," *Hermes,* LXIX (1934), 64 ff.

11. For more details see Julius Kaerst, *Die antike Idee der Oekumene in ihrer politischen und kulturellen Entwicklung* (Leipzig, B. G. Teubner, 1903).

"demon," says Marcus Aurelius, lives in harmony with the universe.[12] The personal and the universal order are but different manifestations of a common underlying principle.

That this view was pregnant with the most important practical consequences becomes evident in the treatment of the problem of slavery. No Stoic writer could accept the saying of Aristotle that there are slaves "by nature." "Nature" means ethical freedom, not social bondage. It is not nature but fortune that makes a man a slave. "It is a mistake," says Seneca, "to imagine that slavery pervades a man's whole being; the better part of him is exempt from it: the body indeed is subjected and in the power of a master, but the mind is independent, and indeed is so free and wild, that it cannot be restrained even by this prison of the body, wherein it is confined." The mind remains free, independent, sui juris.[13] The history of Stoic thought confirms and elucidates this maxim. Of the great Stoic thinkers one, Marcus Aurelius, was the Emperor of Rome, whereas another, Epictetus, was a slave.

This Stoic conception of man became one of the firmest bonds between ancient and medieval thought, a link that was even stronger than that of classical Greek philosophy. The early Middle Ages knew very little of the works of Plato and Aristotle. What Augustine knew of Aristotle was only a Latin translation of the *Organon*. But he himself has told what a deep influence the study of Cicero's *Hortensius* exerted upon his mind. It was here that he first found the Stoic ideal of the sage. Throughout the whole Middle Ages Cicero and Seneca remained the great authorities of ethical thought. The Christian writers were very much surprised to find in these pagan writers their own religious views. The Stoic maxim of the fundamental equality of men was generally and easily accepted and it became one of the cardinal points of the medieval theory. It was not only taught by the Christian Fathers; it was also established and confirmed by the Roman Jurists of the *Digests* and *Institutes*. On this point there was scarcely any disagreement between the various trends of thought and the philosophic schools of the Middle Ages. All of them could coöperate with each other in a common task. It was a general

12. Cf. also *The Communings with Himself of Marcus Aurelius Antoninus*, II, 13, 17. English trans. by C. R. Haines (Loeb Classical Library, 1916), pp. 37, 41.
13. Seneca, *De beneficiis*, III, 20. English trans. by Aubrey Stewart (London, G. Bell & Sons, 1900), p. 69.

maxim of medieval theology and jurisprudence that according to "nature" and in the original order of things all men are free and equal. "Omnes namque homines natura aequales sumus," said Gregory the Great. "Quod ad jus naturale attinet omnes homines aequales sunt," said Ulpian.[14] The Stoic conception that all men are free because they are all endowed with the same reason found its theological interpretation and justification in the added dictum that this very reason is the image of God. "Signatum est super nos lumen vultus tui, Domine," says the book of Psalms.[15] Augustine declared in the *City of God* that God had made man the master of the animals but had given him no power over other human souls. Every attempt to usurp such a power would be an intolerable arrogance. Here as well as in Stoic thought every soul is declared to be *sui juris;* it cannot lose or renounce its original freedom.[16]

It follows that the authority of no political power can ever be absolute. It is always bound to the laws of justice. These laws are irrevocable and inviolable because they express the divine order itself, the will of the supreme lawgiver. It is true that from Roman law the conclusion could be drawn, as was later done, that the sovereign is free from all legal bonds. But in medieval thought the principle of the divine right of kings was always subject to certain fundamental limitations. Both the theologians and the Roman lawyers interpreted the maxim *Princeps legibus solutus* in the sense that the prince is free from legal coercion, but that this freedom does not discharge him from any of his duties and obligations. The sovereign is not under any external compulsion to obey the laws; but the power and authority of the "natural law" remains unbroken. The saying *Rex nihil potest nisi quod jure potest* always was in full force. There seems to be no evidence that it was ever doubted or seriously attacked by any medieval writer. Thomas Aquinas starts from the principle that the law should bind the sovereign *quoad vim directivam* but not *quoad vim coactivam.*[17] He explained this principle in a special treatise *De regimine principum* where he was led to very bold conclusions which in the system of a medieval thinker are rather surprising

14. For a full discussion and documentation see Carlyle, *op. cit.,* Vol. I, Pt. II, chaps. VI, VII, 63–79.

15. Psalms 4.6.

16. See Augustine, *City of God,* Bk. XIX, chap. XV. Dods trans., II, 323 f.

17. See *Summa theologica,* Prima Secundae, Quaest. XCVI, art. 5.

and contain a revolutionary element. In medieval philosophy a right of open resistance against the ruler could not be admitted. If the prince derives his authority directly from God, any resistance becomes an open revolt against the will of God and, therefore, a mortal sin. Even the unjust ruler does not cease to be the representative of God and he must therefore be obeyed. Thomas Aquinas could not deny or overthrow this argument. Yet though accepting the current opinion *de jure,* he gave it an interpretation by which it practically changed its sense. He declared that men are bound to obey the secular authorities, but that this obedience is restricted by the laws of justice, and that, therefore, subjects are under no obligation to obey an unjust or usurped authority. Sedition is, indeed, forbidden by the divine law; but to resist an unjust or usurped authority, to disobey a "tyrant," does not have the character of revolt or sedition but is rather a legitimate act.[18] All this shows very clearly that in spite of the incessant conflicts between the Church and the state, between the spiritual and the secular order, both orders are united by a common principle. The power of the king is, as Wyclif said, a "potestas spiritualis et evangelica." [19] The secular order is not merely "temporal"; it has a true eternity, the eternity of the law and, therefore, a spiritual value of its own.

18. *Idem,* Secunda Secundae, Quaest. XLII, art. 2.
19. *De officio regis,* chap. I, pp. 4, 10 ff., quoted from J. Hashagen, *Staat und Kirche vor der Reformation* (Essen, G. D. Baedeker, 1931), p. 539.

IX

NATURE AND GRACE IN MEDIEVAL PHILOSOPHY

THE medieval theory of the state was a coherent system based upon two postulates: the contents of Christian revelation and the Stoic conception of the natural equality of men. From these postulates all its consequences could be derived in thoroughly logical order. Nevertheless the system was open to a fundamental objection. Its form was correct and unassailable; but in a material sense it seemed to lack all foundations. The postulate of the equality of men was constantly contradicted by the facts of history and human society. At all times the theory of the natural freedom and the natural rights of man was confronted with this flagrant contradiction. "Man is born free, and everywhere he is in chains," says Rousseau in the beginning of his *Social Contract.* "Many a one believes himself the master of others, and yet he is a greater slave than they. How has this change come about? I do not know. What can render it legitimate? I believe I can settle this question." [1]

In order to answer this question Rousseau himself had to build up a very complicated theory. He had to go a long way that led him from his first negative attitude toward human society to a new, positive, and constructive principle. He had to pass from one pole to the other: from his first *Discours* to his *Contrat social.*[2] To a medieval thinker such a change of attitude was neither possible nor necessary. To him Rousseau's question was answered even before it could be raised. For he had no need, like Rousseau, to reconcile two opposite principles. He did not have to solve the problem of how the obvious evils of human society, the corruption, tyranny, enslavement, are compatible with the "original goodness" of man. Medieval philosophy could easily account for all the inherent and necessary defects of the social order. For in spite of its great ethical task the state itself could never be regarded as an absolute good. The medieval thinkers could quite

1. Rousseau, *Contrat social*, Liv. I, chap. 1.
2. See my *Philosophie der Aufklärung* (Tübingen, Mohr, 1932), chap. vi, "Recht, Staat und Gesellschaft."

well accept the Stoic doctrine that there is one great republic—
the same for God and men. They were convinced, too, that the
spiritual and the secular order, notwithstanding their differences,
form an organic unity. The early Church had not developed a
uniform social philosophy. The social structure within the Church
and the social structure outside it were separated by a wide gulf.[3]
But in the progress of medieval thought this gulf was bridged.
More and more the *corpus Christianum* was conceived as an unbroken whole. The *corpus morale et politicum* was at the same
time a *corpus mysticum.* In spite of the differences and oppositions between its parts there was, as Thomas Aquinas said, an
ordinatio ad unum and the different and conflicting forces were
directed to a common end. This *principium unitatis* was never
forgotten. The totality of mankind appeared as a single state
founded and monarchically governed by God himself and every
partial unity, ecclesiastic or secular, derived its right from this
primeval unity.[4]

Dante gave to this conception its clearest and most striking
expression. In his treatise *De monarchia* the state was elevated to
the highest rank. It was not only justified but extolled and glorified. It was declared to be necessary for the safety and advantage
of the world.[5] But, within the limits of the medieval system, all
these pretensions remained in a sense vain. They could not be
fully realized. For there was always a fundamental obstacle that
could not be completely overcome. The state was good in its purpose, in its administration of justice. But, according to the Christian dogma, it was bad in its origin. It was the result of the original sin and the fall of man. In this regard there was complete
agreement among all the early Christian thinkers. We find the
same conception in Irenaeus in the second century, in Augustine
in the fifth century, in Gregory the Great in the sixth century.
Government, says Irenaeus, was made necessary because men de-

3. See Ernst Troeltsch, *Die Soziallehren der christlichen Kirchen und Gruppen,*
in "Gesammelte Schriften," I (Tübingen, Mohr, 1912), 286 ff. English trans. by
Olive Wyon, *The Social Teaching of the Christian Churches* (London, George
Allen & Unwin; and New York, Macmillan, 1931), I, 280 ff.

4. For a full discussion of this problem see Otto von Gierke, *Johannes Althusius
und die Entwicklung der naturrechtlichen Staatstheorie* (3d ed. Breslau, M. and H.
Marcus, 1913). English trans. by Bernard Freyd, *The Development of Political
Theory* (New York, W. W. Norton & Co., 1939), Pt. II, chap. I, "Religious Elements in the Theory of the State," 69 ff., and the texts quoted on p. 80, n. 12.

5. See Dante, *De monarchia,* Lib. I, cap. III and cap. V–IX.

parted from God, and hated their fellow men and fell into confusion and disorder of every kind. And so God set men over each other, imposing the fear of man upon men, that by this means they might be compelled to some measure of righteousness and just dealing.[6]

This doctrine of the Fathers of the Church was diametrically opposed to the Greek ideal of the polis. Augustine admitted that Plato's theory of the state was philosophically true. Plato was right but as a philosopher, as a man who spoke out of reason, not out of revelation, he was bound to ignore and neglect the principal thing. By his revelation God has destroyed the wisdom of the wise and brought to nothing the understanding of the prudent. Human reason is corrupt; and this corrupt reason will never find the only true state, the City of God. True justice, said Augustine, reigns only in that state whose founder and ruler is Christ.

Plato had not only praised the goodness of his ideal state but also admired its beauty. To him the state was not only one beautiful thing among others; it was, in a sense, beauty itself. What the multitude knows of beauty is only a deception. Even the artists and poets have only a faint image of it. It is for the philosophers to discover that real archetype, that paragon of beauty represented by the ideal state. For can there be a higher beauty than that of order, justice, right proportion?

Your lovers of sights and sounds delight in beautiful tones and colours and shapes and in all the works of art into which these enter; but they have not the power of thought to behold and to take delight in the nature of Beauty itself. That power to approach Beauty and behold it as it is in itself, is rare indeed. Now if a man believes in the existence of beautiful things, but not of Beauty itself, and cannot follow a guide who would lead him to a knowledge of it, is he not living in a dream?[7]

After having given his picture of the ideal state Plato exclaims triumphantly: "We have given to each its portion and thus have made the whole beautiful."

Such a conception of the state was not admissible in early Christian thought. The state could be justified to a certain extent, but it could never be rendered beautiful. It could not be conceived as pure and immaculate; for it always bore the mark of

6. Irenaeus, *Adversus haereticos*, Bk. V, chap. xxiv, quoted from Carlyle, *op. cit.*, I, 129.
7. *Republic*, 476. Cornford trans., p. 179.

its origin. The stigma of the original sin was indelibly branded on it. That makes the sharp difference between classical Greek and early Christian thought. On this point no compromise was possible. Neo-Platonism was one of the first and most essential constructive elements in medieval thought. The pseudo-Dionysian writings about the celestial and ecclesiastic hierarchy had a deep and permanent influence that extended over all the systems of scholastic philosophy. In the ninth century Scotus Erigena wrote his book *De divisione naturae* that explained the whole Christian dogma in terms of Neo-Platonism.[8] Yet on the other side the very founder of the Neo-Platonic system had launched a vigorous attack against the Christian gnostics. He charged them with impiety because they failed to see and to recognize the beauty of the world. "Again, to despise the world," says Plotinus,

and the gods and other beautiful natures that are contained in it, is not to become a good man. . . . For he who loves any being, is delighted with every thing which is attached to the object of his love. For he also loves the children of the father whom he loves. . . . For how could this world, or the gods in it, be separated from the intelligible world? . . . Nor is it the province of a wise man to investigate things of this kind, but of one who is mentally blind, who is entirely destitute both of sense and intellect, and who being very remote from a knowledge of the intelligible world does not look to the sensible universe. For what musician is there, who, on perceiving the harmony in the intelligible world, is not moved when he hears the harmony arising from sensible sounds? Or what skilled geometrician or arithmetician, when he beholds through his eyes that which is commensurate, analogous and orderly, is not delighted with the view? . . . But his mind must be dull and sluggish in the extreme, and incapable of being incited to any thing else, who on seeing all the beautiful objects in the sensible world, all this symmetry and great arrangement of things, and the form apparent in the stars though so remote, is not from this view mentally agitated, and does not venerate them as admirable productions of still more admirable causes?[9]

If this holds for the physical world it must, a fortiori, hold for the world of law and order. The more the medieval thinkers be-

8. See Saint René Taillandier, *Scot Érigène et la philosophie scolastique* (Strasbourg, 1843).
9. Plotinus, "Against the Gnostics," in *Enneads*, II, 9, chap. XVI. English trans. by Thomas Taylor, "Select Works of Plotinus" (London, G. Bell & Sons, 1914), pp. 72–75. I have made a few slight alterations.

came acquainted with the works of the ancient thinkers, especially with the works of Aristotle, the less they could persevere in their merely negative attitude toward the social order. With the eleventh century there begins a slow and tenacious struggle. From the point of view of our general problem this struggle is extremely interesting and of paramount importance. Here was a definite mythical element that could not be openly attacked. To doubt the fact of the original sin was impossible for any medieval thinker. On the other hand the dogma of the fall of man obviously defied all efforts of dialectic thought. It was impenetrable and recalcitrant to rational explanation. Yet the scholastic thinkers would not admit such a defeat of reason. None of them thought and spoke of philosophy as a mere *ancilla theologiae*. They had a very high conception of the task and the dignity of philosophy. Hence they tried to restate the problem, and by this restatement to find a solution of the antinomy, to restore reason to its right and dignity.

The fall of man always remained a mystery; but the mystery itself was now seen in a new light and not considered to be unfathomable. Reason is not entirely and irretrievably corrupted. It has preserved a right of its own and a sphere of its own. It was for philosophy to secure this right and to define this sphere. All the scholastic systems, from the eleventh century on—those of Anselm of Canterbury, Abélard, Albert the Great, Thomas Aquinas —concentrated upon and coöperated in this problem. The physical as well as the political theories were under the influence of this general trend of thought. It is true that in the eleventh century there were still many thinkers who severely criticized and condemned the new tendency. They continued to speak of human society as being the result of human vice and sin. About seven centuries later Augustine's thesis was still repeated by Gregory VII. He declared that the state was a work of Sin and the Devil.[10] On the other hand, even this radical theory had to make some allowances for the earthly state. It had to admit that the political order possesses at least a conditional value. Although worthless in itself it fulfils, within its limits, a positive and indispensable role. It cannot lead us to the true end but it saves

10. Gregory VII, *Epistulae*, Lib. VIII, epist. xxi, in Jaffé, *Monum. Gregor.*, p. 456, quoted from von Gierke, *op. cit.*, English trans., p. 72; cf. Augustine, *City of God*, Bk. IV. chap. i.

men from the greatest evil—the evil of anarchy. The evil of the state, lodged as it is in the original sin of man, is deep and incurable; but it is only a relative evil. When it is compared with the highest, absolute, religious truth the state proves to be at a very low level; but it is still good in comparison to our common human standards which, without the state, would lead us to chaos. Besides, the state contains the remedy for its own inherent defects. Being a punishment for human vices and failures, it is a sort of divine cure that takes away the most disastrous effects of these failures. In a corrupted and disorganized world the earthly state is the only force which can maintain an equilibrium, a certain proportion and balance.[11]

In the system of Thomas Aquinas the evaluation of the social and political order has completely changed. Of course Thomas Aquinas never doubted any dogma of the Christian Church. But besides the Church he had found a new teacher and a new authority. To Thomas Aquinas, as well as to Dante, Aristotle was *il maestro di color che sanno*—the master of the knowing ones. And Aquinas wished not only to believe but also to know. According to him there is no contradiction between these two desires—they are not only compatible but complement each other. Since reason and revelation are two different expressions of one and the same truth, the truth of God, no disagreement between them is possible. If such a disagreement appears it must depend upon merely subjective causes. In this case it is for philosophy to discover these causes and to remove them. Reason may err; revelation is infallible. If there seems to be any discord and discrepancy between the two we may, therefore, from the first be convinced that the error is on the side of reason and we must try to find out and to correct this error. That is the true relation between philosophy and theology.[12] In all our philosophical efforts we must always be guided and enlightened by the revealed truth. Yet when accepting this guide, reason may trust its own forces. The two spheres thus become clearly distinguished. There can be no confusion between the realms of nature and grace. Each of them has its own objects and its own rights: impossibile est quod de eodem sit fides et scientia.[13]

11. For the development of this theory in the early Church see Ernst Troeltsch, *op. cit.* English trans., I, 145 ff.

12. Thomas Aquinas, *Summa contra gentiles*, Lib. I, cap. 1, 2, 9.

13. See Thomas Aquinas, *De veritate*, Quaest. xiv, art. 9.

This general principle stamps both Thomas Aquinas' natural philosophy and his social philosophy. Physics becomes independent; it can follow its own way; it is no longer under the control of theological thought. This "declaration of independence" had already been made in the work of Albert the Great, the teacher of Thomas Aquinas. Albert the Great leaves no doubt that we cannot decide any physical question upon the mere authority of theological thought or by the force of mere syllogisms. In all questions concerning particular natural phenomena experience can be our only guide. To account for any special phenomenon by referring to theological arguments and to the will of God would be absurd. On the strength of this maxim Albert the Great developed his own theory of nature with many original features. He became one of the pioneers of a new theory of motion that, in some respects, prepared the dynamics of Galileo.[14] Thomas Aquinas followed the same method. Since God is the creator of all things it is a matter of course that we have always to regard him as the first and principal cause. This general principle is confirmed both by the Christian revelation and by the authority of Aristotle. In the very beginning of his *Summa theologica* and his *Summa contra gentiles* Thomas starts from the definition of Aristotle that the subject-matter of metaphysics or "first philosophy" is the study of the first causes of things.[15] On the other hand it would be a grave error to regard the first cause as the only cause. If God acts, he does not act by a mere display of his will but in a regular way and by intermediary causes. It is the task of physics to study these intermediary causes. Without an insight into the *causae secundae* the physical world would be incomprehensible; it would be a constant miracle. To deny or minimize the secondary causes does not mean to extol the greatness and glory of God. On the contrary it detracts from his glory: "Detrahere rationes proprias rebus est divinae bonitati derogare." All finite, sensible, empirical things are the creation and the work of God; but it is precisely for this reason that they partake in his perfection—that they have an order and a beauty of their own. It is true that this order and beauty, being a beauty by participa-

14. About Albert the Great's contributions to physics and his general methods see Pierre Duhem, *Le système du monde* (Paris, A. Hermann, 1917), Tome V, chap. xi, 412 ff.

15. *Summa theologica*, Pars Prima, Quaest. i, art. 6; *Summa contra gentiles*, Lib. I, cap. i.

tion, can never attain the perfection of the original; nevertheless it holds its ground and is perfect within its own limitations. There is, therefore, one original goodness and beauty, the same for all things, that leaves room for innumerable particular goodnesses— between the two there can be no possible contradiction.[16]

This new valuation of the empirical world and of scientific thought would not have been possible without a complete reorientation of the general theory of knowledge. On the authority of Plato and Augustine all the previous systems of medieval philosophy had started from the sharp difference between the intellectual world and the world of sense-experience. Between these two realms there was a wide gulf. The one is the realm of being, the other that of becoming; the one gives us truth, the other gives us mere shadows. This severance of the two types of knowledge had its metaphysical roots in the radical dualism between body and soul. Body and soul do not belong to the same world. By its nature and essence the soul is opposed to the body. If it lives in it, it lives in it like a stranger and a prisoner. It is one of the highest tasks of philosophy to break this chain. But sense-experience has the opposite effect. Every new step in our sense-experience adds a new link to the chain. To free ourselves from this constraint, to get rid of the fetters of the body, is the highest aim of knowledge. "When does the soul attain to truth?" asks Plato.

For when it tries to consider anything in company with the body it is evidently deceived by it. In thought, then, if at all, something of the realities becomes clear to it. But it thinks best when none of these things troubles it, neither hearing nor sight . . . but it is, so far as possible, alone by itself, and takes leave of the body, and avoiding, so far as it can, all association or contact with the body, reaches out toward the reality.[17]

Thomas Aquinas reverses this conception. To him the body is no longer an obstacle to the activity of the soul. It is, on the contrary, the only means by which the activity of true thought can be actualized in the human world. Following his Aristotelian view Thomas Aquinas had to explain the union between body and soul in a way that was diametrically opposed to the doctrine of Augus-

16. *Summa theologica*, Pars Prima, Quaest. VI, art. 4.
17. Plato, *Phaedo*, 65 B, C. English trans. by H. N. Fowler (Loeb Classical Library), I, 227.

tine and the early Church. Man is not a *mixtum compositum*—a mere compound of two different and disparate elements. He is an organic unity and acts as such. Hence we cannot separate his rational activities from the act of perception. All forms of human knowledge, the higher and the lower ones, are linked together and directed to the same end. Far from being an obstacle to intellectual knowledge, sense-experience is the beginning and prerequisite of it: "principium nostrae cognitionis est a sensu." [18]

Thomas Aquinas' moral and political philosophy follows the same line of thought. The structure of the moral world is of the same type as that of the physical world. God is not only the creator of the physical universe; he is, first and foremost, the lawgiver, the origin of the moral law. Yet here too we must bear in mind the general principle that it is no increase of the glory of God but rather a detraction from this glory to overlook the *causae secundae* or to deny their effectiveness. We must give their due to these "second causes." God is the first cause and the ultimate end. But the moral order is a human order that can only be brought about by the free coöperation of man. It is not impressed upon us by a superhuman power; it depends on our own free acts. Hence Thomas Aquinas could not accept the current theological doctrine that the state is a divine institution appointed by God merely as a remedy for human sin.

As an Aristotelian Aquinas had to derive the social order from an empirical not from a transcendent principle. The state originates in the social instinct of man. It is this instinct that first leads to family-life and from there, in a continuous development, to all the other and higher forms of commonwealth. It is, therefore, neither necessary nor possible to connect the origin of the state with any supernatural event. The social instinct is common to men and animals; but in man it assumes a new shape. It is not only a natural but also a rational product, depending upon a free and conscious activity. Of course God remains, in a sense, the cause of the state; but here as well as in the physical world he works only as a *causa remota* or *causa impulsiva*. This original impulse does not relieve man himself of his fundamental obligation. He must by his own efforts build up an order of right and justice. It is this organization of the moral world and the state by

18. For a detailed historical discussion of this problem see E. Gilson, *Le Thomisme* (Nouvelle éd. Paris, Vrin, 1922), chap. IX, 138 ff.

which he proves his freedom. Here the chasm between the two realms, the realm of nature and the realm of grace, is not bridged. The two are fused together into a perfect unity. The power of grace is not enfeebled.

Thomas Aquinas is convinced that the highest good, the *summum bonum* of the ancient philosophers, cannot be attained bv reason alone. The *visio beatifica*, the mystical vision of God remains the absolute goal—and this goal always depends upon a free gift of divine grace.[19] But man himself must begin the work and prepare for this event. The divine right does not abrogate the human right which originates in reason.[20] Grace does not destroy nature; it perfects nature (*Gratia naturam non tollit, sed perficit*). Despite the Fall, therefore, man has not lost the faculty of using his forces in the right way and thus of preparing for his own salvation. He plays no passive role in the great religious drama; his active contribution is required and is, indeed, indispensable.[21] In this conception man's political life has won a new dignity. The earthly state and the City of God are no longer opposite poles; they are related to each other and complement each other.

19. *Summa theologica*, Prima Secundae, Quaest. xci, art. 4.
20. *Idem*, Prima Secundae, Quaest. x and xi.
21. *Idem*, Prima Secundae, Quaest. xci, art. 3.

X

MACHIAVELLI'S NEW SCIENCE OF POLITICS

The Machiavelli Legend

IN THE whole history of literature the fate of Machiavelli's *Principe* is the best witness to the truth of the saying: "Pro captu lectoris habent sua fata libelli." [1] The fame of the book was unique and unprecedented. This was no mere scholastic treatise to be studied by scholars and commented on by philosophers of politics. The book was not read for the satisfaction of an intellectual curiosity. In the hands of its first readers Machiavelli's *Prince* was immediately put into action. It was used as a powerful and dangerous weapon in the great political struggles of our modern world. Its effects were clear and unmistakable. Yet its *meaning* remained, in a sense, a secret. Even now, after the book has been approached from every angle, after it has been discussed by philosophers, by historians, by politicians and sociologists, this secret has not yet been completely revealed. From one century to another, almost from one generation to another, we find not only a change but a complete reversal in the judgments about *The Prince.* The same things hold for the author of the book. Confused by party love and party hatred the portrait of Machiavelli in history has varied; and it is extremely difficult to recognize behind all these variations the true face of the man and the theme of his book.

The first reaction was one of fear and horror. "We doubt," wrote Macaulay in the beginning of his essay on Machiavelli,

whether any name in literary history be so generally odious as that of the man whose character and writings we now propose to consider. The terms in which he is commonly described would seem to import that he was the Tempter, the Evil Principle, the discoverer of ambition and revenge, the original inventor of perjury, and that, before the publication of his fatal Prince, there had never been a hypocrite, a tyrant, or a traitor, a simulated virtue or a convenient crime. . . . Out

1. "The fortune of a book depends upon the capacity of its readers" (Terentianus Maurus, *De litteris, syllabis et metris,* v. 1286).

of his surname they have coined an epithet for a knave, and out of his Christian name a synonyme for the Devil.[2]

Later on this judgment was turned upside down. To a period of excessive blame there followed another of excessive praise. Reprobation and severe condemnation were turned into a kind of awe and veneration. Machiavelli, the counsellor of tyrants, became a martyr of freedom; the incarnate devil became a hero and almost a saint.

In a case like Machiavelli's both attitudes are inadequate and misleading. I do not say that we should not read and judge his book from a moral point of view. In the face of a work that had such tremendous moral effects such a judgment is unavoidable and is, indeed, imperative. But we should not *begin* with reprobation of approbation; with denouncement or applause. In regard to no other writer is it more necessary, perhaps, to remember the maxim of Spinoza: "Non ridere, non lugere neque detestari, sed intelligere." We should try to understand before we give a judgment on the man and his work. But this intellectual attitude has been counteracted by the influence of the two Machiavelli legends. When studying *The Prince* we must constantly be on our guard against them: the legend of hatred and the legend of love. The first was created in England during the seventeenth century. Not only the politicians or philosophers but also the great English poets had their share in the propagation of the Machiavelli myth. There is hardly one famous author of the Elizabethan period who does not mention Machiavelli's name and who does not give some verdict on his political theory. In his book *Machiavelli and the Elizabethan Drama* [3] Eduard Meyer noted no less than 395 references to Machiavelli in Elizabethan literature. And everywhere—in the plays of Marlowe, Ben Jonson, Shakespeare, Webster, Beaumont and Fletcher—Machiavellism means the incarnation of cunning, hypocrisy, cruelty and crime. The villain of the piece usually describes himself as a Machiavellian.[4] Perhaps the most striking expression of this general feeling is to be

2. Macaulay, *Critical, Historical and Miscellaneous Essays* (New York, 1860), I, 267 f.

3. "Literarhistorische Forschungen," Band I (Weimar, 1907).

4. For the evidence see the book of Mario Praz, *Machiavelli and the Elizabethans*, "Proceedings of the British Academy," Vol. XVIII (London, 1928).

found in the monologue of Richard, Duke of Gloucester, in the
Third Part of Shakespeare's *King Henry the Sixth:*

> "Why, I can smile and murder whiles I smile,
> And cry Content to that which grieves my heart,
> And wet my cheeks with artificial tears,
> And frame my face to all occasions.
> I'll drown more sailors than the mermaid shall;
> I'll slay more gazers than the basilisk;
> I'll play the orator as well as Nestor,
> Deceive more slily than Ulysses could;
> And, like a Sinon, take another Troy.
> I can add colours to the chameleon,
> Change shapes with Proteus for advantages,
> And set the murderous Machiavel to school." [5]

That Richard III should speak of Machiavelli was, of course,
an anachronism; but this anachronism was hardly noticed by
Shakespeare and his audience. For when Shakespeare wrote his
play the name of Machiavelli had almost lost its historical individuality. It was used for the description of a type of thought.
Even later the word Machiavelli or Machiavellism was always
surrounded with a demonic aura of hatred and abomination. In
Lessing's *Emilia Galotti* the minister and counsellor of the prince,
Marinelli, still embodies many features of the legendary Machiavelli. "Is it not enough," exclaims the prince at the end of Lessing's
tragedy, "that monarchs are men? Must devils disguise themselves in their friends?" [6]

Yet in spite of this hate and contempt Machiavelli's *theory*
never lost its ground. It was in the center of the general interest.
Curiously enough, its most resolute and implacable enemies often
contributed very much to strengthen this interest. The abomination was always mingled with a kind of admiration and fascination. The same men who were diametrically opposed to Machiavelli's political system could not refrain from paying homage to
his political genius. "Unius tamen Machiavelli ingenium non con-
temno," wrote Justus Lipsius in his *Politics,* "acre, subtile, ig-
neum." [7] In this regard there was hardly a difference between

5. *King Henry the Sixth,* Third Part, Act III, sc. 2.
6. Lessing, *Emilia Galotti,* Act V, sc. 8.
7. Justus Lipsius, *Politicorum sive civilis doctrinae libri sex* (Antwerp, 1599),
pp. 8 f.

Machiavelli's adherents and his fiercest adversaries. This strange alliance became one of the principal causes of the abiding power of Machiavellism in our modern political thought. Machiavelli was dead; but his theory appeared in ever new reincarnations. Marlowe in the prologue to his *Jew of Malta* introduces Machiavelli as saying:

> "Albeit the world thinks Machiavel is dead,
>   Yet was his soul but flown beyond the Alps;
>   And now the Guise is dead, is come from France,
>   To view this land, and frolic with his friends.
>   To some perhaps my name is odious,
>   But such as love me guard me from their tongues;
>   And let them know that I am Machiavel,
>   And weigh not men, and therefore not men's words.
>   Admired I am of those that hate me most.
>   Though some speak openly against my books,
>   Yet they will read me, and thereby attain
>   To Peter's chair: and when they cast me off,
>   Are poisoned by my climbing followers."

It took a long time before this legendary picture of Machiavelli was overthrown. The philosophers of the seventeenth century were the first to attack that popular judgment. Bacon found in Machiavelli a kindred spirit; he saw in him the philosopher who had broken away from all scholastic methods and tried to study politics according to empirical methods. "We are much beholden to Machiavelli and other writers of that class," says Bacon, "who openly and unfeignedly declare or describe what men do, and not what they ought to do." [8]

Yet none of the great modern thinkers has done more to revise the judgment on Machiavelli and to purge his name from obloquy than Spinoza. In the pursuit of this aim Spinoza was led to a curious hypothesis. He had to account for the fact that Machiavelli, who was regarded by him as a champion of freedom, could write a book that contained the most dangerous maxims of tyranny. That seemed understandable only on the assumption that *The Prince* had a hidden meaning. "What means a prince whose sole motive is lust of mastery should use to establish and maintain his dominion," says Spinoza in his *Tractatus politicus*,

8. Bacon, *De augmentis scientiarum*, Lib. VII, cap. II, sec. 10.

the most ingenious Machiavelli has set forth at large; but with what design one can hardly be sure. . . . He perhaps wished to show how cautious a free multitude should be of entrusting its welfare absolutely to one man, who . . . must be in daily fear of plots, and so is forced to look chiefly after his own interest, and, as for the multitude, rather to plot against it than consult its good. And I am the more led to this opinion concerning that most farseeing man, because it is known that he was favourable to liberty, for the maintenance of which he has besides given the most wholesome advice.[9]

Spinoza propounded this explanation only in a tentative way. He spoke rather hesitatingly; he was not too sure of his own hypothesis. And as a matter of fact he was mistaken in one point. He was in a certain sense still under the same illusion which he tried to destroy. For to him Machiavelli was not only a very ingenious and penetrating but also a very cunning writer. He looked upon him as a master of craftiness. This judgment is, however, not in keeping with the historical facts. If Machiavellism means deception or hypocrisy Machiavelli was no Machiavellian. He never was a hypocrite. When reading his familiar letters we are surprised to find a Machiavelli widely different from our conventional conceptions and prejudices; a man who speaks frankly, open-mindedly and with a certain ingenuousness. And what holds for the man, holds also for the author. This great teacher of political trickery and double crossing was perhaps one of the most sincere political writers. Talleyrand's famous saying, "La parole a été donnée à l'homme pour déguiser sa pensée," has often been admired as the very definition of the art of diplomacy. If this be true Machiavelli was anything but a diplomat. He never disguised himself nor did he conceal his opinions and judgments; he spoke his mind firmly and bluntly. The boldest word was to him always the best word. His thoughts and his style show us no ambiguity; they are clear, sharp, unmistakable.

The thinkers of the eighteenth century, the philosophers of the Enlightenment came to see the character of Machiavelli in a more favorable light. In a sense Machiavelli seemed to be their natural ally. When Voltaire launched his attack upon the Roman Church, when he spoke his famous *Écrasez l'infâme*, he could believe himself to be continuing the work of Machiavelli. Had not

9. Spinoza, *Tractatus theologico-politicus*, cap. v, sec. 5. English trans. by R. H. M. Elmes (Bohn's Philosophical Library, London, G. Bell and Sons, 1900), "Works," I, 315.

Machiavelli declared that the Church was chiefly responsible for all the misery of Italy? "To the Church of Rome and to its priests," he had said in his *Discorsi*, "we Italians owe this first debt, that through them we have become wicked and irreligious. And a still greater debt we owe them for what is the immediate cause of our ruin, namely, that by the Church our country is kept divided." [10] Words like these were grist to the mills of the French philosophers. On the other hand they never could agree with Machiavelli's theories. In his preface to the first edition of Frederick II's *Anti-Machiavelli* Voltaire still spoke of the "poisonous Machiavelli." [11] Frederick II who wrote his treatise as the young crown prince of Prussia, expressed in it the general feeling and judgment of the thinkers of the Enlightenment. "I shall venture to enter the lists," he said, "in defence of humanity against this monster, this declared enemy to it, and arm myself with reason and justice against sophisms and iniquitous argumentation . . . that so the reader may be immediately provided in one with an antidote for the poison which he finds in the other." [12]

These words were written in 1739, but in the following generation we hear quite a different tone. The judgment about Machiavelli changes completely and abruptly. In his *Letters for the Advancement of Humanity* Herder declared that it was a mistake to regard Machiavelli's *Prince* either as a satire or as pernicious book on politics or as a hybrid of these two things. Machiavelli was an honest and upright man, a sharp observer, a devoted friend of his country. Every line of his book proves that he was no traitor to the cause of humanity. The mistake of his book was due to the fact that nobody saw it in its right environment. The book is neither a satirical work nor a textbook of morality. It is a political masterpiece written for the contemporaries of Machiavelli. It was never the intention of Machiavelli to give a *general* theory of politics. He simply portrayed the customs, the ways of thinking and acting of his own times.[13]

This judgment was accepted by Hegel. And he spoke in a much

10. *Discourses on the First Decade of Titus Livy,* Bk. I, chap. xii. English trans. by N. H. Thomson (London, 1883), pp. 56 f.
11. An English translation of Voltaire's Preface was given by Ellis Farneworth, "The Works of Nicholas Machiavel" (2d ed. London, 1775), II, 181–186.
12. *Anti-Machiavel,* Preface, Farneworth, *op. cit.,* II, 178 f.
13. Herder, *Briefe zur Beförderung der Humanität,* Brief 58, "Werke," ed. B. Suphan, XVII, 319 ff.

more decisive tone. He became the first eulogist of Machiavelli. In order to understand this fact we must bear in mind the special conditions under which Hegel studied Machiavelli's political theory. It was in the times of the Napoleonic Wars—after Francis II had renounced the crown of the German Empire. The political collapse of Germany seemed to be an accomplished fact. In an unpublished treatise on the *Constitution of Germany*, written in 1801, Hegel begins with the words: "Germany has ceased being a state." In this frame of mind, in a political situation that seemed to be entirely desperate, Hegel read Machiavelli's *Prince*. And then he seems to have found the clue to this much denounced and much applauded book. He found an exact parallel between German public life in the nineteenth century and Italian national life in the period of Machiavelli. A new interest and a new ambition were roused in him. He dreamed of becoming a second Machiavelli—the Machiavelli of his own time. "In a period of misfortune," says Hegel,

when Italy was hastening towards her ruin and was the battlefield of wars carried on by foreign princes, when she was offering the means for these wars and was, at the same time, the prize of them, when Germans, Spanish, French and Swiss stripped her, and foreign governments decided on the destiny of this nation—in the deep feeling of this general misery, of hatred, of disorder and blindness, an Italian politician conceived with cold circumspection the necessary conception of the delivery of Italy by the union in one State. It is most unreasonable to treat the development of an idea which was formed by observing the conditions of Italy as a disinterested summary of moral and political principles, fit for all conditions and therefore for no condition. One has to read the Prince taking into consideration the history of the centuries preceding Machiavelli and the contemporary history of Italy, and then this book is not only justified, but it will appear as a highly magnificent and true conception of a genuine political genius of the greatest and noblest mind.

That was, indeed, a new step, and a step of high importance for the development of political thought in the nineteenth century. "It was new and it was a monstrosity," says Friedrich Meinecke, "when Machiavellism was inserted into an idealistic system that tried to embrace and support all ethical values whereas, hitherto, it had existed only outside the ethical cosmos. What happened here was almost to be compared to the legitimization of a bastard."[14]

The same tendency appears in the development of Fichte's political philosophy. In 1807 Fichte published an essay on Machiavelli in the review *Vesta* at Königsberg.[15] As he declared, his remarks were destined to contribute to the "Ehrenrettung eines braven Mannes"—to save the reputation of a righteous man. What we find here is a Fichte far different from our traditional view. We think of him as an advocate of the sternest moral rigorism. But in his judgment of Machiavelli there is nothing of the kind. He praised Machiavelli's political realism and tried to exculpate him from all moral blame. He admitted that Machiavelli professed a resolute paganism, that he had spoken of Christian religion with hatred and contempt. But all this did not change his judgment nor did it diminish his admiration for Machiavelli as a political thinker.

This interpretation of Machiavelli's work prevailed in the nineteenth century. From then on the roles were changed. Machiavelli's name which formerly had been an abusive word suddenly became a sort of *epitheton ornans*. Two strong powers, an intellectual and a social power, contributed to produce this effect. In the culture of the nineteenth century history began to take the leading part. After a short time it had replaced and almost eclipsed all the other intellectual interests. From this new perspective the former judgments on Machiavelli's *Prince* were unacceptable; for they had completely failed to see the historical background of the book. On the other hand nationalism had, since the beginning of the nineteenth century, become the strongest impulse and driving force of political and social life. These two movements had a deep repercussion upon the appreciation of Machiavelli's theory. In the literature of the seventeenth century Machiavelli had been described as an incarnation of the devil; and then, in a curious hyperbole, the devil himself was sometimes styled a Machiavellian and tinged with Machiavellism.[16] But two hundred years later there was the complete reversal of this judg-

---

14. *Die Idee der Staatsräson in der neueren Geschichte* (München and Berlin, R. Oldenbourg, 1925), p. 435.

15. Later reprinted in Fichte, "Nachgelassene Werke" (Bonn, 1835), III, 401–453.

16. See Mario Praz, *op. cit.*, p. 37.

ment. The devilization of Machiavelli was superseded by a sort of deification. The Italian patriots always hailed with enthusiasm the last chapter of Machiavelli's *Prince*. When Vittorio Alfieri published his work *Del Principe e delle lettere* he did not hesitate to speak of the "divino Machiavelli." He inserted into the work a special chapter that was meant to be an exact parallel to Machiavelli's famous exhortation to liberate Italy from the barbarians.[17]

I think, however, that in this case our "historism" and our nationalism have done much more to confuse our judgment than to clarify it. Since the times of Herder and Hegel we have been told that it is a mistake to regard Machiavelli's *Prince* as a systematic book—as a *theory* of politics. Machiavelli, it is said, never meant to offer such a theory; he wrote for a special purpose and for a small circle of readers. "The *Prince*," says L. Arthur Burd in the introduction to his edition of Machiavelli's work, "was never meant except for Italians, and Italians too of a given period; indeed, we may go further, and ask whether it was ever intended even for all Italians." [18] But is there any evidence that this current opinion is a correct expression of Machiavelli's own views and of his principal purpose? Had Machiavelli no other interest, and no other ambition, than to act as a spokesman of Italy, and were all his counsels restricted to a special moment in Italian history? Was he convinced that these views were not applicable to the political life and problems of future generations?

I am unable to find a single conclusive proof of this thesis. I fear lest we are suffering from a sort of optical illusion when judging in this way. We are liable to a mistake that may be called "the historian's fallacy." We are lending our own conceptions of history and historical method to an author to whom these conceptions were entirely unknown and to whom they would have been hardly understandable. To us it seems to be quite natural to envisage everything in its own surroundings. We consider this maxim to be a sort of categorical imperative for every sound interpretation of human actions and the phenomena of culture. Accordingly we have developed a feeling about the individuality

17. "Così intitolò il divino Machiavelli il suo ultimo capitolo del *Principe;* e non per altro si è qui ripetuto se non per mostrare che in diversi modi si può attenere lo stesso effetto." Alfieri, *Del Principe e delle lettere Libri III*, Cap. XI, "Opere di Vittorio Alfieri" (Italia, 1806), I, 244.

18. Niccolò Machiavelli, *Il Principe,* ed. L. Arthur Burd (Oxford, Clarendon Press, 1891), p. 14.

of things and the relativity of judgments that often makes us oversensitive. We hardly dare to make a general statement; we mistrust all clear-cut formulae; we are skeptical of the possibility of eternal truths and universal values. But this was not the attitude of Machiavelli nor was it that of the Renaissance. The artists, the scientists, the philosophers of the Renaissance did not know of our modern historical relativism; they still believed in an absolute beauty and an absolute truth.

In the case of Machiavelli himself there was a further and special reason that would forbid all those restrictions of his political theory which have been introduced by his modern commentators. He was a great historian; but his conception of the task of history was widely different from ours. He was interested in the statics not in the dynamics of historical life. He was not concerned with the particular features of a given historical epoch but sought for the recurrent features, for those things that are the same at all times. Our way of speaking of history is individualistic; Machiavelli's way was universalistic. We think that history never repeats itself; he thinks that it always repeats itself. "Anyone comparing the present with the past," he says,

will soon perceive that in all cities and in all nations there prevail the same desires and passions as always have prevailed; for which reason it should be an easy matter for him who carefully examines past events, to foresee those which are about to happen in any republic, and to apply such remedies as the ancients have used in like cases. . . . But these lessons being neglected or not understood by readers, or if understood by them, being unknown to rulers, it follows that the same disorders are common to all times.[19]

He who would forecast what is about to happen should, therefore, always look to what has been; for all human events, whether present or to come, have their exact counterpart in the past. "And this, because these events are brought about by men, whose passions and dispositions remaining in all ages the same, naturally give rise to the same effects." [20]

It follows from this static view of human history that all historical events are interchangeable. Physically they have a definite place in space and time; but their meaning and their character remain invariable. Now the thinker who could expound his own

19. *Discourses*, Bk. I, chap. xxxix. English trans., p. 125.
20. *Discourses*, Bk. III, chap. xliii. English trans., p. 475.

political maxims and theories in a commentary on the work of
Titus Livy certainly did not share the conception of our modern
historians that every epoch is to be measured by its own standards. To him all men and all ages were on the same level. Machiavelli does not make the slightest distinction between the examples
taken from the history of Greece or Rome and those taken from
contemporary history. He speaks in the same tone of Alexander
the Great and Cesare Borgia, of Hannibal and Lodovico il Moro.
In the same chapter in which he deals with the "new principalities" of the Renaissance he speaks of Moses, Cyrus, Romulus,
Theseus.[21] Even Machiavelli's own contemporaries, the great historians of the Renaissance, noticed and criticized this defect of
his method; Guicciardini especially made very interesting and
pertinent remarks to this point.[22]

If a thinker of this type undertook to build up a new constructive theory, a real science of politics, he certainly could not mean
to restrict this science to special cases. However paradoxical it
may sound, we must say that in this case our own modern historical sense has blinded us and prevented us from seeing the plain
historical truth. Machiavelli wrote not for Italy nor even for his
own epoch, but for the world—and the world listened to him.
He would never have agreed at all with the judgment of his
modern critics. What they praised in him would have been regarded by him as a defect. He looked upon his political work as
Thucydides did upon his historical work. He saw in it a κτῆμα ἐς ἀεί,
an everlasting possession, not an ephemeral thing. Machiavelli
was, in fact, overconfident in all his judgments. He was very fond
of the boldest generalizations. From a few examples taken from
ancient or modern history, he immediately drew the most far-
reaching conclusions. This deductive way of thinking and arguing must always be taken into consideration if we are to understand the results of Machiavelli's theory. It was not his intention
to describe his own personal experiences or to speak to a special
public. Of course he made use of his own experience. In the dedi-
cation of his *Discourses* he tells his friends, Zanobi Buondelmonte
and Cosimo Ruccellai, that the work which he offers to them contains all the political knowledge that he had collected from much

21. See *The Prince*, chap. VI.
22. See Guicciardini, "Considerazioni intorno ai Discorsi del Machiavelli,"
Opere inedite di F. Guicciardini (2d ed., Florence, 1857), I, 3–75.

reading and long experience in the affairs of the world. Yet Machiavelli's rather scanty experience of the affairs of the world would never have enabled him to write a work of the stature and importance of *The Prince*. For this quite different intellectual powers were needed, the power of logical deduction and analysis and that of a really comprehensive mind.

There is still another prejudice that has prevented many modern writers from seeing Machiavelli's *Prince* in its true light. Most of these writers, if not all of them, began with a study of Machiavelli's life. Here they hoped to find the clue to his theory of politics. It was taken for granted that a full knowledge of the *man* Machiavelli was enough to give us a full insight into the meaning of his work. Thanks to modern biographical research the Machiavelli of former times, the "murderous" Machiavelli of the Elizabethan drama has completely disappeared. We see Machiavelli as he really was, as an honest and upright man, a fervent patriot, a conscientious servant of his country, a loyal friend, and a man devoted to his wife and children.[23] Yet if we read all these personal qualities into his book we are mistaken. We fail to see both its fundamental merits and defects. It is not only the hypertrophy of our historical but also that of our psychological interest that has often confused our judgment. Former generations were interested in a book itself and studied its contents; we begin with psychoanalyzing its author. Instead of analyzing and criticizing Machiavelli's *thoughts* most of our modern commentators only ask for his *motives*. An amazing effort has been made to clear these motives; the question has become one of the most warmly debated in the whole literature on the subject.

I do not intend to go into the details of this discussion. The question of motives is always a difficult and precarious one—only in a few cases can it be decided with absolute certainty. But even if we could answer it in a clear and satisfactory way, that would not help us very much. The motives of a book, and the purpose for which it was written, are not the book itself. They are only the occasional cause; they do not make us understand its systematic purport. Earlier times suffered from a certain lack of biographical material; we perhaps suffer from the very contrary. We

23. For all details see the standard work on the subject, Pasquale Villari, *Niccolò Machiavelli e i suoi tempi* (Florence, 1877–82). 3 vols. English trans. (London, Kegan Paul, Trench & Co., 1878). 4 vols.

have read Machiavelli's intimate letters; we have studied his political career in every detail; we have read not only *The Prince* but all his other writings. But when it comes to the decisive point of judging *The Prince* both in its systematic meaning and its historical influence we are at a loss. Many modern students of Machiavelli are so very much absorbed in the particulars of his life that they begin to lose a grip on the whole; they do not see the wood for the trees. In order to save the reputation of the author they minimize the importance of his work. "What was there in the *Prince*," asks a recent biographer,

to occasion so much feeling and controversy? . . . The answer to the query now as it always has been in reality is—*Nothing*. There is nothing in the *Prince* to justify the hatred, the contempt, the loathing and horror that it called forth, just as there is nothing in it to merit the praise awarded by its enthusiasts who have read into it an interpretation of their own deeds and ideals. The prince himself, the procedure he is recommended to follow, the aims he is taught to keep in view, are all the products of the age, and the counsel offered by Machiavelli is that which experience had taught him to regard as the best one for the times—the only one likely to be understood and respected in that era.[24]

If this judgment were true the whole fame of Machiavelli would, to a large degree, be due to a mistake. Not Machiavelli himself, but his readers created his fame, and they could only do so by entirely misunderstanding the sense of his work.

That seems to me to be a very poor escape from the dilemma. The dilemma really exists. There seems to be a flagrant contradiction between Machiavelli's political doctrine and his personal and moral character. But we must certainly seek for a better explanation of the problem than to deny the originality or the universality of Machiavelli's theory. If this interpretation were right, we could of course, still regard Machiavelli as a great publicist and as the spokesman and propagandist for special political and national interests. Yet we could not see in him the founder of a new science of politics—the great constructive thinker whose conceptions and theories revolutionized the modern world and shook the social order to its foundations.

24. Jeffrey Pulver, *Machiavelli, the Man, His Work and His Times* (London, Herbert Joseph, 1937), p. 227.

XI

THE TRIUMPH OF MACHIAVELLISM
AND ITS CONSEQUENCES

Machiavelli and the Renaissance

NOTWITHSTANDING the widely different opinions about Machiavelli's work and his personality there is at least one point in which we find a complete unanimity. All authors emphasize that Machiavelli is "a child of his age," that he is a typical witness to the Renaissance. This statement is, however, of no avail as long as we have no clear and unambiguous conception of the Renaissance itself. And in this regard the situation seems to be hopelessly confused. In the last decades the interest in Renaissance studies has steadily increased. We are now provided with an astoundingly rich material, with new facts collected by political historians and by historians of literature, art, philosophy, science, and religion. But as to the main question, the question of the "meaning" of the Renaissance, we still seem to be in the dark. No modern writer could repeat the famous formulae by which Jakob Burckhardt tried to describe the civilization of the Renaissance. On the other hand all those descriptions that have been given by the critics of Burckhardt's work are equally objectionable. There are many scholars, and scholars of high authority in their special fields, who decided to cut the Gordian knot. They warn us against the use of the very term "Renaissance." "What is the use in questioning the Renaissance," wrote Lynn Thorndike in a recent discussion of the subject. "No one has ever proved its existence, no one has really tried to." [1]

But we should not discuss merely names and terms. That the Renaissance is not a mere *flatus vocis*, that the term corresponds to a historical reality, is undeniable. If we were in need of proving this reality it would be enough to summon two classical witnesses and to point to two works: Galileo's *Dialogues Concerning Two New Sciences* and Machiavelli's *Prince*. To connect these two

1. *Journal of the History of Ideas*, IV, No. 1 (January, 1943), with contributions by Hans Baron, Ernst Cassirer, Francis R. Johnson, Paul Oskar Kristeller, Dean P. Lockwood, and Lynn Thorndike.

works may, at first sight, appear to be very arbitrary. They deal with entirely diverse subjects; they belong to different centuries, they were written by men who were widely divergent in their thoughts, in their scientific interests, in their talents, and in their personalities. Nevertheless the two books have something in common. In both of them we find a certain trend of thought which marks them as two great and crucial events in the history of modern civilization. Recent research has taught us that both Machiavelli and Galileo had their precursors. Their works have not jumped, ready made and in full armor, out of the heads of their authors. They needed a long and careful preparation. But all this does not detract from their originality. What Galileo gave in his *Dialogues* and what Machiavelli gave in his *Prince* were really "new sciences." "My purpose," said Galileo, "is to set forth a very new science dealing with a very ancient subject. There is, in nature, perhaps nothing older than motion concerning which the books written by philosophers are neither few nor small; nevertheless I have discovered by experiment some properties of it which are worth knowing and which have not hitherto been either observed or demonstrated." [2] Machiavelli would have been perfectly entitled to speak of his book in the same way. Just as Galileo's Dynamics became the foundation of our modern science of nature, so Machiavelli paved a new way to political science.

In order to understand the novelty of both these works we must begin with an analysis of medieval thought. That in a mere chronological sense we cannot separate the Renaissance from the Middle Ages is obvious. By innumerable visible and invisible threads the Quattrocento is connected with scholastic thought and medieval culture. In the history of European civilization there never was a break of continuity. To seek for a point in this history in which the Middle Ages "end" and the modern world "begins" is a sheer absurdity.[3] But that does not do away with the necessity of looking for an *intellectual* line of demarcation between the two ages.

The medieval thinkers were divided into various schools. Between these schools, the dialecticians and the mystics, the realists

2. Galileo, *Dialogues Concerning Two New Sciences,* Third Day. English trans. by H. Crew and Alfonso de Salvio (New York, The Macmillan Co., 1914; now Evanston and Chicago, Northwestern University, 1939), p. 153.

3. In the following paragraphs I have repeated some remarks contained in a paper, "The Place of Vesalius in the Culture of the Renaissance," *The Yale Journal of Biology and Medicine,* XVI, No. 2 (December, 1943), 109 ff.

and the nominalists, there were interminable discussions. Nevertheless there was a common center of thought that remained firm and unchangeable for many centuries. To grasp the unity of medieval thought there is perhaps no better and easier way than to study the two books Περὶ τῆς οὐρανίας ἱεραρχίας and Περὶ τῆς ἐκκλησιαστικῆς ἱεραρχίας (*On the Celestial Hierarchy* and *On the Ecclesiastical Hierarchy*). The author of these books is unknown. In the Middle Ages they were generally attributed to Dionysius Areopagita, the disciple of St. Paul, who was converted and baptized by him. But this is only a legend. The books were probably written by a Neo-Platonic writer, a disciple of Proclus. They presuppose the theory of emanation that had been developed by Plotinus, the founder of the Neo-Platonic school. In order to understand a thing we must, according to this theory, always go back to its first principle and we must show in what way it has evolved from this principle. The first principle, the cause and origin of all things is the One, the Absolute. This absolute One develops into the multiplicity of things. But that is not a process of evolution, in our modern sense, it is rather a process of degradation. The whole world is held together by a golden chain—that *aurea catena* of which Homer spoke in a famous passage of his *Iliad*. All things whatsoever, spiritual and material things, the archangels, the angels, the seraphim and cherubim and all the other celestial legions, man, organic nature, matter, all of them are bound in this golden chain about the feet of God. There are two different hierarchies; the hierarchy of existence and that of value. But they are not opposed to each other; they correspond to each other in perfect harmony. The degree of value depends on the degree of being. What is lower in the scale of existence is also lower in the ethical scale. The more a thing is remote from the first principle, from the source of all things, so much the less is its grade of perfection.

The pseudo-Dionysian books about the celestial and ecclesiastic hierarchies were widely and eagerly studied throughout the Middle Ages. They became one of the principal sources of scholastic philosophy. The system developed in these books not only influenced the thoughts of men but was also connected with their deepest feelings, and it was expressed, in different ways, in the whole ethical, religious, scientific, and social order. In Aristotelian cosmology God is described as the "unmoved mover" of the universe. He is the ultimate source of motion—being at rest himself. He transmits his moving force first to the things that are next to him: to the highest celestial spheres. From here this force descends, by different degrees, to our own world, to the earth, the sublunar world, the world below the moon. But here we no longer find the same perfection. The higher world, the world of the celestial bodies, is made of an imperishable and incorruptible substance—the ether or the *quinta essentia,* and the movements of these bodies are eternal. In our world everything is perishable and liable to decay; and every movement comes, after a short time, to its standstill. There is a sharp discrimination between the lower and the higher worlds; they do not consist of the same substance and they do not follow the same laws of motion. The same principle holds for the structure of the political and social world. In religious life we find the ecclesiastical hierarchy that reaches from the Pope as the summit, to the cardinals, the archbishops, the bishops down to the lower degrees of the clergy. In the state the highest power is concentrated in the Emperor, who delegates this power to his inferiors, the princes, the dukes, and all the other vassals. This feudal system is an exact image and counterpart of the general hierarchical system; it is an expression and a symbol of that universal cosmic order that has been established by God and which, therefore, is eternal and immutable.

This system prevailed throughout the Middle Ages and proved its force in all spheres of human life. But in the first centuries of the Renaissance, in the Quattrocento and Cinquecento, it changed its form. The change did not come all of a sudden. We do not find a complete breakdown, an abrogation or an open denial of the fundamental principles of medieval thought. Nevertheless, one breach after another is made in the hierarchical system that seemed to be so firmly established and that had governed the thoughts and feelings of men for many centuries. The system was not destroyed; but it began to fade away and lose its unquestioned authority.

The Aristotelian cosmological system was replaced by the astronomical system of Copernicus. In the latter we no longer find a distinction between the "higher" and the "lower" world. All movements whatever, the movements of the earth and those of the celestial bodies, obey the same universal rules. According to Giordano Bruno, who was the first thinker to give a metaphysical interpretation of the Copernican system, the world is an infinite whole, pervaded and animated by the same infinite divine spirit. There are no privileged points in the universe, no "above" or "below." In the political sphere, too, the feudal order dissolved and began to crumble. In Italy new political bodies of a quite different type appeared. We find the Renaissance tyrannies, created by individual men, the great *condottieri* of the Renaissance, or by great families, the Visconti or Sforzas in Milan, the Medici in Florence, the Gonzagas in Mantua.

The Modern Secular State

That scene was the general political and intellectual background of Machiavelli's *Prince,* and if we approach his book from this angle, we have no difficulty in determining its meaning and its right place in the development of European culture. When Machiavelli conceived the plan of his book the center of gravity of the political world had already been shifted. New forces had come to the fore and they had to be accounted for—forces that were entirely unknown to the medieval system. When studying Machiavelli's *Prince* we are surprised how much his whole thought is concentrated upon this new phenomenon. If he speaks of the usual forms of government, of the city-republics or of the hereditary monarchies, he speaks very briefly. It is as if all these old and time-honored forms of government could hardly arouse Machiavelli's curiosity—as if they were unworthy of his scientific interest. But when Machiavelli begins to describe the new men and when he analyzes the "new principalities," he speaks in an entirely different tone. He is not only interested but captivated and fascinated. We feel this strong and strange fascination in every word about Cesare Borgia. Machiavelli's narration of the method taken by Cesare Borgia to rid himself of his enemies, is, both in style and thought, one of his most characteristic writings.[4] And long after the fall of Cesare Borgia he still felt the same way. The "Duca Valentino" always remains his classical example. He frankly confesses that, if he had to found a new state, he would always follow the famous model of Cesare Borgia.[5]

4. *Descrizione del modo tenuto dal duca Valentino nell' ammazzare Vitellozzo Vitelli,* etc. English trans. by Farneworth, "The Works of Nicholas Machiavel," II, 481–490.

5. *Lettere familiari,* CLIX, ed. Ed. Alvisi (Florence, 1883), p. 394.

All this cannot be explained by a personal sympathy for Cesare Borgia. Machiavelli had no reason to love him; on the contrary he had the strongest reasons to fear him. He always objected to the temporal power of the Pope, in which he saw one of the greatest dangers for Italy's political life. And nobody had done more to extend the temporal dominion of the Church than Cesare Borgia. On the other hand Machiavelli knew very well that the triumph of Cesare Borgia's politics would have meant the ruin of the Florentine Republic. How was it that, in spite of all this, he spoke of this enemy of his native city not only with admiration but with a kind of awe—with a reverence that perhaps no other historian ever felt for Cesare Borgia? This is only understandable if we bear in mind that the real source of Machiavelli's admiration was not the man himself but *the structure of the new state* that had been created by him. Machiavelli was the first thinker who completely realized what this new political structure really meant. He had seen its origin and he foresaw its effects. He anticipated in his thought the whole course of the future political life of Europe. It was this realization that induced him to study the form of the new principalities with the greatest care and thoroughness. He was perfectly aware that, when compared to former political theories, this study was to be regarded as a certain anomaly—and he apologized for the unusual course of his thought. "It ought not to appear strange to anyone," he says in the sixth chapter of *The Prince,*

if in what I am going to say concerning Principalities and Princes and States, altogether new, I shall quote great and eminent examples . . . I say then, that the possession of a Principality newly acquired by one who was not a Prince before, is more or less difficult to be maintained, in proportion to the abilities of the person that acquires it. Now as it argues a great share of valour and conduct, or good fortune at least, to raise one's self from a private condition to the rank of a Prince; either that valour and conduct, or that good fortune, in all probability, will enable the same person to surmount many other ensuing difficulties.[6]

Of those states that are based upon mere tradition and the principle of legitimacy Machiavelli speaks with a certain disdain or with an open irony. The ecclesiastic principalities, he declares, are very fortunate; for as they are fortified by religious constitutions

6. *The Prince.* chap. VI, *op. cit.,* II, 223 f.

of ancient and venerable authority they maintain themselves easily. "But as they are under the immediate superintendence and direction of an Almighty Being who both raised and supports them, and whose operations are far above the comprehension of our weak understanding, it would be rash and presumptuous in any mortal man that should pretend to account for these things: and therefore I may very well be excused from entering into any solution of that kind." [7] To attract Machiavelli's interest something different from these quiet and peaceful forms of commonwealth was needed—a body politic that had been created by force and was to be maintained by force.

Yet this political aspect is not the only one. In order to understand the whole purport of Machiavelli's theory we must see it in a much broader perspective. To the political we must add the philosophical point of view. This aide of the problem has been unduly neglected. Politicians, sociologists, and historians have vied with each other in analyzing, commenting, and criticizing Machiavelli's *Prince*. Yet in our textbooks of the history of modern philosophy we find no chapter on Machiavelli. That is in a sense understandable and justifiable. Machiavelli was no philosopher in the classical or medieval sense of this term. He had no speculative system, not even a system of politics. Nevertheless his book had a very strong indirect influence upon the general development of modern philosophical thought. For he was the first who, decidedly and unquestionably, broke away from the whole scholastic tradition. He destroyed the cornerstone of this tradition—the hierarchic system.

Time and again the medieval philosophers had quoted the saying of St. Paul that all power is of God.[8] The divine origin of the state was generally acknowledged. In the beginning of the modern era this principle was still in full vigor; it appears, for instance, in its full maturity in the theory of Suárez.[9] Even the strongest champions of the independence and sovereignty of the temporal power did not dare to deny the theocratic principle. As to Machiavelli he does not even attack this principle; he simply ignores it. He speaks from his political experience; and his experi-

7. *Idem,* chap. xi, *op. cit.,* II, 281.
8. See St. Paul, Romans, 13.1.
9. See von Gierke, *op. cit.,* quoted above (Chapter IX, p. 107, n. 4). English trans., pp. 71 ff.

ence had taught him that power, real and factual political power, is anything but divine. He had seen the men who were the founders of the "new principalities" and he had keenly studied their methods. To think that the power of these new principalities was of God was not only absurd, it was even blasphemous. As a political realist Machiavelli had, once for all, to give up the whole basis of the medieval political system. The pretended divine origin of the rights of kings seemed to him to be entirely fantastic. It is a product of imagination, not of political thought. "It now remains to show," says Machiavelli in the fifteenth chapter of *The Prince*,

in what manner a prince should behave to his subjects and friends: but as many have written upon this head already, it may seem arrogant in me, perhaps, to offer any thing further, especially as I shall differ widely in my opinion from that of others. However, since I write only for the instruction of such, as I would have thoroughly acquainted with the nature of things, I thought it better to represent them as they really are in fact, than to amuse the imagination with visionary models of Republics and Principalities (as several have done) which never did nor can exist.[10]

Machiavelli does not follow the usual ways of a scholastic disputation. He never argues about political doctrines or maxims. To him the facts of political life are the only valid arguments. It is enough to point to "the nature of things" to destroy the hierarchic and theocratic system.

Here too we find a close connection between the new *cosmology* and the new *politics* of the Renaissance. In both cases the difference between the "lower" and the "higher" world vanishes. The same principles and natural laws hold for the "world below" and the "world above." Things are on the same level both in the physical and in the political order. Machiavelli studied and analyzed political movements in the same spirit as Galileo, a century later, did the movement of falling bodies. He became the founder of a new type of science of a political static and a political dynamics.

On the other hand it would be incorrect to say that the only aim of Machiavelli was to describe certain political facts as clearly and exactly as possible. In this case he would have acted as a historian not as a theoretician of politics. A theory demands much

10. *The Prince, op. cit.,* II, 320.

more; it needs a constructive principle to unify and synthesize the facts. The secular state had existed long before the times of Machiavelli. One of the earliest examples of a complete secularization of political life is the state founded by Frederick II in the south of Italy; and this state had been created three hundred years before Machiavelli wrote his book. It was an absolute monarchy in the modern sense; it had emancipated itself from any influence of the Church. The officials of this state were not clerics but laymen. Christians, Jews, Saracens had an equal share in the administration; nobody was excluded for merely religious reasons. At the court of Frederick II a discrimination between sects, between nations or races was unknown. The paramount interest was that of the secular, the "earthly" state.

That was an entirely new fact, a fact that had no equivalent in medieval civilization. But this fact had not yet found a theoretical expression and justification. Frederick II was always regarded as an arch heretic. He was twice excommunicated by the Church. Dante, who felt a great personal admiration for him and saw in him the very model of a great monarch, nevertheless condemned him in his *Inferno* to the flaming sepulchers of the heretics.[11] The Lawbook of Frederick II has been styled "The Birth Certificate of Modern Bureaucracy." Yet although modern in his political actions Frederick was by no means modern in his thoughts. When he speaks about himself and about the origin of his empire he speaks not as a skeptic or heretic but as a mystic. He always claims an immediate personal relation to God. It is this personal relation that makes him entirely independent of all ecclesiastic influences and demands. As his biographer describes his thoughts and feelings,

divine Providence had singled him out, him only, and elevated him directly to the throne, and the marvel of her grace had enveloped the last of the Hohenstaufens in a mist of magic glory far beyond that of any other prince, far from the ken of the profane. The purposeful active Foresight of God did not enshroud the Emperor but revealed herself in him as the highest Reason: "Leader in Reason's path" he has been called.[12]

11. Dante, *Inferno*, X, 119 ff.
12. See Ernst Kantorowicz, *Frederick the Second*. English version by E. O. Lorimer (London, Constable & Co., 1931), p. 253. For all details see chap. v, pp. 215–368.

Religion and Politics

To Machiavelli all such mystical conceptions had become entirely unintelligible. In his theory all the previous theocratic ideas and ideals are eradicated root and branch. Yet he never meant on the other hand to separate politics from religion. He was an opponent of the Church but he was no enemy of religion. He was, on the contrary, convinced that religion is one of the necessary elements of man's social life. But in his system this element cannot claim any absolute, independent, and dogmatic truth. Its worth and validity depend entirely on its influence on political life.

By this standard, however, Christianity occupies the lowest place. For it is in strict opposition to all real political *virtù*. It has rendered men weak and effeminate. "Our religion," says Machiavelli, "instead of heroes canonizes those only that are meek and lowly" whereas the "Pagans deified none but men full of worldly glory, such as great commanders and illustrious governors of commonwealths." [13] According to Machiavelli this pagan use of religion was the only rational use. In Rome religion could become, instead of a source of weakness, the chief source of the greatness of the state. The Romans always availed themselves of religion in reforming their state, in prosecuting their wars, and in composing tumults.[14] Whether they did this in good faith or by calculation is of no importance. It was a proof of great political wisdom in Numa Pompilius that he derived his laws from a supernatural source and that he convinced the people of Rome that these laws had been inspired by his conversations with the nymph Egeria.[15] Even in Machiavelli's system, therefore, religion is indispensable. But it is no longer an end in itself; it has become a mere tool in the hands of the political rulers. It is not the foundation of man's social life but a powerful weapon in all political struggles. This weapon must prove its strength in action. A merely passive religion, a religion that flees the world instead of organizing it, has proved to be the ruin of many kingdoms and states. Religion is only good if it produces good order; and good order

13. *Discourses*, Bk. II, chap. II.
14. *Idem*, Bk. I, chap. XIII.
15. *Idem*, Bk. I, chap. XI.

is generally attended with good fortune and success in any undertaking.[16] Here the final step has been taken. Religion no longer bears any relation to a transcendent order of things and it has lost all its spiritual values. The process of secularization has come to its close; for the secular state exists not only *de facto* but also *de jure;* it has found its definite theoretical legitimization.

16. *Ibid.*

XII

IMPLICATIONS OF THE NEW THEORY
OF THE STATE

The Isolation of the State and Its Dangers

THE whole argument of Machiavelli is clear and coherent. His logic is impeccable. If we accept his premises we cannot avoid his conclusions. With Machiavelli we stand at the gateway of the modern world. The desired end is attained; the state has won its full autonomy. Yet this result has had to be bought dearly. The state is entirely independent; but at the same time it is completely isolated. The sharp knife of Machiavelli's thought has cut off all the threads by which in former generations the state was fastened to the organic whole of human existence. The political world has lost its connection not only with religion or metaphysics but also with all the other forms of man's ethical and cultural life. It stands alone—in an empty space.

That this complete isolation was pregnant with the most dangerous consequences should not be denied. There is no point in overlooking or minimizing these consequences. We must see them face to face. I do not mean to say that Machiavelli was fully aware of all the implications of his political theory. In the history of ideas it is by no means unusual that a thinker develops a theory, the full purport and significance of which is still hidden to himself. In this regard we must, indeed, make a sharp distinction between Machiavelli and Machiavellism. There are many things in the latter that could not be foreseen by Machiavelli. He spoke and judged from his own personal experience, the experience of a secretary of the State of Florence. He had studied with the keenest interest the rise and fall of the "new principalities." But what were the small Italian tyrannies of the Cinquecento when compared to the absolute monarchies of the seventeenth century and with our modern forms of dictatorship? Machiavelli highly admired the methods used by Cesare Borgia to liquidate his adversaries. Yet in comparison with the later much more developed technique of political crimes these methods appear to be only child's play. Machiavellism showed its true face and its real danger when its principles were later applied to a larger scene and to entirely new political conditions. In this sense we may say that the consequences of Machiavelli's theory were not brought to light until our own age. Now we can, as it were, study Machiavellism in a magnifying glass.

There was still another circumstance that prevented Machiavellism from coming to its full maturity. In the centuries that followed, in the seventeenth and eighteenth centuries, his doctrine played an important role in practical political life; but, theoretically speaking, there were still great intellectual and ethical forces which counterbalanced its influence. The political thinkers of this period, with the single exception of Hobbes, were all partisans of the "Natural Right theory of the state." Grotius, Pufendorf, Rousseau, Locke looked upon the state as a means, not as an end in itself. The concept of a "totalitarian" state was unknown to these thinkers. There was always a certain sphere of individual life and individual freedom which remained inaccessible to the state. The state and the sovereign in general were *legibus solutus*. But this meant only that they were free from legal coercion; it did not mean that they were exempt from moral obligations. After the beginning of the nineteenth century, however, all this was suddenly called in question. Romanticism launched a violent attack against the theory of natural rights. The romantic writers and philosophers spoke as resolute "spiritualists." But it was precisely this metaphysical spiritualism that paved the way for the most uncouth and uncompromising materialism in political life. In this regard it is a highly interesting and remarkable fact that the "idealistic" thinkers of the nineteenth century, Fichte and Hegel, became the advocates of Machiavelli and the defenders of Machiavellism. After the collapse of the theory of natural rights the last barrier to its triumph was removed. There was no longer any great intellectual or moral power to check and counterbalance Machiavellism; its victory was complete and seemed to be beyond challenge.

The Moral Problem in Machiavelli

That Machiavelli's *Prince* contains the most immoral things and that Machiavelli has no scruples about recommending to the ruler all sorts of deception, of perfidy, and cruelty is incontestable. There are, however, not a few modern writers who deliberately shut their eyes to this obvious fact. Instead of explaining it they make the greatest efforts to deny it. They tell us that the measures recommended by Machiavelli, however objectionable in themselves, are only meant for the "common good." The ruler has to respect this common good. But where do we find this mental reservation? *The Prince* speaks in quite a different, in an entirely uncompromising way. The book describes, with complete indifference, the ways and means by which political power is to be acquired and to be maintained. About the *right use* of this power it does not say a word. It does not restrict this use to any consideration for the commonwealth. It was only centuries later that the Italian patriots began to read into Machiavelli's book all their own political and national idealism. In any word of Machiavelli, declared Alfieri, we find the same spirit, a spirit of justice, of passionate love for freedom, of magnanimity and truth. He who understands Machiavelli's work in the right way must become an ardent enthusiast for liberty and an enlightened lover of all political virtues.[1]

This is, however, only a rhetorical answer to our question, not a theoretical one. To regard Machiavelli's *Prince* as a sort of ethical treatise or a manual of political virtues is impossible. We need not enter here into a discussion of the vexed problem whether the last chapter of *The Prince*, the famous exhortâtion to deliver Italy out of the bonds of barbarians, is an integral part of the book or a later addition. Many modern students of Machiavelli have spoken of *The Prince* as if the whole book were nothing but a preparation for this closing chapter, as if this chapter were not only the climax but also the quintessence of Machiavelli's political thought. I think this view to be erroneous, and, as far as I see, the *onus probandi* rests in this case with the advocates of the

---

1. "Chiunque ben legge e nell' autore s'immedesima non può riuscire se non un focoso entusiasta di libertà, e un illuminatissimo amatore d' ogni politica virtù." Alfieri, *Del Principe e delle lettere,* cap. VIII.

thesis. For there are obvious differences between the book taken as a whole and the last chapter, differences of thought and differences of style. In the book itself Machiavelli speaks with an entirely detached mind. Everyone may hear him and make what use he will of his advice which is available not only to the Italians but also to the most dangerous enemies of Italy. In the third chapter Machiavelli discusses at great length all the errors committed by Louis XII in his invasion of Italy. Without these errors, he declares, Louis XII would have had no difficulty in attaining his end, which was to subjugate the whole of Italy. In his analysis of political actions Machiavelli never gives vent to any personal feeling of sympathy or antipathy. To put it in the words of Spinoza he speaks of these things as if they were lines, planes, or solids. He did not attack the principles of morality; but he could find no use for these principles when engrossed in problems of political life. Machiavelli looked at political combats as if they were a game of chess. He had studied the rules of the game very thoroughly. But he had not the slightest intention of changing or criticizing these rules. His political experience had taught him that the political game never had been played without fraud, deception, treachery, and felony. He neither blamed nor recommended these things. His only concern was to find the best move —the move that wins the game. When a chess champion engages in a bold combination, or when he tries to deceive his partner by all sorts of ruses and stratagems, we are delighted and admire his skill. That was exactly Machiavelli's attitude when he looked upon the shifting scenes of the great political drama that was played before his eyes. He was not only deeply interested; he was fascinated. He could not help giving his opinion. Sometimes he shook his head at a bad move; sometimes he burst out with admiration and applause. It never occurred to him to ask by whom the game was played. The players may be aristocrats or republicans, barbarians or Italians, legitimate princes or usurpers. Obviously that makes no difference for the man who is interested in the game itself—and in nothing but the game. In his theory Machiavelli is apt to forget that the political game is not played with chessmen, but with real men, with human beings of flesh and blood; and that the weal and woe of these beings is at stake.

It is true that in the last chapter his cool and detached attitude gives way to an entirely new note. Machiavelli suddenly shakes off the burden of his logical method. His style is no longer analytical but rhetorical. Not without reason has that last chapter been compared to Isocrates' exhortation to Philip.[2] Personally we may prefer the emotional note of the last chapter to the cold and indifferent note of the rest of the book. Yet it would be wrong to assume that in the book Machiavelli has concealed his thoughts; that what is said there was only a sham. Machiavelli's book was sincere and honest; but it was dictated by his conception of the meaning and task of a *theory* of politics. Such a theory must describe and analyze; it cannot blame or praise.

No one has ever doubted the patriotism of Machiavelli. But we should not confuse the philosopher with the patriot. *The Prince* was the work of a political thinker—and of a very radical thinker. Many modern scholars are liable to forget or, at least, to underrate this radicalism of Machiavelli's theory. In their efforts to purge his name from all blame they have obscured his work. They have portrayed a harmless and innocuous but at the same time a rather trivial Machiavelli. The real Machiavelli was much more dangerous—dangerous in his thoughts, not in his character. To mitigate his theory means to falsify it. The picture of a mild or lukewarm Machiavelli is not a true historical portrait. It is a "fable convenue" just as much opposed to the historical truth as the conception of the "diabolic" Machiavelli. The man himself was loath to compromise. In his judgments about political actions he warned over and over again against irresolution and hesitation. It was the greatness and the glory of Rome that in Roman political life all half measures were avoided.[3] Only weak states are always dubious in their resolves, and tardy resolves are always hateful.[4] It is true that men, in general, seldom know how to be wholly good or wholly bad. Yet it is precisely this point in which the real politician, the great statesman, differs from the average man. He will not shrink from such crimes as are stamped with an inherent greatness. He may perform many good actions, but when circumstances require a different course he will be "splendidly wicked."[5] Here we hear the voice of the real Machiavelli, not of the conventional one. And even if it were true that

2. See L. A. Burd's notes in his edition of "*Il Principe*," p. 366.
3. *Discourses*, Bk. II, chap. xxiii.
4. *Idem*, Bk. II, chap. xv; Bk. I, chap. xxxviii.
5. *Idem*, Bk. I, chap. xxvii.

all the advice of Machiavelli was destined only for the "common good," who is the judge of this common good? Obviously no one but the prince himself. And he will always be likely to identify it with his private interest: he will act according to the maxim: *L'état c'est moi.* Moreover, if the common good could justify all those things that are recommended in Machiavelli's book, if it could be used as an excuse for fraud and deception, felony, and cruelty, it would hardly be distinguishable from the common evil.

It remains, however, one of the great puzzles in the history of human civilization how a man like Machiavelli, a great and noble mind, could become the advocate of "splendid wickedness." And this puzzle becomes the more bewildering if we compare *The Prince* with Machiavelli's other writings. There are many things in these other writings that seem to be in flagrant contradiction with the views exposed in *The Prince.* In his *Discourses* Machiavelli speaks as a resolute republican. In the struggles between the Roman aristocracy and the plebeians his sympathy is clearly on the side of the people. He defends the people against the reproach of inconstancy and fickleness; [6] he declares that the guardianship of public freedom is safer in the hands of the commons than in those of the patricians.[7] He speaks in a very disparaging tone of the *gentiluomini,* of those men who live in opulence and idleness on the revenues of their estates. Such persons, he declares, are very mischievous in every republic or country. But even more mischievous are those who are lords of strongholds and castles besides their estates, and who have vassals and retainers who render them obedience. Of these two classes of men the Kingdom of Naples, the Romagna and Lombardy were full; and hence it happened that in these provinces no commonwealth or free form of government ever existed; because men of this sort are the sworn foes to all free institutions.[8] Taking everything into consideration, declares Machiavelli, the people are wiser and more constant than a prince.[9]

In *The Prince* we hear very little of these convictions. Here the fascination of Cesare Borgia is so strong that it seems completely to eclipse all republican ideals. The methods of Cesare Borgia be-

6. *Idem,* Bk. I, chap. LVIII.
7. *Idem,* Bk. I, chaps. IV, V.
8. *Idem,* Bk. I, chap. LV.
9. *Idem,* Bk. I, chap. LVIII.

come the hidden center of Machiavelli's political reflections. His thought is irresistibly attracted to this center. "Upon a thorough review of the Duke's conduct and actions," says Machiavelli,

I see nothing worthy of reprehension in them; on the contrary, I have proposed them and here propose them again as a pattern for the imitation of all such as arrive at dominion by the arms or fortune of others. For as he had a great spirit and vast designs, he could not well have acted otherwise in his circumstances: and if he miscarried in them, it was entirely owing to the sudden death of his father, and the desperate condition in which he happened to lie himself at that critical juncture.[10]

If Machiavelli reprehends anything in Cesare it is not his character; it is not his ruthlessness, his cruelty, his treachery and rapacity. For all this he has no word of blame. What he blames in him is the only grave error in his political career: the fact that he allowed Julius II, his sworn enemy, to be elected Pope after the death of Alexander VI.

There is a story according to which Talleyrand, after the execution of the Duke of Enghien by Napoleon Bonaparte, exclaimed: "C'est plus qu'un crime, c'est une faute!" If this anecdote be true then we must say that Talleyrand spoke as a true disciple of Machiavelli's *Prince*. All judgments of Machiavelli are political and moral judgments. What he thinks to be objectionable and unpardonable in a politician are not his crimes but his mistakes.

That a republican could make the Duca Valentino his hero and model seems to be very strange: for what would have become of the Italian Republics and all their free institutions under a ruler like Cesare Borgia? There are however two reasons that account for this seeming discrepancy in Machiavelli's thought: a general and a particular one. Machiavelli was convinced that all his political thoughts were entirely realistic. Yet when studying his republicanism we find very little of this political realism. His republicanism is much more "academic" than practical; more contemplative than active. Machiavelli had served, sincerely and faithfully, the cause of the city-state of Florence. As a secretary of the state he had combated the Medici. But when the power of the Medici was restored he hoped to retain his post; he made the

10. *The Prince*, chap. VII (VI in Farneworth trans. is a misprint), cf. chap. XIII. Farneworth trans., p. 247, cf. p. 304.

greatest efforts to make his peace with the new rulers. That is easily understandable. Machiavelli did not swear by the words of any political program. His was not a stern unyielding and uncompromising republicanism. He could readily accept an aristocratic government; for he had never recommended an ochlocracy, a dominion of the populace. It is not without reason, he declares, that the voice of the people has been likened to the voice of God.[11] But on the other hand he is convinced that to give new institutions to a commonwealth, or to reconstruct old institutions on an entirely new basis, must be the work of one man.[12] The multitude is helpless without a head.[13]

Yet if Machiavelli admired the Roman plebs, he had not the same belief in the power of the citizens of a modern state to rule themselves. Unlike many other thinkers of the Renaissance he did not cherish the hope of restoring the life of the ancients. The Roman Republic was founded upon the Roman virtù—and this virtù is lost, once for all. The attempts to resuscitate ancient political life appeared to Machiavelli as idle dreams. His was a sharp, clear, and cool mind; not the mind of a fanatic and enthusiast like Cola di Rienzi. In Italian life of the fifteenth century Machiavelli saw nothing to encourage his republican ideals. As a patriot he felt the strongest sympathies for his fellow citizens, but as a philosopher he judged them very severely; his feeling bordered on contempt. Only in the North he was still able to find some traces of love of freedom and the ancient virtù. The nations of the North, he says, have to a certain degree been saved because they did not learn the manners of the French, the Italians, or the Spaniards—this corruption of the world.[14] This judgment about his own times was irrevocable. Machiavelli did not even admit that it could be questioned by anyone. "I know not," he says,

whether I may not deserve to be reckoned in the number of those who deceive themselves, if, in these discourses of mine, I render excessive praise to the ancient times of the Romans while I censure our own. And, indeed, were not the excellence which then prevailed and the

11. *Discourses,* Bk. I, chap. LVIII.
12. *Idem,* Bk. I, chap. IX.
13. *Idem,* Bk. I, chap. XLIV.
14. *Idem,* Bk. I, chap. LV. "Perchè non hanno possuto pigliare i costumi, nè franciosi, nè spagnuoli, nè italiani; le quali nazioni tutte insieme sono la corruttela del mondo."

corruption which prevails now clearer than the sun. I should proceed more guardedly in what I have to say. . . . But since the thing is so plain that everyone sees it, I shall be bold to speak freely all I think, both of old times and of new, in order that the minds of the young who happen to read these my writings may be led to shun modern examples, and be prepared to follow those set by antiquity whenever chance affords the opportunity.[15]

Machiavelli was by no means especially fond of the *principati nuovi*, of the modern tyrannies. He could not fail to see all their defects and evils. Yet under the circumstances and conditions of modern life these evils seemed to him to be unavoidable. There is no doubt that Machiavelli personally would have abhorred most of the measures he recommended to the rulers of the new states. He tells us in so many words that these measures are most cruel expedients, repugnant not merely to every Christian, but to every civilized rule of conduct and such as every man should shun, choosing rather to lead a private life than to be a king on terms so hurtful to mankind. But, as he adds very characteristically, whoever will not keep to the fair path of virtue, must, to maintain himself, enter the path of evil.[16] *Aut Caesar aut nihil*—either to lead a private, harmless and innocuous life, or to enter the political arena, struggle for power, and maintain it by the most ruthless and radical means. There is no choice between these two alternatives.

When speaking of Machiavelli's "immoralism" we must, however, not understand this term in our modern sense. Machiavelli did not judge human actions from a standpoint "beyond good and evil." He had no contempt for morality; but he had very little esteem for men. If he was a skeptic, his skepticism was a human rather than a philosophical skepticism. The best proof of this ineradicable skepticism, of this deep mistrust of human nature, is to be found in his comedy *Mandragola*. This masterpiece of comic literature reveals perhaps more of Machiavelli's judgment about his contemporaries than all his political and historical writings. For his own generation and his own country he saw no hope. And in his *Prince* he tried to inculcate the same conviction of the deep moral perversion of men upon the minds of the rulers of states.

15. *Idem*, Bk. II, Preface. Thomson trans., p. 191.
16. *Idem*, Bk. I, chap. XXVI.

This was an integral part of his political wisdom. The first condition for ruling men is to understand man. And we shall never understand him as long as we are suffering from the illusion of his "original goodness." Such a conception may be very humane and benevolent; but in political life it proves to be an absurdity. Those that have written upon civil government lay it down as first principle, says Machiavelli, and all historians demonstrate the same, that whoever would found a state, and make proper laws for the government of it, must presuppose that all men are bad by nature, and that they will not fail to show that natural depravity of heart, whenever they have a fair opportunity.[17]

This depravity cannot be cured by laws; it must be cured by force. Laws are, indeed, indispensable for every commonwealth —but a ruler should use other and more convincing arguments. The best foundations of all states, whether new, old, or mixed, says Machiavelli, are good laws and good arms. But since good laws are ineffective without arms, and since, on the other hand, good arms will always give due weight to such laws, I shall here no longer argue about laws but speak about arms.[18] Even the "saints," the religious prophets have always acted according to this principle as soon as they became rulers of states. Without this they were lost from the very beginning. Savonarola failed to attain his end, because he had neither power to keep those steady in their persuasion who acknowledged his mission nor to make others believe who denied it. Hence it comes that all the prophets who were supported by an armed force succeeded in their undertakings, whereas those that had not such a force to rely on were defeated and destroyed.[19]

Of course Machiavelli prefers by far the good, the wise, and noble rulers to the bad and cruel ones; he prefers a Marcus Aurelius to a Nero. Yet if you write a book that is destined solely for these good and just rulers, the book itself may be excellent but it will not find many readers. Princes of this kind are the exception, not the rule. Everyone admits how praiseworthy it is in a prince to keep faith, and to live with integrity. Nevertheless, as matters stand, a prince has also to learn the opposite art: the art of craft and treachery.

17. *Idem*, Bk. I, chap. III.
18. *The Prince*, chap. XII.
19. *Idem*, chap. VI.

A prince ought to know how to resemble a beast as well as a man, upon occasion: and this is obscurely hinted to us by ancient writers who relate that Achilles and several other princes in former times were sent to be educated by Chiron the Centaur; that as their preceptor was half-man and half-beast, they might be taught to imitate both natures since one cannot long support itself without the other. Now, because it is so necessary for a prince to learn how to act the part of a beast sometimes, he should make the lion and the fox his patterns: for the lion has not cunning enough of himself to keep out of snares and toils; nor the fox sufficient strength to cope with a wolf: so that he must be a fox to enable him to find out the snares, and a lion in order to terrify the wolves.[20]

This famous simile is highly characteristic and illuminating. Machiavelli did not mean to say that a teacher of princes should be a brute. Yet he has to do with brutal things and must not recoil from seeing them eye to eye and from calling them by their right names. Humanity alone will never do in politics. Even at its best politics still remains an intermediary between humanity and bestiality. The teacher of politics must therefore understand both things: he must be half man, half beast.

No political writer before Machiavelli had ever spoken in this way. Here we find the clear, the unmistakable and ineffaceable difference between his theory and that of all his precursors—the classical as well as the medieval authors. Pascal says that there are certain words which, suddenly and unexpectedly, make clear the sense of a whole book. Once we meet with these words we no longer can have any doubt about the character of the book: all ambiguity is removed. Machiavelli's saying that a teacher of princes must be *un mezzo bestia e mezzo uomo* is of such a kind: it reveals, as in a sudden flash, the nature and purpose of his political theory. No one had ever doubted that political *life,* as matters stand, is full of crimes, treacheries, and felonies. But no thinker before Machiavelli had undertaken to teach the *art* of these crimes. These things were done, but they were not taught. That Machiavelli promised to become a teacher in the art of craft, perfidy, and cruelty was a thing unheard of. And he was very thorough in his teaching. He did not hesitate or compromise. He tells the ruler that since cruelties are necessary they should be done quickly and mercilessly. In this case, and in this

20. *Idem,* chap. xviii, *op. cit.,* II, 340.

case alone, they will have the desired effect: they will prove to be *crudeltà bene usate*. It is no use postponing or mitigating a cruel measure; it must be done at one blow and regardless of all human feelings. A usurper who has won the throne must not allow any other man or woman to stand in his way; he must extirpate the whole family of the legitimate ruler.[21] All these things may be called shameful; but in political life we cannot draw a sharp line between "virtue" and "vice." The two things often change places: if everything is considered we shall find that some things that seem to be very virtuous, if they are turned into actions, will be ruinous to the prince, whereas others that are regarded as vicious are beneficial.[22] In politics all things change their place: fair is foul, and foul is fair.

It is true that there are some modern students of Machiavelli who see his work in quite a different light. They tell us that this work was by no means a radical innovation. It was, after all, a rather commonplace thing; it belonged to a familiar literary type. *The Prince*, these writers assure us, is only one of the innumerable books that, under various titles, had been written for the instruction of kings. Medieval and Renaissance literatures were full of these treatises. Between the years 800 and 1700 there were accessible some thousand books telling the king how to conduct himself so that he may be "clear in his great office." Everyone knew and read these works: *De officio regis, De institutione principum, De regimine principum*. Machiavelli simply added a new link to this long list. His book is by no means *sui generis;* it was rather a typical book. There is no real novelty in *The Prince*—neither a novelty of thought nor a novelty of style.[23]

Against this judgment we can, however, appeal to two witnesses: to the witness of Machiavelli himself and to that of his readers. Machiavelli was deeply convinced of the originality of his political views. "Prompted by that desire which nature has implanted in me fearlessly to undertake whatsoever I think offers a common benefit to all," he wrote in the Preface to his *Discourses*, "I enter on a path which, being untrodden by any though it involve me in trouble, may yet win me thanks from those who

---

21. *Discourses*, Bk. III, chaps. IV, XXX; cf. *The Prince*, chap. III: "a possederli sicuramente basta avere spenta la linea del principe che li dominava."

22. *The Prince*, chap. XV.

23. See Allan H. Gilbert, *Machiavelli's "Prince" and Its Forerunners. "The Prince" as a Typical Book "de Regimine Principum"* (Duke University Press, 1938).

judge my efforts in a friendly spirit." [24] This hope was not disappointed: Machiavelli's readers judged likewise. His work was read not only by scholars or by students of politics. It had a much wider circulation. There is hardly one of the great modern politicians who did not know Machiavelli's book and who was not fascinated by it. Among its readers and admirers we find the names of Catarina de' Medici, Charles V, Richelieu, Queen Christina of Sweden, Napoleon Bonaparte. To these readers the book was much more than a book; it was a guide and lodestar in their political actions. Such a deep and permanent influence of *The Prince* would hardly be understandable if the book were only a specimen of a well-known literary type. Napoleon Bonaparte declared that of all political works those of Machiavelli were the only ones worth reading. Can we think of a Richelieu, a Catarina de' Medici, a Napoleon Bonaparte as enthusiastic students of works such as Thomas Aquinas' *De regimine principum*, Erasmus' *Institutio principis Christiani* or Fénélon's *Télémaque?*

In order to show the striking contrast between *The Prince* and all the other works *De regimine principum* we need, however, not rely on personal judgments. There are other and better reasons to prove that there is a real gulf between Machiavelli's views and those of all previous political writers. Of course *The Prince* had its forerunners; what book has not? We may find in it many parallels to other writers. In Burt's edition most of these parallels have been carefully collected and annotated. But literary parallels do not necessarily prove parallels of thought. *The Prince* belongs to a "climate of opinion" quite different from that of previous writers on the subject. The difference may be described in two words. The traditional treatises *De rege et regimine, De institutione regis, De regno et regis institutione* were *pedagogical* treatises. They were destined for the education of princes. Machiavelli had neither the ambition nor the hope of being equal to this task. His book was concerned with quite different problems. It only tells the prince how to acquire his power and how, under difficult circumstances, to maintain it. Machiavelli was not naïve enough to assume that the rulers of the *principati nuovi*, that men like Cesare Borgia, were apt subjects for "education." In earlier and later books that called themselves *The King's Mirror* the monarch was supposed to see, as in a mirror, his fundamental duties

24. Thomson trans., p. 3.

and obligations. But where do we find such a thing in Machiavelli's *Prince?* The very term "duty" seems to be missing in his
book.

The Technique of Politics

Yet if *The Prince* is anything but a moral or pedagogical treatise, it does not follow that, for this reason, it is an immoral book.
Both judgments are equally wrong. *The Prince* is neither a moral
nor an immoral book: it is simply a technical book. In a technical
book we do not seek for rules of ethical conduct, of good and evil.
It is enough if we are told what is useful or useless. Every word
in *The Prince* must be read and interpreted in this way. The book
contains no moral prescripts for the ruler nor does it invite him
to commit crimes and villainies. It is especially concerned with
and destined for the "new principalities." It tries to give them all
the advice necessary for protecting themselves from all danger.
These dangers are obviously much greater than those which
threaten the ordinary states—the ecclesiastic principalities or the
hereditary monarchies. In order to avoid them the ruler must
take recourse to extraordinary means. But it is too late to seek for
remedies after the evil has already attacked the body politic.
Machiavelli likes to compare the art of the politician with that
of a skilled physician. Medical art contains three parts: diagnosis,
prognosis, and therapy. Of these a sound diagnosis is the most
important task. The principal thing is to recognize the illness at
the right moment in order to be able to make provision against
its consequences. If this attempt fails the case becomes hopeless.
"The physicians," says Machiavelli,

say of hectic fevers, that it is no hard task to get the better of them in
their beginning, but difficult to discover them: yet in course of time,
when they have not been properly treated and distinguished, they are
easily discovered, but difficult to be subdued. So it happens in political
bodies; for when the evils and disturbances that may probably arise
in any government are foreseen, which yet can only be done by a
sagacious and provident man, it is easy to ward them off; but if they
are suffered to sprout up and grow to such a height that their malig-
nity is obvious to every one, there is seldom any remedy to be found
of sufficient efficacy to repress them.[25]

25. *The Prince,* chap. III, *op. cit.,* II, 200 f.

All the advice of Machiavelli is to be interpreted in this spirit. He foresees the possible dangers that threaten the different forms of government and provides for them. He tells the ruler what he has to do in order to establish and to maintain his power, to avoid inner discords, to foresee and prevent conspiracies. All these counsels are "hypothetical imperatives," or to put it in the words of Kant, "imperatives of skill." "Here," says Kant, "there is no question whether the end is rational and good, but only what one must do in order to attain it. The precepts for the physician to make his patient thoroughly healthy, and for a poisoner to ensure certain death, are of equal value in this respect, that each serves to effect its purpose perfectly." [26] These words describe exactly the attitude and method of Machiavelli. He never blames or praises political actions; he simply gives a descriptive analysis of them—in the same way in which a physician describes the symptoms of a certain illness. In such an analysis we are only concerned with the truth of the description, not with the things spoken of. Even of the worst things a correct and excellent description can be given. Machiavelli studied political actions in the same way as a chemist studies chemical reactions. Assuredly a chemist who prepares in his laboratory a strong poison is not responsible for its effects. In the hands of a skilled physician the poison may save the life of a man—in the hands of a murderer it may kill. In both cases we cannot praise or blame the chemist. He has done enough if he has taught us all the processes that are required for preparing the poison and if he has given us its chemical formula. Machiavelli's *Prince* contains many dangerous and poisonous things, but he looks at them with the coolness and indifference of a scientist. He gives his political prescriptions. By whom these prescriptions will be used and whether they will be used for a good or evil purpose is no concern of his.

What Machiavelli wished to introduce was not only a new science but a new *art* of politics. He was the first modern author who spoke of the "art of the state." It is true that the idea of such an art was very old. But Machiavelli gave to this old idea an entirely new interpretation. From the times of Plato all great po-

26. See Kant, *Fundamental Principles of the Metaphysics of Morals.* English trans. by T. K. Abbott, *Kant's Critique of Practical Reason and Other Works on the Theory of Ethics* (6th ed. New York and London, Longmans, Green & Co., 1927), p. 32.

litical thinkers had emphasized that politics cannot be regarded as mere routine work. There must be definite rules to guide our political actions; there must be an art (*technē*) of politics. In his dialogue *Gorgias* Plato opposed his own theory of the state to the views of the sophists—of Protagoras, Prodikos, Gorgias. These men, he declared, have given us many rules for our political conduct. But all these rules have no philosophical purport and value because they fail to see the principal point. They are abstracted from special cases and concerned with particular purposes. They lack the essential character of a technē—the character of universality. Here we grasp the essential and ineradicable difference between Plato's technē and Machiavelli's *arte dello Stato*. Plato's technē is not "art" in Machiavelli's sense; it is knowledge (*epistēmē*) based on universal principles. These principles are not only theoretical but practical, not only logical but ethical. Without an insight into these principles no one can be a true statesman. A man may think himself to be an expert in all problems of political life, because he has, by long experience, formed right opinions about political things. But this does not make him a real ruler; and it does not enable him to give a firm judgment, because he has no "understanding of the cause." [27]

Plato and his followers had tried to give a theory of the *Legal* State; Machiavelli was the first to introduce a theory that suppressed or minimized this specific feature. His art of politics was destined and equally fit for the illegal and for the legal state. The sun of his political wisdom shines upon both legitimate princes and usurpers or tyrants, on just and unjust rulers. He gave his counsel in affairs of state to all of them, liberally and profusely. We need not blame him for this attitude. If we wish to compress *The Prince* into a short formula we could perhaps do no better than to point to the words of a great historian of the nineteenth century. In the introduction to his *History of English Literature* Hippolyte Taine declares that the historian should speak of human actions in the same way as a chemist speaks of different chemical compounds. Vice and virtue are products like vitriol or sugar and we should deal with them in the same cool and detached scientific spirit. That was exactly the method of Machiavelli. To be sure he had his personal feelings, his political ideals, his national aspirations. But he did not allow these things to affect his

27. See Plato, *Republic*, 533 B; cf. above, Chapter VI, p. 70.

political judgment. His judgment was that of a scientist and a technician of political life. If we read *The Prince* otherwise, if we regard it as the work of a political propagandist, we lose the gist of the whole matter.

The Mythical Element in Machiavelli's Political Philosophy: Fortune

Machiavelli's political science and Galileo's natural science are based upon a common principle. They start from the axiom of the uniformity and homogeneity of nature. Nature is always the same; all natural events obey the same invariable laws. This leads, in physics and cosmology, to the destruction of the distinction between the "higher" and the "lower" world. All physical phenomena are on the same level: if we have found a formula that describes the movements of a falling stone we may apply it to the movements of the moon around the earth and to the remotest fixed stars. In politics, too, we find that all ages are of the same fundamental structure. Whoever knows one age, knows them all. The politician who is confronted with a concrete actual problem will always find in history an analogous case, and by this analogy he will be able to act in the right way. The knowledge of the past is a sure guide; he who has won a clear insight into past events will understand how to cope with the problems of the present and how to prepare the future. There is no greater danger for a prince, therefore, than to neglect the examples of history. History is the clue to politics. "It ought not to appear strange to anyone," says Machiavelli in the beginning of his work,

if in what I am going to say concerning principalities and princes and states, altogether new, I shall quote great and eminent examples; for mankind in general are apt to tread in the footsteps and imitate the actions of others. . . . A wise man ought always to follow the traces of those illustrious personages whose actions are most worthy of his imitation: so that if he cannot equal, he may at least in some measure resemble them.[28]

Yet, in the field of history, this resemblance has its definite limits. In physics we may always argue upon the principle that the same causes must have the same effects. We may predict with

28. *The Prince*, chap. VI, *op. cit.*, II, 223 f.

absolute certainty a future event: for instance, an eclipse of the sun or the moon. But when it comes to human actions all this seems suddenly to be called into question. We can, to a certain degree, anticipate the future, but we cannot foretell it. Our expectations and hopes are frustrated; our actions, even the best planned actions, fail to have their effect. How is this difference to be accounted for? Shall we give up the principle of universal determinism in the field of politics? Shall we say that here things are incalculable; that there is no necessity in political events; that, as contrasted with the physical world, the human and social world is governed by mere chance?

This was one of the great puzzles that Machiavelli's political theory had to solve. On this matter he found his political *experience* in flagrant contradiction with his general scientific principles. Experience had taught him that even the best political advice is often ineffective. Things will go their own way; they will thwart all our wishes and purposes. Even the most artful and cunning schemes are liable to failure; they may, suddenly and unexpectedly, be crossed by the course of events. This uncertainty in the affairs of men seems to make all political science impossible. Here we are living in an inconstant, irregular, capricious world that defies all our efforts of calculation and prediction.

Machiavelli saw this antinomy very clearly, but he could not solve it and he could not even express it in a scientific way. His logical and rational method deserted him at this point. He had to admit that human things are not governed by reason, and that, therefore, they are not entirely describable in terms of reason. We must have recourse to another—to a half-mythical power. "Fortune" seems to be the ruler of things. And of all things Fortune is the most whimsical. Every attempt to reduce it to certain rules is bound to fail. If Fortune is an indispensable element in political life, it is absurd to hope for a science of politics. To speak of a "science of Fortune" would be a contradiction in terms.

Here the theory of Machiavelli had come to a crucial point. Yet Machiavelli could not accept this seeming defect of rational thought. His was not only a very clear, but also a very energetic and tenacious mind. If Fortune plays a leading part in human things, it is for the philosophic thinker to understand the part. For this reason Machiavelli had to insert into his *Prince* a new chapter—one of the most curious of the book. What is Fortune and what does it mean? What relation does it bear to our own human forces, to the intellect and will of man?

Machiavelli was by no means the only thinker of the Renaissance who wrestled with this problem, for the question itself was familiar to all the thinkers of his age. It pervaded the whole cultural life of the Renaissance. Artists, scientists, and philosophers were eagerly concerned to find an answer to it. In the literature and poetry of the Renaissance the theme occurs over and over again; in the fine arts we find innumerable symbols of Fortune.[29] On the reverse of a Portrait Medal of Cesare Borgia there was such a symbol.[30] But Machiavelli's *treatment* of the problem proves once again his great originality. According to his predominant interest he approaches the question from the angle of public instead of private life. Fortune becomes an element in his philosophy of history. It is the power of Fortune that brings to the fore now one nation, then another nation and gives it the dominion of the world. At all times, says Machiavelli in the Preface to the second book of his *Discourses*, the world has always been pretty much the same. There has at all times been nearly the same portion of good and evil in it; but this good and evil have sometimes changed their stations, and passed from one empire to another. Virtue which once seemed to have fixed itself in Assyria afterward removed its seat to Media, from thence into Persia, and at last came and settled amongst the Romans. Nothing under the sun is stable and ever will be. Evil succeeds good, good succeeds evil, and the one is always the cause of the other. Yet that does not mean that man has to give up his struggle. Quietism would be the deathblow of an active life—the only life worthy of man. The Renaissance was, in its feelings and its thoughts, under the strong pressure of astrology. With the sole exception of Pico della Mirandola no Renaissance thinker could avoid or overcome this pressure. The life of such a great and noble mind as Ficino was still filled with superstitious astrological fears.[31] Even Machiavelli

29. For a detailed account see the third chapter "Freiheit und Notwendigkeit in der Philosophie der Renaissance," of my book *Individuum und Kosmos in der Philosophie der Renaissance*, "Studien der Bibliothek Warburg" (Leipzig, B. G. Teubner, 1927), X, 77–129.

30. A reproduction of this medal is to be found in the book of Mrs. D. Erskine Muir, *Machiavelli and His Times* (New York, E. P. Dutton and Co., 1936), p. 150.

31. See Cassirer, *op. cit.*, pp. 105 ff., and *Journal for the History of Ideas*, III, Nos. 2 and 3 (1942), 123–144 and 319–346. About Ficino's attitude toward

could not entirely free himself from astrological conceptions. He thought and spoke in the manner of his age and contemporaries. We see from many instances both in ancient and modern history, he said in his *Discourses,* that before any great misfortune happens to a state, it is commonly foretold either by soothsayers, or revelations, or signs in the heavens. He confesses his ignorance as to the explanation of the fact; but the fact itself is not denied.[32] Nevertheless Machiavelli does not yield to any sort of fatalism. The adage *Sapiens vir dominabitur astris* was often quoted in the Renaissance.[33] Machiavelli gave a new turn to this adage. To overcome the inimical influence of the stars strength and will power are needed in addition to wisdom. The power of Fortune is great and incalculable, but it is not irresistible. If it seems to be irresistible it is the fault of man who does not use his own forces, who is too timid to take arms against Fortune.

There have been many, I know, and still are some, who think the affairs of this world are governed either by divine providence, or Fortune, in such a manner, that human wisdom has no share at all in them: from whence they infer, that it is best not to give ourselves any trouble about them, but to leave every thing to its natural tendency. . . . And indeed, when I sometimes seriously consider these things, I am almost persuaded to think so myself. Nevertheless, that our free will may not be absolutely overruled, it seems as if Fortune had reserved the direction of one half of our actions to herself, and left the other in a great measure to our own management.

Fortune may be compared to a rapid river which when it overflows its banks breaks all resistance. This ought not, however, to discourage us from throwing up mounds and cutting trenches, and making other due provisions whilst the season is favorable to guard against it in such a manner, when it swells again, that if the current cannot be wholly stemmed, it may at least be divided into other channels, and the impetuosity of the current in some measure restrained.[34]

That is said in a merely metaphorical, in a poetical or mythical way. Yet under the cover of this mythical expression we find the

astrology see Paul Oskar Kristeller, *The Philosophy of Marsilio Ficino* (New York, Columbia University Press, 1943), pp. 310 ff.

32. See *Discourses,* Bk. I, chap. LVI.

33. See Jakob Burckhardt, *Die Kultur der Renaissance in Italien.* English trans. by S. G. C. Middlemore (New York, Oxford University Press, 1937), p. 269.

34. *The Prince,* chap. XXV, *op. cit.,* II, 411 f.

tendency that determines and pervades Machiavelli's thought. For what is given here is nothing but a *secularization* of the symbol of Fortune. Even in medieval literature this symbol was quite familiar. But with Machiavelli it has undergone a characteristic change of meaning. The classical expression of the role that Fortune had in the medieval system is to be found in a famous passage of Dante's *Inferno*. It is Virgil who teaches Dante the true nature and function of Fortune. Men, he explains to him, are in the habit of speaking of Fortune as if she were an independent being. But such a conception is a mere result of human blindness. Whatever Fortune does she does not in her own name but in that of a higher power. Men praise Fortune as long as they are favored by her; they insult her as soon as they find themselves insulted by her. Both attitudes are foolish. Fortune can neither be blamed nor extolled; for she has no power of her own but is only the agent of a higher principle. If she acts she acts under the control of divine providence which has assigned to her the task she has to perform in human life. Therefore she is far superior to the judgment of men; she is impregnable to blame and praise.[35] This Christian element is removed in Machiavelli's description. He goes back to the Greek and Roman, the pagan conception. Yet, on the other side, he introduces a new element of thought and feeling which is specifically modern. The conception that Fortune is the ruler of the world is true; but it is only half of the truth. Man is not subdued to Fortune; he is not at the mercy of winds and waves. He must choose his course and steer his course. If he fails to perform this duty Fortune scorns and deserts him.

In the twenty-fifth chapter of *The Prince* Machiavelli explains the tactical rules for this great and continual battle against the power of Fortune. These rules are very involved and it is not easy to use them in the right way. For they contain two elements that seem to exclude each other. The man who wishes to stand his ground in this combat must combine in his character two opposite qualities. He must be timid and courageous; reserved and impetuous. Only by such a paradoxical mixture can he hope to win the victory. There is no uniform method to be followed at all times. At this moment we must be on our guard, again we must dare everything. We must be a sort of Proteus who, from one mo-

35. See Dante, *Inferno*, VII, 67 ff.

ment to another, can change his shape. Such a talent is very rare in men.

There is no person, let him be ever so wise, that can perfectly accommodate himself to all changes; for one man cannot well tell how to act contrary to what, perhaps, he is powerfully inclined by nature; and another cannot easily persuade himself to quit a course of life in which he has always succeeded before. So that when it is necessary to proceed with vigour and expedition, a cool and deliberate man, not knowing how to act that part, is generally undone: whereas if he would alter his conduct, according to the times, he would have no reason to complain that Fortune had deserted him.[36]

He who enters the lists against Fortune must know both ways: he must understand defensive and offensive warfare and he must, suddenly and unexpectedly, change from one to the other. Personally Machiavelli is more in favor of the offensive. "It is better," he says, "to be bold than bashful: for Fortune is like a woman who must be teased and treated in a Cavalier manner by those that expect to prevail over her." [37]

The Machiavelli who gives us his theory of Fortune seems to be a person quite different from the author of the preceding chapter. What we find here is not his usual clear logical style but an imaginative and rhetorical style. Nevertheless even the theory of Fortune does not lack philosophical importance. It is not a mere diversion but is connected with the whole of the work. Machiavelli tries to convince his reader that, in the struggle against Fortune, it is not enough to rely upon material weapons. Assuredly he did not underrate these weapons. Throughout his book he admonished the prince not to neglect the art of war. A prince ought to turn all his thoughts and care and application to the art of war.[38] If his arms are good he need not care for the judgment of the world; he can always act upon the principle: *Oderint dum metuant*.[39] He can cope with all dangers if he is well armed and has good allies: and such he will always be sure to have whilst his arms are respectable.[40] Here Machiavelli speaks as a champion of militarism; we may even see in him the first philosophical advo-

36. *The Prince,* chap. xxv, *op. cit.,* II, 414.
37. *Idem, op. cit.,* II, 416.
38. *Idem,* chap. xvi.
39. *Idem,* chap. xvii: "It is safer to be feared than beloved, if one side or other of the question must necessarily be taken."
40. *Idem,* chap. xi.

cate of a resolute militarism. He wrote a special treatise on the art of war in which he dealt with many technical details: with the dangers in using mercenaries, with the requirement of military service for all citizens, with the superiority of infantry over cavalry and artillery. Yet all this has only a biographical not a systematic interest. In his *Art of War* Machiavelli could only speak as a simple amateur. His experience in this field was scanty and inadequate. A man who for a few years had been the commander of the Florentine militia could not very well speak and judge as an expert in the art of war. When compared to the whole of his work this factor appears as a negligible quantity. But there was another thing that was much more important. Machiavelli discovered an entirely new *type* of strategy—a strategy based upon mental weapons instead of physical weapons. No other author before him had taught this strategy. It was a compound of two elements: it was created by a clear, cool, and logical mind and by a man who could make use of both his rich personal experience in the affairs of the state and his deep knowledge of human nature.

XIII

THE RENAISSANCE OF STOICISM AND "NATURAL RIGHT" THEORIES OF THE STATE

The Theory of the Social Contract

THE fifteenth and sixteenth centuries were the period of the labor pains of the modern world. In all branches of human culture, in religion, art, philosophy, a new spirit began to arise and to prove its strength. But this spirit was still in a chaotic state. The philosophy of the Renaissance is rich in new and fruitful impulses but filled with the grossest contradictions. The modern mind had begun to find its way; but it did not yet understand it. Side by side with a great gift for empirical observation we find a new flowering of all the "occult sciences." Magic, alchemy, astrology were held in the highest esteem. Giordano Bruno was the first philosophical spokesman of the Copernican system. He is usually reckoned among the pioneers and martyrs of modern science. But if we study his work we find a quite different picture. His faith in magic is unshaken; his logic is an imitation of the *Great Art* of Raymundus Lullus. Here as elsewhere everything is still in a state of uncertainty; philosophical thought is divided within itself and tending to opposite directions.

The great scientists and philosophers of the seventeenth century were the first to put an end to this confusion. Their work may be condensed in two great names—Galileo and Descartes. Galileo began his investigations of natural phenomena with a general statement of the task of science and philosophy. Nature, he declared, is not wrapped in mystery; nor is it an involved and complicated thing. Philosophy is written in that vast book of the universe that constantly lies before our very eyes. But the human mind must learn how to decipher and interpret this book. It is written in mathematical language; its characters are not ordinary sense perceptions, but triangles, circles, and other geometrical figures. If we fail to grasp this geometrical language it is impossible to understand a single word of the book of nature.[1] Descartes' physics is in many regards, both in its explanation of special phenomena and in its general conception of the laws of motion, opposed to Galileo's views.[2] But it is an offspring of the same philosophic spirit. Physics is no special branch of human knowledge. It is part and parcel of a comprehensive and universal science—of that *Mathesis universalis* that deals with all things whatever, so far as these things are capable of order and measure. Descartes had begun with his universal doubt. It was not a skeptical but a methodological doubt. It became the "Archimedean point," the fixed and immobile center of a new world of philosophic truth. With Descartes and Galileo a new age began of "clear and distinct ideas." In the sharp and bright light of Galileo's "two new sciences" and of Descartes' geometrical and logical analysis the "occult sciences" of the Renaissance were fading away. The period of fermentation was succeeded by the period of maturity. The modern spirit became aware of its creative energies; it began to form and understand itself. The divergent and incoherent tendencies of the Renaissance were thus bound together by a superior intellectual force. They were no longer isolated and dispersed but directed to a common center. In Descartes' philosophy the modern mind came of age; it stood its ground and defended its right against all traditional concepts and external authorities.

But if the physical world had become transparent to the human mind, was the same thing possible in an entirely different field? If knowledge means *mathematical* knowledge, can we hope for any *science of politics?* The very concept and ideal of such a science seems, at first sight, to be a mere utopia. Galileo's saying that philosophy is written in geometrical characters may apply to nature; but it does not apply to man's social and political life, which is not to be described and explained in mathematical terms. It is a life of emotions and passions. No mere effort of abstract thought seems to be able to rule these passions, to set them definite boundaries, and to direct them to a rational end.

1. Galileo, *Il saggiatore*, "Opere" (Edizione nazionale, Tipografia di G. Barbèra, Florence, 1890–1909), VI, 232. 20 vols. For a detailed discussion of Galileo's concept of nature see E. Cassirer, *Individuum und Kosmos in der Philosophie der Renaissance, op. cit.*, pp. 165 ff., 177 ff.

2. An excellent account of the relation between Galileo's and Descartes' physics has been given by A. Koyré, *Études Galiléennes*, III, "Galilée et la loi d'inertie" (Paris, Hermann, 1940).

The thinkers of the seventeenth century however did not give way before this obvious objection. All of them were determined rationalists. They had an almost unbounded faith in the power of human reason. In this regard we can scarcely find any difference between the various philosophical schools. Hobbes and Hugo Grotius are the two opposite poles of the seventeenth century's political thought. They disagree in their theoretical presuppositions and in their political demands. Nevertheless they follow the same way of thinking and arguing. Their method is not historical and psychological, but analytical and deductive. They derive their political principles from the nature of man and the nature of the state. And in this they follow the same great historical example of Galileo. We have a letter written by Hugo Grotius in which he expresses the greatest admiration for Galileo's work.[3] The same holds for Hobbes. From the first beginning of his philosophy it was his great ambition to create a theory of the body politic equal to the Galilean theory of physical bodies—equal in clarity, in scientific method, and in certainty. In the introduction to his work *De jure belli et pacis* Hugo Grotius expressed the same conviction. According to him it is by no means impossible to find a "mathematics of politics." Man's social life is not a mere mass of incoherent and haphazard facts. It is based upon judgments which are of the same objective validity and are capable of the same firm demonstration as any mathematical proposition. For they are not dependent on accidental empirical observations; they have the character of universal and eternal truths.

In this respect all the political theories of the seventeenth century, however divergent in their aims and means, have a common metaphysical background. Metaphysical thought definitely takes precedence over theological thought. But metaphysics itself would be powerless without the help of mathematics. The boundary between these two fields becomes almost imperceptible. Spinoza develops a system of ethics according to a geometrical method. Leibniz goes even farther. He does not hesitate to apply the general principles of his *Scientia generalis* and his *Characteristica universalis* to concrete and special political problems. When Leibniz was invited to give his opinion on the question who of

3. Hugo Grotius, *Epistolae,* No. 654 (Amsterdam, 1687), p. 266; for more details see E. Cassirer, "Wahrheitsbegriff und Wahrheitsproblem bei Galilei," *Scientia* (Milano, October, 1937), p. 188.

all the rivals for the Polish throne had the best claim, he wrote a paper in which he tried to prove his point—the election of Stanislaus Letizinsky—by formal arguments.[4] Leibniz' disciple Christian Wolff, who followed the example of his master, was the first to write a textbook on natural law according to a strict mathematical method.[5]

But here arose another question that was of vital importance for the further development of political thought. Granted that it is possible, and even necessary, to demonstrate a political or ethical truth in the same way as a mathematical truth—where can we find the *principle* of such a demonstration? If there is a "Euclidean" method of politics we must assume that, in this field too, we are in possession of certain axioms and postulates that are incontrovertible and infallible. Thus it became the first aim of any political theory to find out and to formulate these axioms. That may seem to us a very difficult and intricate problem. But the thinkers of the seventeenth century did not feel it so. Most of them were convinced that the question had been solved even before it was raised. We need not seek for the first principles of man's social life. They have been found long ago. It is enough to reassert and reformulate them, to express them in logical language, the language of clear and distinct ideas. According to the philosophers of the seventeenth century the task is a negative rather than a positive one. All we have to do is to dispel the clouds that hitherto have obscured the clear light of reason—to forget all our preconceived opinions and prejudices. For reason, says Spinoza, has this peculiar power to illuminate itself and its contrary; to discover both truth and falsehood.

The political rationalism of the seventeenth century was a rejuvenation of Stoic ideas. This process began in Italy, but after a short time it spread over the whole of European culture. In rapid progress Neo-Stoicism passed from Italy to France; from France to the Netherlands; to England, to the American colonies. The best-known political books of this period show the clear and unmistakable imprint of the Stoic mind. These books were not only studied by scholars or philosophers. Works like Pierre Charron's

4. See Leibniz, *Historisch-politische und staatswissenschaftliche Schriften*, ed. Onno Klopp (Hanover, 1864 ff.), II, 100 ff.

5. Christian Wolff, *Jus gentium methodo scientifica pertractatum* (Halle, 1749, new ed. Oxford, Clarendon Press; London, Humphrey Milford, 1934).

De la sagesse, du Vair's treatise *De la constance et consolation ès calamitez publiques,* Justus Lipsius' *De constantia* or *Philosophia et physiologia Stoica* became a sort of lay breviary in ethical wisdom. The influence of these books was so strong that it made itself felt even in the field of practical political problems. In the education of princes and princesses the medieval treatises *De rege et regimine,* or *De institutione principum* were replaced by these modern treatises. We know from the example of Queen Christina of Sweden that her first teachers knew no better way to introduce her to the problems of politics than through the study of Lipsius and of the classic Stoic writers.[6]

When Thomas Jefferson, in 1776, was asked by his friends to prepare a draft of the American Declaration of Independence he began it by the famous words: "We hold these truths to be self-evident, that all men are created equal; that they are endowed by their Creator with certain unalienable rights; that among these are life, liberty, and the pursuit of happiness. That, to secure these rights, governments are instituted among men, deriving their just powers from the consent of the governed." When Jefferson wrote these words he was scarcely aware that he was speaking the language of Stoic philosophy. This language could be taken for granted; for since the times of Lipsius and Grotius it had a common place with all the great political thinkers. The ideas were regarded as fundamental axioms that were not capable of further analysis and in no need of demonstration. For they expressed the essence of man and the very character of human reason. The American Declaration of Independence had been preceded and prepared by an even greater event: by the intellectual Declaration of Independence that we find in the theoreticians of the seventeenth century. It was here that reason had first declared its power and its claim to rule the social life of man. It had emancipated itself from the guardianship of theological thought; it could stand its own ground.

The history of the great intellectual movement that culminated in the American Bill of Rights and in the French Declaration of the Rights of Man and the Citizen has been studied in all its details. We seem now to be in full possession of all the facts of this history. But it is not enough to know the facts. We must try to un-

6. See my essay, "Descartes und Königin Christina von Schweden," *Descartes* (Stockholm, Bermann-Fischer, 1939), pp. 177–278.

derstand them; we must inquire into their reasons. And these reasons are by no means obvious. So far the question does not seem to have found a satisfactory answer. How was it that the same ideas that had been known for two thousand years and had been discussed ever since, were suddenly seen in an entirely new light? For the influence of Stoic thought had been unbroken and continuous. We can trace it in Roman jurisprudence, in the Fathers of the Church, in scholastic philosophy.[7] But all this then had a theoretical interest rather than an immediate practical effect. The tremendous practical significance of this great stream of thought did not appear until the seventeenth and eighteenth centuries. Henceforward the theory of the natural rights of man was no longer an abstract ethical doctrine but one of the mainsprings of political action. How was this change brought about? What gave to the old Stoic ideas their freshness and novelty, their unprecedented strength, their importance for the formation of the modern mind and the modern world?

Taken at its face value the phenomenon appears, indeed, paradoxical. It seems to contradict all our current opinions about the general character of the seventeenth century. If there is any feature that is characteristic of this age and that may be regarded as the distinctive mark of the whole epoch, it is its intellectual courage, its radicalism of thought. Descartes' philosophy had begun with a general postulate. Once in his life every man has to forget all that he has learned before. He has to reject all authorities and to defy the power of tradition. This Cartesian demand led to a new logic and epistemology, to a new mathematics and metaphysics, to a new physics and cosmology. But seventeenth century's *political* thought seems, at first sight, to have been untouched by the new Cartesian ideal. It does not enter upon an entirely new route. On the contrary, it seems to continue a time-honored tradition. How can we account for this fact? Obviously the general background of the civilization of the seventeenth century was not the same as that of Graeco-Roman culture. The intellectual, religious, social and economic conditions were widely different. How could any serious thinker ever try to solve the problems of this age, the problems of the modern world, by speaking in terms and thinking in concepts that had been coined two thousand years before?

7. See above Chapter VIII, p. 102 ff.

There is a double reason that may explain this fact. What matters here is not so much the content of the Stoic theory as the function that this theory had to fulfil in the ethical and political conflicts of the modern world. In order to understand this function we must go back to the new conditions created by the Renaissance and the Reformation. All the great and undeniable progress made by the Renaissance and the Reformation were counterbalanced by a severe and irreparable loss. The unity and the inner harmony of medieval culture had been dissolved. Assuredly the Middle Ages were not free from deep conflicts. The struggle between the Church and the State never came to an end; the discussions about logical, metaphysical, and theological problems seemed to be interminable. But the ethical and religious foundation of medieval civilization was not seriously affected by these discussions. Realists and nominalists, rationalists and mystics, philosophers and theologians had a common basis that never was called into question. After the fifteenth and sixteenth centuries this basis was shaken; it could never regain its former solidity. The hierarchic chain of being that gave to everything its right, firm, unquestionable place in the general order of things was destroyed. The heliocentric system deprived man of his privileged condition. He became, as it were, an exile in the infinite universe. The schism within the Church endangered and undermined the foundation of the Christian dogma. Neither the religious nor the ethical world seemed to possess a fixed center. During the seventeenth century theologians and philosophers still cherished the hope of finding such a center again. One of the greatest thinkers of the age incessantly worked on this problem. Leibniz made the most serious efforts to find a formula for the reunion of the different Christian churches. But all these attempts were made in vain. It became clear that, within the Church itself, the former "catholicity" could not be restored. If there was to be a really universal system of ethics or religion, it had to be based upon such principles as could be admitted by every nation, every creed, and every sect. And Stoicism alone seemed to be equal to this task. It became the foundation of a "natural" religion and a system of natural laws. Stoic philosophy could not help man to solve the metaphysical riddles of the universe. But it contained a greater and more important promise: the promise to restore man to his ethical dignity. This dignity, it asserted, cannot be lost; for it does not depend on a dogmatic creed or on any outward revelation. It rests exclusively on the moral will—on the worth that man attributes to himself.

That was the great and, indeed, invaluable service which the theory of natural rights had to render to the modern world. Without this theory there seemed to be no escape from a complete moral anarchy. Bossuet, one of the greatest theologians of the seventeenth century, still represents the tradition of the Catholic Church in its inner unity and old strength. But he too had to make all sorts of accommodations. These accommodations were inevitable if the Christian dogma was to be maintained in a new age, in the world of Louis XIV. Louis XIV was praised and admired as the protector and defender of Christian religion; he was styled the *rex Christianissimus*. But his court was scarcely a place where the old Christian ideals could thrive and subsist.

The hidden conflict of the *Siècle de Louis XIV* suddenly came into the open in the struggle between Jansenism and Jesuitism. At first sight it is extremely difficult to grasp the real meaning and purport of this struggle. If a modern reader tries to study Jansen's great work on St. Augustine he is completely at a loss to understand how a book like this ever could arouse such a storm of the most violent passions. How was it that a work of scholastic theology, a work dealing with the most abstruse and obscure dogmatic questions could shake the whole moral and social order and have such a tremendous effect upon French public life?

We find the answer to this question when reading one of the greatest books of French literature in the seventeenth century. In his *Lettres provinciales* Pascal too begins with a discussion of the subtlest problems of dogmatic theology—with the distinction between "sufficient" and "efficacious" grace, between the "real" and the "proximate" power of the human will to observe the divine precepts. But all this is only a prelude. Suddenly and unexpectedly Pascal changes his problem and his tactics. He attacks his adversaries from another side and at a much more vulnerable point. He denounces the ambiguity and perversity of the Jesuitic system of morality. Pascal did not speak as a theologian. His was a logical and a mathematical rather than a theological mind. He could, therefore, not content himself with stigmatizing the moral theology of the Jesuits. He had to seek for the hidden motives, both the logical and the moral. What was it that had incited the authors of Jesuitic casuistry to write and to propagate their books? According to Pascal the answer to this question may be given in one word. The Jesuits were members of the *Ecclesia militans.* With the utmost exertion they strove to maintain the absolute authority of the Pope and the Catholic Church. No price seemed to be too high for this purpose. Now in the modern world, in the century of Louis XIV, the old stern and austere Christian ideals had no place. They had to be sacrificed. A new morality, the *morale relâchée* of the Jesuits, seemed to be the only means to save the Church or, what was the same thing to the Jesuit writers, to save Christian religion. These were the premises of the Jesuitic system that were uncovered by Pascal's sharp and relentless logical analysis. Jesuitic morality was shown to be the necessary outcome of Jesuitic policy.

"Their object is not to corrupt morals," declared Pascal,

that is not their design. But neither is it their sole purpose to reform them: this would be bad policy. Their intention is this: They have such a good opinion of themselves as to believe that it is useful, and in some sort essentially necessary to the good of religion, that their reputation should extend everywhere, and that they should govern all consciences. And as the severe maxims of the Gospel are apt to govern some people, they make use of them whenever the occasion favors it. But as these maxims do not accord with the views of the great majority of the people, they waive them in regard to such persons, for the sake of affording universal satisfaction. On this account, having to deal with persons of every condition in life and of all different nations, it is necessary to have casuists assorted to match this whole diversity. . . . They have a few for the select few, while the multitude of lax casuists offer their services for the multitude that prefer laxity. In this manner they have spread over the whole earth, by *the doctrine of probable opinions,* which is the source and the basis of all this disorder . . . for they make no secret of it . . . , with this difference only that they veil their human and political prudence under the pretext of divine and Christian prudence, as if faith, supported by tradition, were not always one and the same and invariable at all times and in all places; as if it were the part of the rule to bend to the accommodation of the person who was to submit to it.[8]

This was the wide and deep gulf that divided the theologian writers into two opposite camps. Once this gulf had been clearly

8. Pascal, *Lettres provinciales,* V. English trans. (New York, J. Leavitt; Boston, Crocker & Brewster, 1828), pp. 69–71.

seen it was impossible to fill it. After the publication of Pascal's *Lettres provinciales* no reconciliation and no compromise was possible. There was only one alternative left. In his moral conduct man had to choose between two opposites: between the stern and austere demands of Jansenism and the laxity of the Jesuitic system. But what was the place of *philosophy* in this conflict? Could the contemporaries of Galileo and Descartes be expected to go back to St. Augustine's doctrine of grace and free will? Could the seventeenth century's philosophy—a philosophy of "clear and distinct ideas"—return to the scholastic distinctions between "sufficient" and "efficacious," "concomitant" and "efficient" grace? Or could a humanist and a moral philosopher, a great and noble mind like Hugo Grotius, yield to the *morale relâchée* of the Jesuits? Both ways were impossible. But the philosophic thinkers of the seventeenth century were not in need of a "moral *theology*." They were even convinced that the very concept of such a theology was, in a sense, a contradiction in terms. For they had accepted the Stoic principle of the "autarky" ($αὐτάρκεια$) of human reason. Reason is autonomous and self-dependent. It is not in need of any external help; it could not even accept this help if it were offered. It has to find its own way and to believe in its own strength.

This principle became the cornerstone of all the systems of natural right. It has been expressed in a classical way by Hugo Grotius in the introduction to his work *De jure belli et pacis*. Even the will of an omnipotent being, said Grotius, cannot change the principles of morality or abrogate those fundamental rights that are guaranteed by natural laws. These laws would maintain their objective validity even if we should assume—*per impossibile*—that there is no God or that he does not care for human affairs.[9]

The rational character of the seventeenth century's political philosophy becomes even clearer if, instead of analyzing its first principles, we look at its general method. As to the question of the principles of the social order we find a sharp opposition between the systems of absolutism—the systems of Bodin or Hobbes—and the defenders of popular rights and of the sovereignty of the people. But both parties, however combating each other, agree in one point. They try to prove their point by going back to the same fundamental hypothesis. The doctrine of the state-contract be-

9. Grotius, *De jure belli et pacis*, "Prolegomena," sec. 11.

comes in the seventeenth century a self-evident axiom of political thought.

In the history of our problem this fact marks a great and decisive step. For if we adopt this view, if we reduce the legal and social order to free individual acts, to a voluntary contractual submission of the governed, all mystery is gone. There is nothing less mysterious than a contract. A contract must be made in full awareness of its meaning and consequences; it presupposes the free consent of all the parties concerned. If we can trace the state to such an origin, it becomes a perfectly clear and understandable fact.

This rational approach was by no means understood as a *historical* approach. Only a few thinkers were so naïve as to assume that the "origin" of the state, as explained in the theories of the social contract, gave us an insight into its beginnings. Obviously we cannot assign a definite moment of human history at which the state made its first appearance. But this lack of historical knowledge does not concern the theoreticians of the state-contract. Theirs is an analytical, not a historical, problem. They understand the term "origin" in a logical not in a chronological sense. What they are seeking for is not the beginning, but the "principle" of the state—its *raison d'être*.

That becomes particularly clear if we study the political philosophy of Hobbes. Hobbes is a typical example of the general spirit that led to the various theories of the social contract. His results were never generally accepted; they met with opposition. But his method exerted the strongest influence. And this new method was an outcome of Hobbes's logic. The philosophical value of Hobbes's political works consists not so much in their subject-matter as in the form of arguing and reasoning. In the first chapters of his work *De corpore* Hobbes gives us his general theory of knowledge. Knowledge is the inquiry into first principles, or, as he puts it, into "first causes." In order to understand a thing we must begin with defining its nature and essence. Once this definition has been found all its properties can be derived in a strictly deductive way. But a definition is not adequate as long as it contents itself with designating a special quality of the subject. True definitions must be "genetic" or "causal" definitions. They not only have to answer the question *what* a thing is, but *why* it is. In this way alone we can come to a true insight. "Ubi generatio nulla," says Hobbes, ". . . ibi nulla philosophia intellegitur"—where there is no generation, there is no true philosophical knowledge.[10] But this "generation" is not at all understood by Hobbes as a physical or historical process. Even in the field of geometry Hobbes demands a genetic or causal definition. The objects of geometry must be constructed in order to be fully understood. Obviously this constructive act is a mental, not a temporal process. What we are looking for is an origin in reason, not in time. We try to analyze geometrical objects into their first elements and reconstruct them by a synthetic process of thought. The same principle holds for political objects. If Hobbes describes the transition from the natural to the social state, he is not interested in the empirical origin of the state. The point at issue is not the history but the *validity* of the social and political order. What matters alone is not the historical but the legal basis of the state; and it is the question of this legal basis that is answered by the theory of the social contract.

Hobbes's theory culminates in the paradoxical assertion that the legal bond between the ruler and the subjects once it has been tied is indissoluble. The pact of submission by which the individuals renounce all their rights and freedoms is the necessary presupposition, the first step, that leads to a social order. But it is, in a sense, also the ultimate step. Henceforth the individuals no longer exist as independent beings. They have no will of their own. The social will has become incorporated with the ruler of the state. This will is unrestricted; there is no other power beside or above the absolute sovereign.[11] Obviously this was a gratuitous assumption that could not be proved or justified by the general concept of the social contract. For when combined with the Stoic doctrine of natural rights this concept led to the very opposite result. It was clear that the individuals, when entering into an agreement with each other and with the ruler, could only act for themselves. They could not create an absolutely rigid and unchangeable order; they could not bind their posterity. And even from the point of view of the present generation it was not possible to abdicate, unconditionally and absolutely, all rights and

10. See Hobbes, *De corpore*, Pars I, cap. I, sec. 3 ad 8, "Opera Philosophica quae Latine scripsit," ed. W. Molesworth (London, Bohn, 1839), I, 9.
11. See Hobbes, *De cive*, cap. 5–7; *Leviathan*, cap. 17–19.

to transfer them to the ruler. There is, at least, *one* right that cannot be ceded or abandoned: the right to personality. Arguing upon this principle the most influential writers on politics in the seventeenth century rejected the conclusions drawn by Hobbes. They charged the great logician with a contradiction in terms. If a man could give up his personality he would cease being a moral being. He would become a lifeless thing—and how could such a thing obligate itself—how could it make a promise or enter into a social contract? This fundamental right, the right to personality, includes in a sense all the others. To maintain and to develop his personality is a universal right. It is not subject to the freaks and fancies of single individuals and cannot, therefore, be transferred from one individual to another. The contract of rulership which is the legal basis of all civil power has, therefore, its inherent limits. There is no *pactum subjectionis*, no act of submission by which man can give up the state of a free agent and enslave himself. For by such an act of renunciation he would give up that very character which constitutes his nature and essence: he would lose his humanity.

XIV

THE PHILOSOPHY OF THE ENLIGHTENMENT AND ITS ROMANTIC CRITICS

IN THE development of political thought the eighteenth century, the period of the Enlightenment, proved to be one of the most fertile ages. Never before had the philosophy of politics played such an important and decisive role. It was no longer regarded as a special branch but was the very focus of all intellectual activities. All other theoretical interests were directed to and concentrated upon this end. "Of the different works which I had on the stocks," writes Rousseau in his *Confessions,*

the one which I had long had in my head, at which I worked with the greatest inclination, to which I wished to devote myself all my life, and which, in my own opinion, was to set the seal upon my reputation, was my *Institutions Politiques* . . . I had come to see that everything was radically connected with politics, and that, however one proceeded, no people would be other than the nature of its government made it.[1]

Yet in spite of this keen interest in all political problems the period of the Enlightenment did not develop a new political philosophy. When studying the works of the most famous and influential authors we are surprised to find that they do not contain any totally new theory. The same ideas are repeated over and over again—and these ideas had not been created by the eighteenth century. Rousseau is fond of speaking in paradoxes, but when it comes to politics, we hear quite a different and a very sober tone. In Rousseau's conception of the aim and the method of political philosophy, in his doctrine of the indefeasible and inalienable rights of men, there is hardly anything that has not its parallel and model in the books of Locke, Grotius, or Pufendorf. The merit of Rousseau and his contemporaries lies in a different field. They were much more concerned about political *life* than political *doctrine.* They did not want to prove, but to affirm and apply the first principles of man's social life. In matters of politics

1. Rousseau, *Confessions,* Bk. IX (Everyman's Library, New York, E. P. Dutton & Co., 1931), II, 55.

the eighteenth century's writers never had the intention of being original. As a matter of fact they regarded originality in this field as highly suspicious. The French Encyclopedists who were the spokesmen of the age always warned against what they called *l'esprit de système*. They had no ambition to emulate the great systems of the seventeenth century, the systems of Descartes, Spinoza, or Leibniz. The seventeenth century had been a metaphysical century and created a metaphysics of nature and a metaphysics of morals. The period of the Enlightenment had lost its interest in these metaphysical speculations. Its whole energy was concentrated upon another point, not so much an energy of thought as of action. "Ideas" were no longer regarded as "abstract ideas." They were forged into weapons for the great political struggle. The question never was whether these weapons were new but whether they were efficient. And in most cases it turned out that the oldest weapons were the best and most powerful ones.

The writers of the Great Encyclopedia and the fathers of American democracy, men like D'Alembert, Diderot, and Jefferson, would scarcely have understood the question whether their ideas were new. All of them were convinced that these ideas were in a sense as old as the world. They were regarded as something that has been always, everywhere and believed by all: *quod semper, quod ubique, quod ab omnibus*. "La raison," said La Bruyère, "est de tous les climats." "The object of the Declaration of Independence," wrote Jefferson on May 8, 1825, in a letter to Henry Lee,

was not to find out new principles, or new arguments, never before thought of, not merely to say things which had never been said before; but to place before mankind the common sense of the subject, in terms so plain and firm as to command their assent. . . . Neither aiming at originality of principle or sentiment, nor yet copied from any particular and previous writing, it was intended to be an expression of the American mind, and to give to that expression the proper tone and spirit called for by the occasion.[2]

But the principles laid down in the American Declaration of Independence and the French Declaration of the Rights of Man and the Citizen were not only an expression of a general popu-

2. Thomas Jefferson, "Writings," ed. Paul Chester Ford (New York, G. P. Putnam's Sons, 1899), X, 343. Modern Library ed., p. 719.

lar sentiment.[3] Nothing is perhaps so characteristic of the inner unity of the culture of the eighteenth century as the fact that the same principles were maintained and confirmed by the deepest thinker of the age: by the critic of pure reason.

Kant was a fervent admirer of the French Revolution. And it is significant for the strength of his mind and character that he did not change his judgment when the cause of the French Revolution seemed to be lost. His belief in the ethical value of the thoughts expressed in the Declaration of the Rights of Man and the Citizen remained unshaken. "Such an event," he said,

does not consist in important deeds or misdeeds of men, whereby, what had been great, became little among men, or what had been little, became great, and . . . old glorious political edifices disappeared, whereas, in their stead, other ones grew out of the ground. No; nothing of the kind! . . . The revolution of an ingenious people which we have lived to see, may succeed or fail. It may be filled with such calamities and atrocities that a righteous man, even if he could be sure to carry it out luckily, never would decide to repeat the experiment at such a high price. In spite of all this such a revolution finds, in the minds of all spectators, a sympathy very near to enthusiasm. . . . Such a phenomenon in the history of mankind can never be forgotten; because it proves that in human nature there exists an inclination and disposition to the better which no politician ever could have been able to predict by summing up the course of former events.[4]

The spirit of the eighteenth century is usually described as an "intellectualistic" spirit. But if "intellectualism" means a cool and abstract attitude, an aloofness from the actual problems of practi-

3. We need not enter here into the vexed question of the historical origin of the French Declaration. In a paper, published in 1895, Georg Jellinek tried to prove that it is a mistake to regard the Declaration of the Rights of Man and the Citizen as a result of the ideas of the French philosophers of the eighteenth century. According to Jellinek we have to seek the real source of the legal and political ideas of the French Revolution in the American Bills of Rights, especially in the Bill of Right of the State of Virginia. Other authors have emphatically denied this view, see, for instance, V. Marcaggi, *Les origines de la déclaration des droits de l'homme de 1789* (Paris, 1904). But in this case the question of priority is of little interest. It is clear that neither Jefferson and Adams nor Lafayette and Condorcet "invented" the ideas that were incorporated in the Declaration of Rights; they simply expressed the convictions that were held by all the pioneers of the theory of "natural rights."

4. Kant, *Der Streit der Fakultäten* (1798), sec. II, "Werke," ed. E. Cassirer, VII, 397 f., 401.

cal, social, political life, no description could be more inadequate and misleading. Such an attitude was entirely alien to the thinkers of the Enlightenment. All of them would have accepted that principle that was later formulated by Kant as the "primacy of practical reason." They never admitted a clear-cut distinction between theoretical and practical reason. They did not separate speculation from life. There has perhaps never existed a more complete harmony between theory and practice, between thought and life, than in the eighteenth century. All thoughts were immediately turned into actions; all actions were subordinated to general principles and judged according to theoretical standards. It was this feature that gave to the culture of the eighteenth century its strength and its inner unity. Literature and art, science and philosophy had a common center and coöperated with each other to the same end. For this reason the great political events of the age were hailed with such general enthusiasm. "It is not enough," wrote Condorcet, "that they (the original and imprescriptible rights) live in the writings of the philosophers and in the hearts of all righteous men. Ignorant or feeble men must read them in the example of a great nation. America has given us this example. The American Declaration of Independence is a simple and sublime expression of those sacred rights which such a long time had been forgotten." [5]

How was it that all these great achievements were suddenly called into question—that the nineteenth century began with attacking and openly defying all the philosophical and political ideals of the former generation? There seems to be an easy answer to this question. The French Revolution had ended in the period of the Napoleonic Wars. The first enthusiasm was followed by a deep disillusionment and mistrust. In one of his letters, written in the beginning of the French Revolution, Benjamin Franklin had expressed the hope that the idea of the inviolable rights of man would operate in the same way as fire operates on gold: "it will purify without destroying." But this optimistic hope seemed to be frustrated once for all. All the great promises of the French Revolution remained unfulfilled. The political and social order of Europe seemed to be threatened with a complete breakdown.

5. Condorcet, *De l'influence de la révolution d'Amérique sur l'Europe* (1786), chap. I, "Oeuvres complètes" (Brunswick, Vieweg; and Paris, Henrichs, 1804), XI, 249.

Edmund Burke called the French constitution of 1793 a "digest of anarchy" and the doctrine of inalienable rights was to him "an invitation to insurrection and a persistent cause of anarchy." [6] "La raison humaine," wrote Joseph de Maistre in his book *De la papauté,* "est manifestement convaincue d'impuissance pour conduire les hommes . . . en sorte qu'en général il est bien, quoi qu'on dise, de commencer par l'autorité."

These are the obvious reasons for the complete and rapid change of ideas that we meet in the first decades of the nineteenth century. But it is not enough to describe this reaction as merely political. It has other and deeper causes. The German romanticists who began the fighting and were the first heralds in the combat against the philosophy of Enlightenment were not primarily interested in political problems. They lived much more in the world of "spirit"—poetry and art—than in the world of hard political facts. Of course romanticism had not only its philosophy of nature, of art and history, but also its philosophy of politics. But in this field the romantic writers never developed a clear and coherent theory; nor were they consistent in their practical attitude. Friedrich Schlegel was at different times an advocate of conservative and liberal ideas. From republicanism he was converted to monarchism. It seems to be impossible to take a system of definite, fixed, unquestioned political ideas from any romantic writer; in most cases the pendulum swings from one pole to its opposite.

There are, however, two points that are of vital importance in the struggle between romanticism and Enlightenment. The first is the new interest in history; the second the new conception and valuation of myth. As to the first point it became a slogan of all the romantic writers, a sort of war cry that was repeated over and over again, that the period of the Enlightenment was an entirely unhistorical age. A calm and unbiased analysis of the facts by no means confirms this view. It is true that the interest in historical facts was not the same with the thinkers of the Enlightenment as with the early romanticists. They approached the problem from different angles and saw it in a different perspective. Yet that does not mean that the philosophers of the eighteenth century lost sight of the historical world. On the contrary these phi-

6. See Charles Grove Haines, *The Revival of Natural Law Concepts* (Cambridge, Mass., Harvard University Press, 1930), p. 65.

losophers were the first to introduce a new scientific method into the study of history. They were not yet provided with that immense historical material that has since been collected; but they had a clear insight into the importance of historical knowledge. "I believe this to be the historical age and this the historical nation," said David Hume speaking of the English culture of the eighteenth century. Men like Hume, Gibbon, Robertson, Montesquieu, Voltaire cannot be charged with a lack of interest and historical understanding. In his *Siècle de Louis XIV* and in his *Essai sur les mœurs* Voltaire created a new and modern type of the history of civilization.[7]

There is, however, one fundamental difference between the conception of history in the eighteenth and nineteenth centuries. The romantics love the past for the past's sake. To them the past is not only a fact but also one of the highest ideals. This idealization and spiritualization of the past is one of the most distinctive characteristics of romantic thought. Everything becomes understandable, justifiable, legitimated as soon as we can trace it back to its origin. This frame of mind was entirely alien to the thinkers of the eighteenth century. If they looked back to the past they did so because they wanted to prepare a better future. The future of mankind, the rise of a new political and social order, was their great theme and real concern. For this purpose the study of history is necessary, but it is not an end in itself. History may teach us many things but it can only teach us what has been, not what ought to be. To accept its verdict as infallible and definitive would be a crime against the majesty of reason. If history meant a glorification of the past, a confirmation of the *ancien régime*, it was, to the minds of the "philosophers" of the "Great Encyclopedia," doomed from its beginning. It could have no theoretical interest for them because it lacked a real ethical value. According to the principle of the primacy of practical reason both things were correlative and inseparable. The thinkers of the eighteenth century, who by their adversaries were so often accused of intellectualism, never studied history in order to satisfy a merely intellectual curiosity. They saw in it a guide to action, a compass that could lead them to a future and better state of human society. "We have admired our ancestors less," said one of the writ-

7. For more details see E. Cassirer, *Die Philosophie der Aufklärung* (Tübingen, Mohr, 1932), chap. v, "Die Eroberung der geschichtlichen Welt," pp. 263–312.

ers of the eighteenth century, "but we have loved our contemporaries better, and have expected more of our descendants." [8] As Duclos said, our knowledge of history can be no more and no better than an "anticipated experience." [9]

That is the real difference, the deep gulf, between the period of the Enlightenment and German romanticism. "We have sure guides," we read in a political pamphlet written on the eve or immediately after the outbreak of the French Revolution, "older than ancient monuments; guides that exist everywhere and are possessed by all men: reason to govern our thoughts, morality to conduct our feelings, and natural right." [10] But the romantics started from the opposite principle. They not only said that every historical epoch has a right of its own and must be measured according to its own standards but went much farther. The founders of the "Historic Right School" declared that history was the source, the very origin of right. There is no authority above history. Law and the state cannot be "made" by men. They are no products of the human will and they are, therefore, not under the jurisdiction of these wills. They are not bound to nor restricted by the pretended inherent rights of the individuals. Man could not make law any more than he could make language, myth or religion. According to the principles of the Historic Right School, as they were conceived by Savigny and developed in the works of his pupils and followers, human culture is not an offspring of free and conscious human activities. It originates in a "higher necessity." This necessity is a metaphysical one; it is the natural spirit which works and creates unconsciously.

According to this metaphysical conception the *value* of myth is completely changed. To all the thinkers of the Enlightenment myth had been a barbarous thing, a strange and uncouth mass of confused ideas and gross superstitions, a mere monstrosity. Between myth and philosophy there could be no point of contact. Myth ends where philosophy begins—as darkness gives way to

8. Chastellux, *De la félicité publique*, II, 71; quoted from Carl L. Becker, *The Heavenly City of the Eighteenth Century Philosophers* (New Haven, Yale University Press, 1932), pp. 129–130.

9. See Becker, *idem*, p. 95.

10. *Des États-Généraux et principalement de l'esprit qu'on doit y apporter*, par Target (Paris, 1789), quoted from Fritz Klövekorn, *Die Entstehung der Erklärung der Menschen- und Bürgerrechte*, "Historische Studien," XC (Berlin, E. Ebering, 1911), 31, 224, n. 23.

the rising sun. This view undergoes a radical change as soon as we pass to the romantic philosophers. In the system of these philosophers myth becomes not only a subject of the highest intellectual interest but also a subject of awe and veneration. It is regarded as the mainspring of human culture. Art, history, and poetry originate in myth. A philosophy which overlooks or neglects this origin is declared to be shallow and inadequate. It was one of the principal aims of Schelling's system to give myth its right and legitimate place in human civilization. In his works we find for the first time a *philosophy of mythology* side by side with his philosophy of nature, history, and art. Eventually all his interest seems to be concentrated upon this problem. Instead of being the opposite of philosophic thought myth has become its ally; and, in a sense, its consummation.

All this may appear paradoxical; but it follows from the very principles of romantic thought. Schelling only expressed the common convictions of the whole younger generation in Germany. He became the philosophic spokesman of romantic poetry. The deep wish to go back to the sources of poetry accounts for the romantic interest in myth. Poetry must learn to speak a new language, a language not of concepts, of "clear and distinct ideas," but of hieroglyphs, of secret and sacred symbols. That was the language spoken in Novalis' *Heinrich von Ofterdingen*. To Kant's critical idealism Novalis opposed his own "magic idealism"—and it was this new type of idealism that was thought by Schelling and Friedrich Schlegel to be the keystone of philosophy and poetry.

That was a new step in the general history of ideas—a step that was pregnant with the most important consequences which proved to be even more momentous for the further development of political than for that of philosophic thought. In philosophy the influence of Schelling was counterbalanced and soon eclipsed by the appearance of the Hegelian system. His conception of the role of mythology remained only an episode. Nevertheless the way was paved that could lead later to the rehabilitation and glorification of myth that we find in modern politics.

It would, however, be a mistake, and it would not do justice to the romantic spirit, to hold it responsible for this later development. In recent literature we often meet with the view that romanticism was the first and the most prolific source of the myth of the twentieth century. According to many writers it has produced the concept of the "totalitarian state," and has prepared all the later forms of an aggressive imperialism.[11] But judging in this way we are likely to forget the principal and, indeed, the decisive feature. The "totalitarian" view of the romantic writers was, in its origin and meaning, a *cultural* not a political view. The universe they were longing for was a universe of human culture. They never meant to politicize but to "poeticize" the world. To pervade all spheres of human life—religion, history, even natural science—with the "poetic spirit" was declared by Friedrich Schlegel as the highest aim of the romantic movement.[12] Like most of the romantic writers Friedrich Schlegel felt much more at home in the "divine world of science and art" than in the world of politics. It was this attitude that gave romantic nationalism its special tinge and character. Assuredly the romantic poets and philosophers were fervent patriots, and many of them were intransigent nationalists. But their nationalism was not of an imperialistic type. They were anxious to preserve not to conquer. They tried, with the utmost exertion of all their spiritual forces, to maintain the peculiarity of the German character but they never meant to enforce and impose it upon other peoples.

This was a necessary result of the historical origin of German nationalism. This nationalism had been created by Herder—and of all the thinkers and poets of the eighteenth century Herder possessed the keenest sense and the deepest understanding of *individuality*. That individualism became one of the outstanding and most characteristic features of the romantic movement. The romanticists never could sacrifice the particular and specific forms of cultural life, poetry, art, religion, and history, to the "totalitarian" state. They had a deep respect for all the innumerable, subtle differences that characterize the life of individuals and nations. To feel and to enjoy these differences, to sympathize with all forms of national life, was to them the real scope and the greatest charm of historical knowledge. The nationalism of the

11. See, for instance, Peter Viereck, *Metapolitics. From the Romantics to Hitler* (New York, A. A. Knopf, 1941). See also the article by Arthur O. Lovejoy, "The Meaning of Romanticism for the Historian of Ideas," and his very interesting discussion with Leo Spitzer, *Journal of the History of Ideas*, Vol. II, No. 3 (1941) and Vol. V, No. 2 (1944).

12. See Friedrich Schlegel, "Gespräch über die Poesie," *Prosaische Jungendschriften*, ed. Jacob Minor (2d ed. Vienna, Carl Konegen, 1906), II, 338 ff.

romantics was, therefore, no mere particularism. It was the very contrary. It was not only compatible with a real universalism but presupposed it. To Herder every nation was only an individual voice in a universal, all-embracing harmony. In his collection of national songs we find the songs of all peoples, German, Slavic, Celtic, Scandinavian, Lithuanian, and Turkish. And the romantic poets and philosophers were the heirs of Herder and Goethe. Goethe was the first to use the term World Literature (*Welt-literatur*) which became the great passion of all romantic writers. In his lectures on dramatic art, A. W. Schlegel gave a universal survey of the dramatic literature of all ages and he treated them with the same love and the same unbiased sympathy.

This literary universalism was confined and strengthened by a new religious universalism. The early romanticists saw the greatest privilege of medieval culture in the fact that the Middle Ages were held together by a universal religious ideal. Here Christianity was still an undivided whole. Christian society was a mystic body, governed by God and represented in the two correlative orders of the Universal Church and the Universal Empire. The romantic writers were inspired by the wish to return to this golden age of mankind. In this regard they could not think of restricting their cultural and religious ideals to their own country. They strove not only for a unified Germany but also for a unified Europe. In his essay *Christianity or Europe* Novalis praised the beautiful and splendid days when one Christianity inhabited the continent of Europe, when one great interest connected the remotest provinces of this wide spiritual empire.[13] The greatest of the romantic theologians, Friedrich Schleiermacher, went much farther. The universal religion that he developed and defended in his *Reden über die Religion* comprises all sorts of creed and worship. All the "heretics" of former times could be included in this religious ideal. The "atheist" Spinoza was called by Schleiermacher "the great and sainted Spinoza." For truly religious feeling, declared Schleiermacher, all dogmatic differences are irrelevant. Religion is love but it is not love for "this" and "that" or for a finite and special object, but love for the Universe, the Infinite.

That explains further the character of romantic nationalism.

13. Novalis, *Die Christenheit oder Europa* (1799), "Schriften," ed. Jacob Minor (Jena, Diederichs, 1907), II, 23.

This nationalism, too, was a product of love not, as so many later forms of nationalism, of hatred. In Friedrich Schlegel's "Dialogue on Poetry" love had been declared to be the very principle of all romantic poetry. It is like an invisible medium which must penetrate every line and every verse of a true poem. To the poet everything is only an indication of what is higher and really infinite; a hieroglyph of eternal love and of the holy vital power of plastic nature.[14] The political ideals of the early romanticists were pervaded with the same feeling. They had a definitely esthetic or poetic character. Novalis spoke of the state in enthusiastic terms. What he really admired, however, was not its physical power but its beauty. "A true prince," he wrote, "is the artist of artists. Everyone ought to be an artist; everything can become fine art. . . . The prince performs in an infinitely manifold spectacle where the scene and the public, the actors and spectators are one and the same, and where he himself is the author, the dramaturgue and the hero of the play." [15]

It is true that this poetical and esthetic conception was not equal to the task of solving the problems of political life. When these problems became more and more serious and threatening, the theory developed by the first romantic writers could not hold its ground. In the age of the Napoleonic Wars the founders and pioneers of German romanticism began to doubt their own ideal of "poeticizing" political life. They became convinced that, at least in this field, a more "realistic" attitude was imperative and indispensable. Many romantic poets were prepared to offer up their former ideals to the national cause. In poets like Heinrich von Kleist romantic love changed into a bitter and implacable hatred. Even A. W. von Schlegel felt similarly. "As long as our national independence, and even the continuance of our German name, is so seriously threatened," he wrote in 1806, "our poetry might perhaps have to yield entirely to eloquence." [16] But only a few romanticists followed this counsel; even in their extreme nationalism they would not disavow or renounce their universal ideals of human culture.

14. Schlegel, *op. cit.*, II, 370 f.
15. Novalis, *Glauben und Liebe*, sec. 33, "Schriften," II, 162.
16. A. W. von Schlegel, *Letter to Fouqué*, see "Sämtliche Werke," ed. Eduard Böcking (Leipzig, Weidmann, 1846), VIII, 145.

PART III

THE MYTH OF THE TWENTIETH CENTURY

XV

THE PREPARATION: CARLYLE

Carlyle's Lectures on Hero Worship

WHEN Thomas Carlyle on May 22, 1840, began his lectures *On Heroes, Hero Worship and the Heroic in History* he spoke to a large and distinguished audience. A "mob of London society" had assembled to listen to the speaker. The lectures created a sort of sensation; but nobody could have foreseen that this social event was pregnant with great political consequences. Carlyle spoke to Englishmen of the Victorian era. His audience was between two and three hundred in number and "aristocratic in rank and intellect." As Carlyle says in one of his letters "bishops and all kinds of people had appeared; they heard something new and seemed greatly astonished and greatly pleased. They laughed and applauded." [1] But assuredly none of the hearers could think for a moment that the ideas expressed in these lectures contained a dangerous explosive. Nor did Carlyle himself feel this way. He was no revolutionary; he was a conservative. He wished to stabilize the social and political order and he was convinced that for such a stabilization he could recommend no better means than hero worship. He never meant to preach a new political evangelism. To him hero worship was the oldest and firmest element in man's social and cultural life. He saw in it "an everlasting hope for the management of the world." "Had all traditions, arrangements, creeds, societies that men ever instituted, sunk away, this would remain . . . it shines like a pole-star through smoke-clouds, dust-clouds, and all manner of down-rushing and conflagration." [2]

1. A detailed description of Carlyle's lectures has been given by A. MacMeehan in the introduction to his edition (Boston, Ginn & Co., 1891). See also *The Correspondence of Thomas Carlyle and Ralph Emerson, 1834–1872* (Boston, 1894), I, 293 f. 2 vols.

2. *On Heroes, Hero Worship and the Heroic in History*, Lect. vi, p. 195. Centenary ed., V, 202. I quote the lectures from the edition of H. D. Gray in Longman's English Classics (New York, Longmans, Green & Co., 1896). The other works of Carlyle are quoted from the Centenary edition, "The Works of Thomas Carlyle" (30 vols.) first published by H. D. Traill (London, Chapman & Hall,

The effect produced by Carlyle's lectures was, however, far different from the author's expectations. As Carlyle pointed out, the modern world had passed through three great revolutions. First came the Reformation of Luther, then the Puritan revolution, and at last the French Revolution. The French Revolution was properly the third act of Protestantism. This third act we may well call the final one: "for lower than that savage *Sans-culottism* men cannot go." [3] When Carlyle spoke thus he could not know that the very ideas he propounded in his lectures were also the beginning of a new revolution. A hundred years later these ideas had been turned into the most efficient weapons in the political struggle. In the Victorian era nobody could have divined the role that Carlyle's theory was to play in the twentieth century.

In recent literature there is a strong tendency to connect Carlyle's views with our own political problems—to see in him one of those men who had done most for the future "March of Fascism." In 1928 B. H. Lehman wrote a book—*Carlyle's Theory of the Hero. Its Sources, Development, History, and Influence on Carlyle's Work*.[4] This was a merely historical analysis. But it was soon followed by other studies in which Carlyle was, more or less, made responsible for the whole ideology of National Socialism. After Hitler's rise to power H. F. C. Grierson published a lecture that, three years previously, he had delivered on "Carlyle and the Hero" under a new title, *Carlyle and Hitler*. "I have been tempted," he says, "to give it a new, shall I say metonymous, title, so entirely do the recent happenings in Germany illustrate the conditions which lead up to, or at least make possible, the emergence of the Hero, as Carlyle chiefly thought of him, and the feelings, religious and political . . . which raise the wave that washes him into power." [5] It seemed to be not only natural but almost inevitable to attribute to Carlyle all those ideas of political leadership that developed much later and under a quite different "climate of opinion." To the long list of books and articles in which he had studied the philosophy and genealogy of modern imperialism Ernest Seillière added, in 1939, a book on Carlyle.

1831 ff.), then superseded by a new American edition (New York, Charles Scribner's Sons, 1900).

3. *On Heroes*, Lect. vi, p. 229. Centenary ed., V, 237.

4. Durham, N. C., Duke University Press.

5. H. F. C. Grierson, *Carlyle and Hitler* (Cambridge, England, University Press, 1933).

He finds in his works all the characteristics of an "esthetic mysticism" and the first traces of "racial mysticism," and later on, in his book on Frederick the Great, the open defense of Prussian militarism. "The more that, meditating on life's lessons and on the true character of human nature, he approached Toryism, the more room he made for politicians and the military among the delegates of the Most High: it was the Prussian tendency in the heart of German romanticism." [6] Accordingly this Prussification of Carlyle's romanticism was the last and decisive step which led him to a deification of the political leaders and to an identification of might and right.[7]

There is much truth in this description of the effects of Carlyle's theory. Nevertheless it seems to me to be an oversimplification of the matter. Carlyle's conception of the "hero" is very complicated, both in its meaning and in its historical presuppositions. To do full justice to his theory we must study all the diverse and often contradictory elements that formed Carlyle's character, his life, and his work. Carlyle was not a systematic thinker. He did not even try to construct a coherent philosophy of history. To him history was no system—it was a great panorama. History, he declared in his essay on biography, is the essence of innumerable biographies.[8] To read into Carlyle's work, therefore, a definite philosophical construction of the historical process, taken as a whole, or a definite political program is precarious and illusive. Instead of jumping to conclusions about his doctrines we must first try to understand the motives that lay at the bottom of them without a clear insight into which many, if not most, of his ideas remain obscure and ambiguous. Carlyle's conception of history and politics always depends on his own personal history; it is much more biographical than systematic or methodical.

Undoubtedly Carlyle developed in his lectures the idea of "leadership" into its most radical consequences. He identified the whole of historical life with the life of great men. Without them there would be no history; there would be stagnation, and stagnation means death. A mere sequence of events does not constitute history. It consists in deeds and actions, and there are no deeds with-

6. E. Seillière, *Un précurseur du National-Socialisme: L'actualité de Carlyle* (Paris, Éditions de la Nouvelle Revue Critique, 1939), p. 173.

7. *Idem*, pp. 203 ff.

8. "Biography" (1832), *Critical and Miscellaneous Essays*, III, 46. Centenary ed., Vol. XXVIII.

out a doer, without a great, immediate, personal impulse. "Hero Worship," exclaimed Carlyle, "heartfelt prostrate admiration, submission, burning, boundless, for a noblest godlike form of man— is not that the germ of Christianity itself?" [9] This idea was, in a sense, the alpha and omega, the beginning and the end, of his whole philosophy of life and history. He had spoken likewise in his first work. "Well was it written by theologians," he says in *Sartor Resartus*, "a King rules by divine right. He carries in him an authority from God, or man will never give it him. . . . He who is to be my ruler, whose will is to be higher than my will, was chosen for me in Heaven. Neither except in such obedience to the Heaven-chosen is freedom so much as conceivable." [10]

This seems simply to be the language of a theologian who had lost his implicit faith in any dogmatic religion and who, therefore, tried to replace the worship of God by a worship of men. The medieval form of hierarchy was changed into the modern form of "hero-archy." Carlyle's hero is, indeed, a transformed saint, a secularized saint. He need not be a priest or prophet; he may be a poet, a king, a man of letters. But without such temporal saints, Carlyle declares, we cannot live. If hero-archy ever could die out we should have to despair of the world altogether. Without sovereigns, true sovereigns, temporal and spiritual, I see nothing possible but an anarchy, the hatefullest of all things. [11]

But what *is* a hero? There must be a certain standard by which we can recognize him. We must have a touchstone for testing the heroic men, for discerning true gold from base metals. Carlyle knows, of course, that in the history of religion there are true and false prophets and in political life, real and would-be heroes. Is there any criterion by which we know the one from the others? There are heroes who are the representatives of the Divine Idea— there are others who are mere sham heroes. This is a necessary and indestructible feature of human history. For the mass, or, as Carlyle says, "the valets," must have heroes of their own.

Know the men that are to be trusted: alas, this is yet, in these days, very far from us. The sincere alone can recognize sincerity. Not a Hero only is needed, but a world fit for him; a world not of *Valets* . . . The Valet-World has to be governed by the Sham-Hero. . . . It

9. *On Heroes*, Lect. I, p. 11. Centenary ed., V, 11.
10. *Sartor Resartus*, Bk. III, chap. VII, I, 198.
11. *On Heroes*, Lect. IV, p. 120. Centenary ed., V, 124.

is his; he is its! In brief, one of two things: We shall either learn to know a Hero, a true Governor and Captain, somewhat better, when we see him; or else go on to be for ever governed by the Unheroic.[12]

All this is clear and unmistakable. There is nothing that Carlyle hates and abhors more than the "mechanical" theories of political life that he ascribes to the eighteenth century and the philosophers of the Enlightenment. But notwithstanding all his spiritualism he becomes, in matters of politics, one of the most resolute advocates of passive obedience. Carlyle's political theory is, at bottom, nothing short of a disguised and transformed Calvinism. True spontaneity is reserved to the few elect. As to the others, the mass of the reprobates, they have to submit under the will of these elect, the born rulers.

So far we have only received, however, a rhetorical not a philosophical answer. Even if we accept all the premises of Carlyle's theory, the principal question still remains to be answered. Of course, it would be too much to expect from Carlyle a clear definition of what he understands by a hero. Such a definition would be a logical act, and Carlyle speaks with a great contempt of all logical methods. Logic can never penetrate into the secret of reality. The healthy understanding is not the logical and argumentative, but the intuitive. "Consider the old Schoolmen, and their pilgrimage towards truth: the faithfullest endeavour, incessant unwearied motion, often great natural vigour; only no progress: nothing but antic feats of one limb poised against the other; . . . at best gyrated swiftly, with some pleasure, like Spinning Dervishes, and ended where they began." [13] Logic is good, but is not the best; by logic we shall not succeed in understanding life, let alone its highest form: a heroic life. "To know, to get into the truth of anything, is ever a mystic act—of which the best Logics can but babble on the surface." [14] "To attempt *theorizing* on such matters would profit little; they are matters which refuse to be *theoremed* and diagramed; which Logic ought to know that she *cannot* speak of." [15]

But if knowledge, by its nature and essence, is a mystic act, it seems to be a hopeless attempt, to communicate it, to express it

12. *Idem*, Lect. vi, p. 209. Centenary ed., V, 216 f.
13. "Characteristics," *Essays*, III, 6.
14. *On Heroes*, II, 56. Centenary ed., V, 57.
15. *Idem*, I, 25. Centenary ed., V, 26.

in the poor symbols of our human speech, especially, if this communication has to be made in a series of public lectures—delivered before the "mob of London society." How did Carlyle overcome this difficulty; how could he solve this almost impossible task? He could only give an illustration, not a demonstration of his fundamental thesis. It must be admitted that this illustration was vivid and impressive. He had always looked upon history not as an arid textbook, but as a picture gallery. We cannot understand history by mere concepts, we can only understand it by portraits. In his lectures Carlyle tried to cover the whole field of human history. He went from the first rudimentary stages of human civilization to contemporary history and literature. All this had to be combined into one great intuition. Such a synthesis can never be performed by the understanding; it requires other and higher powers. "Not our logical, mensurative faculty, but our imaginative one is king over us; I might say, priest and prophet to lead us heavenward; or magician and wizard to lead us hellward." [16]

Of this imaginative faculty Carlyle made ample use in his lectures. His style is, indeed, that of a prophet who leads us heavenward and of a wizard who leads us hellward. In his description the two directions are sometimes quite undistinguishable. The understanding, he declared, is indeed thy window . . . ; but fantasy is thy eye, with its colour-giving retina, healthy or diseased.[17] Singular men, he had said in a previous essay,[18] are mystic windows through which we glance deeper into the hidden ways of nature. One "mystic window" after another was opened to the hearers of Carlyle's lectures. He could only speak by examples. He felt under no obligation to answer the question: *What* is a hero? But he tried to show, *who* the great heroic men were. His list is long and variegated. Yet he does not admit any specific differences in the heroic character. This character is one and indivisible; it always remains the same. From Norse Odin to English Samuel Johnson, from the divine founder of Christianity to Voltaire, the hero has been worshiped, in one or another form.[19]

By this method the hero of Carlyle became a Proteus that could

16. *Sartor Resartus,* Bk. III, chap. III, I, 176.
17. *Idem,* I, 177.
18. "Peter Nimmo, a Rhapsody."
19. *On Heroes,* Lect. I, p. 14 f. Centenary ed., V, 15.

assume every shape. In every new lecture he shows us a new face. He appears as a mythical god, as a prophet, a priest, a man of letters, a king. He has no limits; nor is he bound to any special sphere of activity.

At bottom the great man, as he comes from the hand of nature, is ever the same kind of thing: Odin, Luther, Johnson, Burns: I hope to make it appear that these are all originally of one stuff. . . . I confess, I have no notion of a truly great man that would not be *all* sorts of men. . . . I cannot understand how a Mirabeau, with that great glowing heart, with the fire that was in it, with the bursting tears that were in it, could not have written verses, tragedies, poems, and touched all hearts in that way, had his course of life and education led him thitherward.[20]

That was a rather paradoxical thesis. Even the strongest imagination will have some difficulties in discovering an identity between a mythical god like Odin and a Rousseau whom Carlyle described as "a morbid, excitable, spasmodic man." [21] And we cannot very well think of a Samuel Johnson, a pedant and schoolmaster, as the writer of the *Divina commedia* or of the plays of Shakespeare. But Carlyle was carried away by the stream of his own eloquence. He spoke of all his heroes with the same enthusiasm. In his "transcendent admiration" [22] of the great men he sometimes seems to lose every sense of proportion. The differences of our lower empirical world were almost forgotten; the most disparate historical characters were put on the same level.

In a writer like Carlyle who had devoted his whole life to historical studies and who in this field possessed a real authority this attitude was rather surprising. But we must not forget the special circumstances under which his lectures were given. Carlyle's style had always been much more oratorical than philosophical. But never before had he made as ample use of mere rhetorical means as in these lectures. As a master in the art of criticism he knew very well how to distinguish between real eloquence and ordinary rhetoric. In the difference between oratory and rhetoric, he declared, we find, as indeed everywhere, that superiority of what is called the natural over the artificial. The orator persuades and

20. *Idem*, Lect. ɪɪ, 41 f., Centenary ed., V, 43; Lect. ɪɪɪ, 76 f., Centenary ed., V, 78 f.

21. *Idem*, Lect. v, 178. Centenary ed., V, 184.

22. *Idem*, Lect. ɪ, 11. Centenary ed., V, 11.

carries all with him, he knows not how; the rhetorician can prove that he ought to have persuaded and carried all with him. "So stands it, in short, with all the forms of intellect, whether as directed to the finding of truth, or to the fit imparting thereof." [23] But this time Carlyle had forgotten this precept. Perhaps he was, unconsciously, influenced by the attitude of his audience that seems to have been very susceptible to the form of his rhetorical style. He spoke to a special public "aristocratic in rank and intellect." He had carefully to weigh his words. He chose his effects and was always sure of them. He tried to capture, to increase and stimulate the interest of his hearers. And he succeeded in this task. Only a few, among them one of his best friends and the most competent critic, John Stuart Mill, seem to have kept their clear critical judgment. When Carlyle spoke of Bentham's theory and declared it to be the most beggarly and falsest view of man, Mill rose from his seat to interrupt the orator and to protest against this description. But the greater part of the audience reacted in quite a different way. The course "On Heroes" became Carlyle's last and greatest public triumph. "The good people sat breathless, or broke out into all kinds of testimonies of good will." [24]

Carlyle himself was critical enough not to be deceived by this success. He was by no means blind to the grave defects of his lectures. He judged them very severely. "Nothing which I have ever written pleases me so ill. They have nothing *new*, nothing that to me is not *old*. The style of them requires to be low-pitched, as like talk as possible." [25] But even the book, as it was published later, is open to the same objections. A great admirer of Carlyle declared that, compared with his masterpieces, the book *On Heroes* is "almost flimsy." [26] It would, therefore, be unfair to judge Carlyle's *thoughts* on hero worship by this book alone. In this regard his previous works were widely superior. To be sure *Sartor Resartus* has not only all the merits but all the defects of his style. It is written in a bizarre and grotesque language; it offends and defies all rules of sound composition. But it is sincere

23. "Characteristics," *Essays*, III, 7.
24. See Carlyle's letters to Margaret Carlyle and to his brother Dr. John Carlyle. Cf. J. A. Froude, *Thomas Carlyle. A History of His Life in London* (New York, Charles Scribner's Sons, 1908), I, 155 ff.
25. See Froude, *idem*, I, 167.
26. See MacMeehan, *op. cit.*, pp. xxxv ff.

in every word; it bears the stamp of Carlyle's personality. In his book on hero worship, which, unfortunately, became his best known and most influential book, he tried much more to persuade than to convince. He had declared the hero to be the "universal man." It was, however, a hard task to prove this universality, not only in the case of a Samuel Johnson or John Knox but even in the case of Luther or Cromwell. Carlyle's exaggerations and inconsistencies are obvious. Yet we should not too much insist upon these inconsistencies. A historian of the rank of Carlyle may lay claim to being judged according to his own conception of a true historical method.

The artist in history may be distinguished from the artisan in history; for here, as in all other provinces, there are artists and artisans; men who labour mechanically in a department, without eye for the Whole, not feeling that there is a Whole; and men who inform and ennoble the humblest department with an Idea of the Whole, and habitually know that only in the Whole is the Partial to be truly discerned. The proceedings and the duties of these two, in regard to history, must be altogether different.[27]

"The Whole" of which Carlyle speaks is not a metaphysical but an individual whole. He is a classical witness to that philosophical attitude that was later styled existential philosophy. We find in him all the characteristics of the type of thought represented by Kierkegaard and his attack against the Hegelian system. We know very little of a thinker, he declares, as long as we know only his concepts. We must know the man before we can understand and appreciate his theories. From German romantic writers, especially from Friedrich H. Jacobi, Carlyle borrowed the term *Lebensphilosophie*.

However it may be with metaphysics and other abstract science originating in the Head (*Verstand*) alone, no Life-Philosophy (*Lebensphilosophie*) . . . which originates equally in the Character (*Gemüt*), and equally speaks thereto, can attain its significance till the Character itself is known and seen; till the author's View of the World (*Weltansicht*) and how he actively and passively came by such view, are clear: in short till a biography of him has been philosophico-poetically written, and philosophico-poetically read.[28]

27. "On History," *Essays*, II, 90.
28. *Sartor Resartus*, Bk. I, chap. xi, I, 59.

In accordance with this maxim Carlyle suddenly interrupted his description of the "philosophy of clothes" that he gave in *Sartor Resartus* in order to insert all sorts of biographical details. In a chapter, "Romance," he tells us a love story of his early youth. He proceeds to that great intellectual crisis in which he saw his "fire baptism." This was not a mere diversion; it was a necessary element of Carlyle's method as a writer and as a thinker. He refused to draw a line of demarcation between a philosophical system and its author. What he called his philosophy always contained an autobiographical element. There can be no doubt of the authenticity of the scene in *Sartor Resartus* in which Carlyle describes the beginning of his *vita nuova,* of his moral and philosophical life. "I remember it well and could go straight to the place where the incident recurred. . . . It is from this hour that I incline to date my spiritual New-birth, or Baphometic Fire-baptism; perhaps I directly thereupon began to be a man." [29]

Philosophical systems belong, roughly speaking, to two different types. They follow an empirical or a rational, an inductive or a deductive method. They are based on facts or they are derived from a priori principles. In order to judge them we must either begin with a study of empirical data or with an analysis of general truths. Yet in the case of Carlyle neither way can lead us to a true insight into the character of his philosophy. His was not an empirical philosophy nor was it a speculative system. He never tried to give more than a "Life-Philosophy," and he never meant to separate this philosophy from his personal experience. In metaphysics as such, as a general system, he could see no more than a perennial disease. In all ages the same questions, the questions of death and immortality, of the origin of evil, of freedom and necessity, have appeared under new forms. Ever and anon must the attempt to shape for ourselves some theorem of the universe be repeated. But all these attempts are doomed to failure; "for what theorem of the Infinite can the Finite render complete?" The mere existence and necessity of a philosophy is an evil. Man is not born to solve the riddles of the universe. What he can do and what he ought to do is to understand himself, his destiny, and his duties. He stands as in the center of nature: "his fraction of time encircled by eternity, his handbreadth of space encircled by

29. *Idem,* Bk. II, chap. vii, I, 135.

infinitude: how shall he forbear asking himself, What am I; and Whence; and Whither?" [30] We must first have Carlyle's answer to all these questions before we can understand any part of his philosophy or any of his theories about man's historical and social life.

The Personal Background of Carlyle's Theory

There is little relation between the ideas of Carlyle and Descartes. They are diametrically opposed both in their results and in their principles; they belong to different hemispheres of the *globus intellectualis*. Nevertheless there is one point of contact—their personal approach to philosophy. Both assert that philosophy begins not with certainty but with doubt. Doubt, in itself, is not to be feared. It is not a subversive but a constructive element in our intellectual life. Metaphysics cannot dispense with it. But ethics is not the same as metaphysics. The ethical life of man begins when he ceases to remain in this "center of indifference" which, in a sense, is the only possible standpoint for metaphysics. Man must learn how to oppose to the "Everlasting No" the "Everlasting Yea." "Having no hope," says Carlyle, speaking of his youth,

neither had I any definite fear. . . . And yet, strangely enough, I lived in a continual, indefinite, pining fear; tremendous, pusillanimous, apprehensive of I knew not what . . . Full of such humour, and perhaps the miserablest man . . . all at once, there arose a thought in me, and I asked myself: "What *art* thou afraid of? Wherefore, like a coward, dost thou forever pip and whimper, and go cowering and trembling? Despicable biped! what is the sum-total of the worst that lies before thee? Death? Well, Death; and say the pangs of Tophet too, and all that the Devil and Man may, will, or can do against thee! Hast thou not a heart; canst thou not suffer whatsoever it be; . . . Let it come, then; I will meet it and defy it!" And as I so thought, there rushed like a stream of fire over my whole soul; and I shook base fear away from me forever. I was strong, of unknown strength; a spirit, almost a god. Ever from that time, the temper of my misery was changed: not fear or whining sorrow was it, but indignation and grim fire-eyed defiance.[31]

30. "Characteristics," *Essays*, III, 25.
31. *Sartor Resartus*, Bk. II, chap. viii, I, 134 f.

Whenever Carlyle, in his later life and work, preached this new gospel of the "Everlasting Yea," he never forgot to mention the name of Goethe. Without this great example, he declared, he could not have found his own way. Goethe's *Wilhelm Meister* had convinced him that "doubt, of whatever kind, can be ended by action alone." [32] Action not speculative thought, ethics not metaphysics is the only means of overcoming doubt and negation. In this way alone we can pass from a science of denial and destruction to a science of affirmation and reconstruction.[33] Such a "science of reconstruction" Carlyle had found in Goethe. It was not the poet Goethe, however, who aroused his highest admiration and was in the focus of his interest. He always spoke of Goethe as a great thinker rather than as a great poet. He even went so far as to call him, in the age of Kant, "*the* Thinker of our time." [34] "We come nearer our meaning," said Carlyle in his second essay on Goethe, "if we say that in Goethe we discover by far the most striking instance, in our time, of a writer who is, in strict speech, what philosophy can call a Man. He is neither noble nor plebeian, neither liberal nor servile, nor infidel nor devotee; but the best excellence of *all* these, joined in pure union, 'a clear and universal Man.'" He stands forth, not only as the literary ornament, but in many respects too as the Teacher and exemplar of his age.[35] His primary faculty, the foundation of all others, was Intellect, depth and force of vision. "A completed man: the trembling sensibility, the wild enthusiasm of a Mignon, can assort with the scornful world-mockery of a Mephistopheles; and each side of manysided life receives its due from him." [36]

From the point of view of literary criticism this characterization may seem to be onesided. The greatest of all lyrical poets was changed by Carlyle into a great teacher, a sage and a didactic poet. Nevertheless it was a great step forward that Carlyle saw Goethe's work in this light. Here he even surpassed the first German apostles of Goethe. To be sure the romantic writers, Novalis, Friedrich Schlegel, Tieck, were much more susceptible to

32. *Past and Present*, Bk. III, chap. xi, X, 198. See Carlyle's trans. of *Wilhelm Meisters Lehrjahre*, Bk. V, chap. xvi, XXIII, 386.
33. *Sartor Resartus*, Bk. I, chap. iii, I, 14.
34. "Diderot," *Essays*, III, 248.
35. "Goethe," *Essays*, I, 208.
36. "Death of Goethe," *Essays*, II, 382.

the charm of Goethe's poetry than was Carlyle. But they did not sympathize with his ethical ideals; they even saw in them a constant danger to the poet Goethe. When Goethe began to publish *Wilhelm Meisters Lehrjahre* those romantic writers were unanimous in their admiration and enthusiasm. Yet when, in the progress of the work, the didactic intention came to the fore, when Goethe began to develop his ideals on education, they were deeply disappointed. Goethe, the man whom Novalis had called "den Statthalter des poetischen Geistes auf Erden," seemed suddenly to have deserted the cause of poetry: he praised the most prosaic and trivial aspect of human life. On the other hand Goethe's work was also open to the opposite objection. Herder, Goethe's friend and the greatest among the German critics, could never become quite reconciled with the moral atmosphere of the first books of *Wilhelm Meisters Lehrjahre*. Characters like Marianne or Philine were intolerable to him; he found in the book a moral indifferentism and a laxity that seemed to him to be unworthy of a great poet.[37]

It was the great merit of Carlyle to see through both errors. One of the paradoxes in the history of modern literature is that this Puritan became the interpreter and defender of Goethe's moral character. If we take into consideration Carlyle's religious and cultural background this was no easy task. Obviously there was no agreement between the ideas of Goethe and Carlyle. The latter had laid aside all dogmatic religion; but he had never completely broken with his Calvinistic credo. Many things in *Wilhelm Meister* must have been repugnant to him. In a letter to James Johnstone he confessed that he felt nothing but disgust for the "players and libidinous actresses" in the story.[38] But after a short time he overcame these moral scruples, for he had found the key to the whole. He began to understand Goethe, and this led him to a better understanding of himself and the great crisis of his early life. "I then felt, and still feel," he wrote later on in his *Reminiscences*, "endlessly indebted to Goethe . . . ; he, in his fashion, I perceived, had travelled the steep rocky road before me—the first of the moderns."[39] He himself had been "in the

---

37. See R. Haym, *Herder* (Berlin, R. Gaertner, 1880), II, 618 f.

38. Letter of September 21, 1823. See *Early Letters*, ed. Charles E. Norton (London, Macmillan & Co., 1886), p. 286.

39. *Reminiscences*, ed. Charles E. Norton (Everyman's Library, London, J. M. Dent & Sons; New York, E. P. Dutton & Co., 1932), p. 282.

very midst of Wertherism, the bleakness and darkness of death." [40]

Carlyle was perhaps the first modern critic who interpreted the subtitle to *Wilhelm Meisters Wanderjahre—Die Entsagenden—* in its right sense. He saw in Goethe's work resignation; but to him this resignation was, at the same time, the highest ethical affirmation. It was not denial but reconstruction. To complain about man's unhappiness, he declared, is mere sentimentalism. "A gifted Byron rises in his wrath; and feeling too surely that he for his part is not 'happy,' declares the same in very violent language, as a piece of news that may be interesting. It evidently has surprised him much. One dislikes to see a man and poet reduced to proclaim on the streets such tidings." [41] Man's unhappiness comes of his greatness; it is the surest proof of an Infinite in him, which with all cunning he cannot quite bury under the Finite. Carlyle spoke here in the style of Pascal. "The fraction of life can be increased in value not so much by increasing your numerator as by lessening your denominator. Nay, unless my Algebra deceive me, *Unity* itself divided by *Zero* will give *Infinity*. Make thy claim of wages a zero then; thou hast the world under thy feet. . . . Close thy Byron; open thy Goethe." [42]

This emphasis on man's activity, on his practical life and practical duties, is the unromantic feature in Carlyle's philosophy. He was a typical romanticist both in his ideas and in their style and expression. But his Philosophy of Life was far different from all the romantic writers. His was a practical not a magical idealism. In his essay on Novalis he spoke of time and space as the deepest of all illusionary appearances. They are not external but internal entities; they are mere forms of man's spiritual being. [43] But this illusionary character of human knowledge disappears as soon as we approach the sphere of action and our ethical life. Only in this sphere do we stand upon firm and unshakeable ground. All skepticism and all theoretical "solipsism" are overcome. We have reached the true reality; we have recognized "the infinite nature of duty." [44] Metaphysics, as such, cannot solve the riddle. We cannot break the spell of skepticism by mere speculation. "There

40. *Lectures on the History of Literature*, ed. J. Reay Greene (New York, Charles Scribner's Sons, 1892), pp. 192 ff.
41. *Past and Present*, Bk. III, chap. IV, X, 154.
42. *Sartor Resartus*, Bk. II, chap. IX, I, 152 f.
43. "Novalis," *Essays*, II, 24 ff.
44. *On Heroes*, Lect. II, p. 73. Centenary ed., V, 75.

is no more fruitless endeavour than this same, which the meta-physician proper toils in: to educe conviction out of negation.
. . . Metaphysical speculation, as it begins in No or Nothingness, so it must needs end in Nothingness; circulates and must circulate in endless vortices, creating, swallowing—itself." [45]

This conviction of the fundamentally ethical character of reality had a double influence upon Carlyle's romanticism. It led not only to a change in his thoughts but also to a change in his style. In *Sartor Resartus* Carlyle deliberately imitated all the characters of the romantic style. Jean Paul became his great model. His manner of writing seemed to defy all logical rules; it was bizarre, fantastic, incoherent. There is, however, one feature of the romantic style that was inconsistent with Carlyle's nature and temperament. We find in him the grotesque humor of Jean Paul, but we do not find the romantic irony. "That faculty of irony," wrote Carlyle in his first essay on Jean Paul Friedrich Richter, "of caricature, which often passes by the name of humour, but consists chiefly in a certain superficial distortion or reversal of objects, and ends at best in laughter, bears no resemblance to the humour of Richter. . . . It is but a poor fraction of humour; or rather, it is the body to which the soul is wanting; any life it has being false, artificial, and irrational." [46] Carlyle could not be ironical. He always spoke in dead earnest. "No Mirabeau, Napoleon, Burns, Cromwell," he said in his lectures on *Hero Worship*, "no man adequate to do anything, but is first of all in right earnest about it. . . . Fearful and wonderful, real as life, real as death, is this universe to him. . . . At all moments the Flame-image glares in upon him; undeniable, there, there!—I wish you to take this as my primary definition of a great man." [47]

To most of the romantic writers this aspect of Carlyle's theory would hardly have been understandable. When Friedrich Schlegel, in his novel *Lucinde*, gave his delineation of a truly romantic life his description ended in praise of idleness. Idleness that commonly is denounced as a vice is, in fact, one of the highest virtues. It is the clue to a poetic conception of the universe; the medium for all imaginative life. Carlyle always spoke of Friedrich Schlegel with great sympathy. But nothing was more remote

45. "Characteristics," *Essays*, III, 27.
46. "Jean Paul Friedrich Richter," *Essays*, I, 16 f.
47. *On Heroes*, Lect. II, p. 44. Centenary ed., V, 45.

from his character and from his doctrine than this theory. He called himself a mystic but his mysticism never led him to any kind of quietism. It was not based upon devotional contemplation. "Virtue, *Vir-tus*, manhood, *hero*-hood . . . is first of all . . . courage and the faculty to *do*." [48] "Labour is life. . . . Properly thou hast no other knowledge but what thou hast got by working: the rest is yet all a hypothesis of knowledge; a thing to be argued of in schools, a thing floating in the clouds, in endless logic-vortices, till we try it and fix it." [49] If this is not worship the more pity for worship. The categorical imperative of Carlyle is Produce, Produce! "Were it but the pitifullest fraction of a product, produce it, in God's name! . . . Work while it is called today; for the night cometh, wherein no man can work." [50]

These last words, like so many others in Carlyle's writings, are a direct quotation from Goethe.[51] In Goethe, not in Novalis or Friedrich Schlegel, could Carlyle find the confirmation of his device *Laborare est orare*.[52] Goethe was to him the Oedipus of the modern world who had solved the riddle of the Sphinx. "From our point of view," he said, "does Goethe rise on us as the Uniter, and victorious Reconciler of the distracted, clashing elements of the most distracted and divided age that the world has witnessed since the introduction of the Christian religion." [53]

In one of his *Maxims and Reflections* Goethe says: "Wie kann man sich selbst kennen lernen? Durch Betrachten niemals, wohl aber durch Handeln. Versuche, deine Pflicht zu tun, und du weisst gleich, was an dir ist." "Was aber ist deine Pflicht? Die Forderung des Tages." [54] This maxim became to Carlyle the true

48. *Idem*, VI, 210. Centenary ed., V, 218.
49. *Past and Present*, Bk. III, chap. xi, X, 197 f.
50. *Sartor Resartus*, Bk. II, chap. ix, I, 157.
51. See Goethe, *West-Oestlicher Divan*, "Buch der Sprüche":
"Noch ist es Tag, da rühre sich der Mann!
Die Nacht tritt ein, wo niemand wirken kann."
52. Cf. Carlyle's letter to Goethe of April 15, 1827: "If I have been delivered from darkness into any measure of light, if I know aught of myself and my duties and destination, it is to the study of your writings more than to any other circumstance that I owe this." *Correspondence between Goethe and Carlyle*, ed. Charles E. Norton (London, Macmillan & Co., 1887), p. 7.
53. "Goethe's Works," *Essays*, II, 434.
54. Goethe, *Maximen und Reflexionen*, herausgegeben von Max Hecker, "Schriften der Goethe-Gesellschaft," Band XXI, Nos. 442, 443 (Weimar, Verlag der Goethe-Gesellschaft, 1907), 93. ("How can we come to know ourselves? Never by speculation, but by action. Try to do your duty and you will know at once what you are worth." "But what is your duty? The demand of the day.")

metaphysics of life, the kernel of his "Life-Philosophy." Self-contemplation, as a mere theoretical act "is infallibly a symptom of disease. . . . There is a self-seeking; an unprofitable looking behind us to measure the way we have made: whereas the sole concern is to walk continually forward, and make more way." [55] For this purpose it is enough to know "the claims of the day"; to fulfil "the task that lies nearest." "Do the duty which lies nearest thee, which thou knowest to be a duty! Thy second duty will already become clearer. . . . You discover, with amazement enough, like the Lothario in *Wilhelm Meister*, that your 'America is here or nowhere.'" [56] "Our works are the mirror wherein the spirit first sees its natural lineaments. Hence, too, the folly of that impossible precept, *Know thyself*; till it be translated into this partially possible one, *Know what thou canst work at*." [57]

This active and energetic conception of man's life necessarily has its repercussion upon our conception of nature. Both questions are closely interwoven; they are only different aspects of one and the same problem. Man will always form his image of nature after his own image. If he fails to see in himself an original and creative power, nature too becomes to him a mere passive thing—a dead mechanism. According to Carlyle this was the fate of the French Encyclopedists and the "philosophers" of the eighteenth century. Their theory of nature was the exact counterpart of their theory of man. Holbach's *Système de la nature* and Lamettrie's *L'homme machine* are closely akin. They express the same skeptical, destructive, negative spirit. The true hero of this philosophy was not Faust, the active and striving man, but Mephisto, "der Geist der stets verneint." Mephisto's maxim is the same as Voltaire's "*N'en croyez rien*." "The shrewd, all-informed intellect he has, is an attorney intellect; it can contradict, but it cannot affirm. With lynx vision he descries at a glance the ridiculous, the unsuitable, the bad; but for the solemn, the noble, the worthy, he is blind as his ancient mother." [58]

How could, indeed, man find greatness in nature after he had lost sight of his own greatness? How could he see in it a great living force when he himself was no longer alive but a mere auto-

55. "Characteristics," *Essays*, III, 7 f.
56. *Sartor Resartus*, Bk. II, chap. x, I, 156.
57. *Idem*, Bk. II, chap. viii, I, 132.
58. "Goethe's Helena," *Essays*, I, 157.

maton? On the other hand the dynamism that we have discovered in ourselves becomes the clue to a new conception of nature. Nature is no great engine moved by outward mechanical forces. It is the symbol and vesture of the Infinite, "the infinite garment of God." That is the very core of that "philosophy of clothes" which Carlyle develops in *Sartor Resartus*. "Alles Vergängliche ist nur ein Gleichnis"—all visible things are emblems. Before this great vision the illusion of a dead nature disappears. "System of Nature! To the wisest man, wide as his vision, nature remains of quite infinite depth." It is incomprehensible and inscrutable as long as we try to stretch it into the Procrustean bed of our poor words or our scientific concepts. We may speak of the "volume of nature"; but "it is a volume written in celestial hieroglyphs, in the true sacred-writing, of which even prophets are happy that they can read here a line and there a line." [59] We must oppose this true synthetic view of nature to the analytical view of the eighteenth century. Then, and then alone, we shall understand the "open secret." [60] We shall no longer see in the physical world a "frightful machine of death" nor hear in it a "monotonous din of a huge mill—a mill as such without millwright or miller." [61]

In all this Carlyle seems simply to reproduce and paraphrase the ideas of Goethe. Yet, on the other hand, he could never accept these ideas in their real and original meaning. Even after he had abandoned his Puritan faith he needed a more personal ideal of the Divine and Infinite than he could find in Goethe's works. There is a constant tendency in Carlyle's writings to suppress or to minimize all the pagan features of Goethe's religion. His own was a moral religion not a religion of nature. In his first lectures on hero worship he tried to do full justice to the different forms of polytheism. The worship of the great natural powers, he said, was the first and inevitable step in religious history. But he could not even understand this step without, unconsciously, modifying

59. *Sartor Resartus*, Bk. III, chap. vin, I, 205 f.

60. *On Heroes*, Lect. iii, p. 78. Centenary ed., V, 80. See Goethe, *Gedichte* (Weimar ed.), III, 88.

> "Müsset im Naturbetrachten
> Immer eins wie alles achten;
> Nichts ist drinnen, nichts ist draussen:
> Denn was innen: das ist aussen.
> So ergreifet ohne Säumnis
> Heilig öffentlich Geheimnis."

61. "Novalis," *Essays*, II, 33; cf. Novalis, *Lehrlinge zu Sais*.

the very character of polytheism. Odin, the highest god of German mythology, became to him simply a man, a great king or priest. We must not think of Odin as a personification of a natural force, but as a real person. He was, first and foremost, a teacher. Had he not solved, for the Norse people, "the sphinx-enigma of this universe"? Existence had become "articulate, melodious by him, he first had made Life alive. We may call this Odin, the origin of Norse mythology: Odin, or whatever name the first Norse thinker bore while he was a man among men." [62]

That was the personal reaction of Carlyle toward paganism, a reaction far different from that of Goethe who sometimes called himself a "decided pagan" and who, in his essay on Winckelmann, had become the interpreter and defender of Winckelmann's paganism.[63] Carlyle was no longer a "theist" in the traditional sense. But if he needed no personal god, he needed, at least, a personal hero. Worship of a natural power was at bottom unintelligible to him. He was deeply impressed by Goethe's doctrine of the "three reverences," the worship of all that is around, above, and below us. But he could never admit a comparison between Goethe's "ethnic religion" and his own religious convictions. To him such a religion was, at best, the "infant thought of man opening itself with awe and wonder, on this ever stupendous universe"—a rude childlike way of recognizing the divineness of nature.[64]

In Eckermann's *Conversations with Goethe* there is a passage that is very suitable to illustrate the fundamental difference between Goethe's religious views and those of Carlyle. He begins by declaring that there are, obviously, some discrepancies and even contradictions between the various texts upon which the Christian revelation is based. Nevertheless we may regard all four gospels as thoroughly genuine. There is in them the reflection of a greatness which emanated from the person of Jesus. "If I am asked," he continues,

whether it is in my nature to pay Him devout reverence, I say—certainly! I bow before Him as the divine manifestation of the highest principle of morality. If I am asked whether it is in my nature to revere the Sun, I again say—certainly! For he is likewise a manifestation of the highest Being, and indeed the most powerful that we chil-

---

62. *On Heroes*, Lect. I, p. 21. Centenary ed., V, 22.
63. Goethe, *Winckelmann und sein Jahrhundert* (Weimar ed.), XLVI, 25 ff.
64. *On Heroes*, Lect. I.

dren of earth are allowed to behold. I adore in him the light and the productive power of God; by which we all live, move, and have our being—we, and all the plants and animals with us.[65]

Carlyle never felt or spoke in this way. To put the reverence of Christ on the same level as the adoration of the Sun would have appeared to him a sacrilege.

There was, however, still another and stronger reason why Carlyle, in his religious conceptions and ideals, could not confine himself to Goethe's works. "I believe in God!" says Goethe in one of his *Maxims*. "That is a fine, a worthy thing to say; but to recognize God where and as he reveals himself, is the only true bliss on earth." [66] According to this dictum Goethe declared himself to be a "pantheist," a "polytheist," and a "theist" at the same time. "As a naturalist," he said, "I am a pantheist; as an artist a polytheist, in my ethical life I am a monotheist." [67]

> "Wie Natur im Vielgebilde
> Einen Gott nur offenbart;
> So im weiten Kunstgefilde
> Webt ein Sinn der ew'gen Art;
> Dieses ist der Sinn der Wahrheit,
> Der sich nur mit Schönem schmückt
> Und getrost der höchsten Klarheit
> Hellsten Tags entgegenblickt." [68]

Yet in this description of the manifestation of the Divine there was one thing missing. Goethe spoke of nature and art, but he did not speak of history. He never could esteem history in the

65. Eckermann, *Conversations with Goethe*, March 11, 1832. English trans. by John Oxenford (Everyman's Library, London, J. M. Dent & Sons; New York, E. P. Dutton & Co., 1930), p. 422.

66. Goethe, *Maximen und Reflexionen*, No. 809, p. 179.

67. *Idem*, No. 807, p. 179.

68. Goethe, "Künstler-Lied," Aus den *Wanderjahren*. Carlyle's trans., XXIV, 329:

> "As all Nature's thousand changes
> But one changeless God proclaim;
> So in Art's wide kingdom ranges
> One sole meaning still the same:
> This is Truth, eternal Reason,
> Which from Beauty takes its dress,
> And serene through time and season
> Stands for aye in loveliness."

same way as nature or art. He did not regard it as an immediate revelation of the Divine—he found it human, all too human. For Goethe historical knowledge was widely inferior to our knowledge of nature. Nature is one great infinite Whole; history gives us, at best, scattered limbs of human life. "Literature," says Goethe, "is the fragment of fragments. The least of what has been spoken was written, the least of what has been written has remained." [69] And even if all sources had been preserved—what would we know of history? What we call historical "facts" are, in most cases, mere legends. Every writer gives us his own distorted image of political events and human characters—according to his taste, his sympathies and antipathies, his national prejudices.[70] Carlyle could not speak of history in so disparaging and skeptical a way. He saw in it, even more than in nature or in art, the "visible garment of God." Great men were to him the inspired speaking and acting texts of that divine book of revelations, whereof a chapter is completed from epoch to epoch, and by some named history. To these inspired texts the more numerous merely talented men are only exegetic commentaries for better or worse. "For my study," he exclaimed, "the inspired texts themselves!" [71] To a true historian history is not, as Goethe says in *Faust,* "ein Kehrichtfass und eine Rumpelkammer." He has not only the power of relating the past; he revivifies it, he makes it present. The genuine historian speaks and acts like Gulliver's conjuror: he brings back "the brave Past, that we might look into it, and scrutinise it at will." [72] For such views Carlyle could find no support in Goethe's works. As a *historian* he had to make a fresh start; he had to find and to pave his own way—and, for this purpose, he had if not completely to change at least to modify his "Life-Philosophy." It was this modification that led him to his theory of hero worship and the heroic in history.

69. *Maximen und Reflexionen,* No. 512, p. 111.
70. For further details see E. Cassirer, *Goethe und die geschichtliche Welt* (Berlin, B. Cassirer, 1932).
71. *Sartor Resartus,* Bk. II, chap. viii, Centenary ed., I, 142.
72. See "Schiller," *Essays,* II, 167.

The Metaphysical Background of Carlyle's Theory and His Conception of History

When Carlyle looked for a guide who could lead him through the labyrinth of history as Goethe had led him through the realms of nature and art, where was he to find him? There was one man who, if anyone, seemed to be fit for this service: Herder. But we have no evidence that Herder ever exerted a decisive influence upon Carlyle's thought. There was, however, another thinker for whom Carlyle had felt a keen interest and a strong admiration from the beginning. In one of his earliest essays, on the state of German literature (1827), he spoke of Fichte as a cold, colossal, adamantine spirit, standing erect and clear, like an elder Cato among degenerate men. So robust an intellect and a soul so calm, so lofty, massive, and immovable, had not mingled in philosophical discussion since the time of Luther. We may accept or reject his opinions; but his character as a thinker can be slightly valued only by such as know it ill. He ranks with a class of men who were common only in better ages than ours.[73]

When judging thus Carlyle hardly thought of Fichte's metaphysics. The first expositions of his metaphysical system that Fichte had given in his *Wissenschaftslehre* are among the most difficult books of philosophical literature. Carlyle would scarcely have been able to study and master them. What he read rather were Fichte's popular books, *Das Wesen des Gelehrten* and, in all probability, *Die Bestimmung des Menschen* and *Die Grundzüge des gegenwärtigen Zeitalters*. Here he could not find the whole of Fichte's metaphysics; but he found the "elder Cato" who spoke of the present age as the "Age of absolute indifference towards all truth, and of entire and unrestrained licentiousness:— the State of completed Sinfulness."[74] As a thinker whose whole interest was concentrated upon moral problems Carlyle must have been deeply impressed by such a judgment. Was it possible to find a remedy for what Fichte had described as the mortal disease of our modern world?

But could Carlyle accept Fichte's views without becoming un-

73. "State of German Literature," *Essays*, I, 77.
74. See Fichte, *Grundzüge des gegenwärtigen Zeitalters*. English trans. by W. Smith, *The Popular Works of Johann Gottlieb Fichte* (4th ed. London, Trübner & Co., 1889), II, 17. Lect. II.

faithful to the man to whom he felt indebted not only as a disciple to his master but as a son to his "spiritual father"? [75] Was it possible to reconcile the Life-Philosophies of Goethe and Fichte? Obviously they are not of the same type. Fichte's "subjective idealism" was, in its very principle, quite incompatible with Goethe's "objective idealism." But of this difference Carlyle does not seem to have been aware. His was not a logical or discursive but an intuitive mind. While he was no mere eclectic who freely borrowed from the most disparate sources, still he easily accepted any theory as long as he could adapt it to his ethical and religious requirements.

And in this respect there was, indeed, a point of contact between the views of Fichte and Goethe. Time and again Carlyle refers to Goethe's words that "doubt of whatever kind can be ended by action alone." This fundamental thesis he could also find in Fichte. Fichte's *Bestimmung des Menschen* is divided into three books. The first is entitled "Doubt," the second "Knowledge," the third "Faith." According to Fichte knowledge is never a mere theoretical act. By logical inferences, by our power of arguing and reasoning, we never can hope to touch reality and truth—let alone, to penetrate into their essence. This way can only lead us to a radical skepticism. If this were the only gateway to truth we should be forever condemned to live as in a dream. What we call the material world has only a shadowy existence; it is a product of the Ego that "posits" the Non-Ego. But there is another way that leads us beyond this world of shadows. The only reality that is clear, certain, unshakable, and admits of no doubt is the reality of our moral life—a "practical" not a merely "theoretical" reality. Here, and here alone, we stand on firm ground. The certainty of the moral law, of the categorical imperative, is the first thing that is given to us—the condition and the foundation of all other knowledge. Not by our intellect but by our will do we grasp reality.

"The reality in which thou didst formerly believe, a material world existing independently of thee, of which thou didst fear to become the slave," says the Spirit in Fichte's *Bestimmung des Menschen*,

has vanished; for this whole material world arises only through knowledge, and is itself our knowledge; but knowledge is not reality, just

75. See *Correspondence with Goethe*, April 15, 1827.

because it is knowledge . . . Thou dost now seek, and with good right as I well know, something real lying beyond mere appearance, another reality than that which has thus been annihilated. But in vain wouldst thou labour to create this reality by means of thy knowledge or out of thy knowledge or to embrace it by thy understanding. If thou hast no other organ by which to apprehend it, thou wilt never find it. But thou hast such an organ. . . . Not merely to know, but according to thy knowledge to do, is thy vocation. . . . Not for idle contemplation of thyself, not for brooding over devout sensations— no, for action art thou here; thine action, and thine action alone, determines thy worth.[76]

All this recurs in Carlyle's writings and is often expressed in the very terms of Fichte. "Not what I Have but what I Do," he says, "is my Kingdom." [77] "Knowledge? The knowledge that will hold good in working, cleave thou to that; for Nature herself accredits that, says Yea to that." [78] If there is any firm and indubitable knowledge it does not belong to the external world, but to our inner life—and to the fixed center of this inner life, the consciousness of ourselves. "Never shall I forget that inward occurrence . . ." says Carlyle, quoting from Jean Paul,

wherein I witnessed the birth of my Self-consciousness, of which I can still give the place and time. One forenoon, I was standing, a very young child, in the outer door, and looking leftward at the stack of the fuel-wood, when all at once the internal vision, "I am a Me" (*ich bin ein Ich*), came like a flash from heaven before me, and in gleaming light ever afterwards continued; then had my Me, for the first time, seen itself, and forever.[79]

But what is this "Self"? "Who am *I;* the thing that can say 'I' (*das Wesen, das sich Ich nennt*)?" [80] How and where can we find it? Obviously it is not a thing among things—an object that can be discovered and described by scientific methods. It cannot be calculated and measured. It is not "given" in the same way as a physical thing; it must be "done." As Fichte said, it is not a *Tatsache* but a *Tathandlung;* it is not a fact but an act. Without the performance of this act the knowledge of ourselves and, ac-

76. Fichte, *Bestimmung des Menschen,* "Sämtliche Werke," ed. J. H. Fichte, II, 246 ff. *Popular Works,* I, 404–406.

77. *Sartor Resartus,* Bk. II, chap. iv, I, 96.

78. *Past and Present,* Bk. III, chap. xi, X, 198.

79. "Jean Paul Friedrich Richter Again," *Essays,* II, 111.

80. *Sartor Resartus,* Bk. I, chap. viii, I, 41.

cordingly, the knowledge of any outward reality, is impossible. With all this Carlyle had found something that he could not find in Goethe's works. Fichte's *Wesen des Gelehrten,* a work that he quoted over and over again, had given a philosophical basis for his conception of the historical world. According to Fichte the historical world is not a mere by-product, a secondary phenomenon, embraced by and, in a sense, forlorn in the great universe of nature. In his system the relation between nature and history had been reversed. As long as we restrict ourselves to the phenomena of nature, declared Fichte, we cannot find the truth nor grasp the "Absolute." The very possibility of a philosophy of nature was passionately and emphatically denied by Fichte. When Schelling developed his philosophy of nature, he was accused by Fichte of high treason to the cause of transcendental idealism. Do not allow yourselves to be blinded and led astray, said Fichte in his second lecture addressing his students, by a philosophy assuming the name *Natur-Philosophie.* Very far from being a step toward truth, that philosophy is but a return to an old and already widespread error.[81]

In this conception of history and the "spiritual" world as the truly, nay only, "Absolute," Carlyle found the first decisive impulse to his theory of heroism and hero worship. Fichte could provide him with a whole *metaphysics* of hero worship.

We must content ourselves with a general delineation of Fichte's system.[82] It may be described as a system of "subjective" idealism. But the term "subjective" is always ambiguous and misleading. It requires a fixation and determination. Fichte's "transcendental subject"—the *Ich* that posits the *Nicht-Ich*—is neither the empirical subject; nor does it coincide with those types of subjectivity that we find in previous philosophical systems. It is neither the logical subject of Descartes nor the psychological subject of Berkeley. It belongs to a different order, the purely ethical order; to the realm of "ends" rather than to the realm of "nature"; to the realm of "values" rather than to that of "being." The first fundamental reality, the condition and prerequisite of anything else that we call "real," is the moral subject. We find this subject

81. Fichte, *Über das Wesen des Gelehrten,* "Sämtliche Werke," VI, 363 f. *Popular Works,* I, 224 f.
82. For a closer analysis of Fichte's *Wissenschaftslehre* see E. Cassirer, *Das Erkenntnisproblem* (Berlin, B. Cassirer, 1920), Vol. III.

not by logical processes such as speculation, contemplation, or demonstration but by an act of our free WILL. In Fichte's philosophy Descartes' *Cogito, ergo sum* is changed to the maxim: *Volo, ergo sum.* But Fichte is neither a "solipsist" nor is he an egotist. The "I" finds itself by a free act—by an original *Tathandlung.* Activity is its very essence and meaning. But it cannot act without a material to act upon. It demands a "world" as the scene of its activity. And in this world it finds other acting and working subjects. It has to respect their rights and their original freedom. Hence it has to restrict its own activity in order to give room to the activity of others. This restriction is not enforced on us by an external power. Its necessity is not that of a physical thing; it is a moral necessity. According to the moral law, the true absolute, we have to coöperate with other subjects and we have to build up a social order. The free act by which we find ourselves is to be completed by another act, by which we recognize other free subjects. This act of recognition is our first and fundamental duty.

Duty and obligation are, therefore, the elements of what we call the "real" world. Our world is the material of our duty, represented in a sensuous form. "Unsere Welt ist das versinnlichte Materiale unserer Pflicht; dies ist das eigentliche Reelle in den Dingen, der wahre Grundstoff aller Erscheinung. Der Zwang, mit welchem der Glaube an die Realität derselben sich uns aufdringt, ist ein moralischer Zwang; der einzige, welcher für das freie Wesen möglich ist." [83]

Yet in this great edifice of our moral world the cornerstone is still missing. Fichte's philosophy begins with the axiom that the basic element of reality, the stuff and material out of which it has been formed, is the moral energy of man. But where do we find this energy? There are some individuals who are so weak that they can hardly raise themselves to the idea of freedom. They have no conception of what a free personality is and means. They do not know and they do not understand that they have a personal, independent being and value, that they are "the thing that can say 'I.'" [84] On the other hand we find other individuals in

83. Fichte, *Über den Grund unseres Glaubens an eine göttliche Weltregierung,* "Sämtliche Werke," V, 185.

84. See Fichte, *Erste Einleitung in die Wissenschaftslehre,* "Sämtliche Werke," I, 434 f. "Was für eine Philosophie man wähle, hängt sonach davon ab, was man für ein Mensch ist . . . Ein von Natur schlaffer . . . Charakter wird sich nie zum Idealismus erheben."

which the moral energy, the consciousness of the "I," appears in its full vigor.

When speaking of the historical and cultural world, we must bear in mind this fundamental difference. The philosophers of the eighteenth century were resolute individualists. They inferred their doctrines of the equal *rights* of men from their implicit faith in the equality of *reason*. Descartes began his *Discourse on Method* by the words: "Good sense is, of all things among men, the most equally distributed; for everyone thinks himself so abundantly provided with it that those even who are the most difficult to satisfy in everything else, do not usually desire a larger measure of this quality than they already possess." Fichte broke with this conception. In his later works, he sees in the thesis of the equality of reason a mere intellectualistic prejudice. If reason means practical reason, if it means the moral will, it is by no means equally distributed. It is not to be found everywhere; it is actually concentrated in a few great personalities. In them the real meaning of the historical process manifests itself in its full and incomparable strength. These are the "heroes," the first pioneers of human culture. "Who, then, in the first place," asks Fichte,

gave to the countries of Modern Europe their present habitable shape, and made them worthy to be the dwelling-place of cultivated men? History answers the question. It was pious and holy men, who, believing it to be God's Will that the timid fugitive of the woods should be elevated to civilized life . . . went forth into the desert wilderness . . . Who has united rude races together, and reduced opposing tribes under the dominion of law? . . . Who has maintained them in this condition, and protected existing states from dissolution through internal disorder, or destruction by outward power? Whatever name they may have borne, it was Heroes, who had left their Age far behind them, giants among surrounding men in material and spiritual power.[85]

I do not mean to say that Carlyle accepted this metaphysical doctrine of Fichte in all its details. Perhaps he could not even understand Fichte's system of transcendental idealism in its full meaning and purport. He had no clear grasp of its theoretical premises or of its implications. Fichte spoke as a metaphysician, Carlyle spoke as a psychologist and historian. Fichte tried to convince by arguments; Carlyle usually contented himself with speaking to the sentiments of his readers and hearers. He simply declared

85. Fichte, *Grundzüge des gegenwärtigen Zeitalters*. See *Popular Works*, II, 47 f. Lect. III.

hero worship to be a fundamental instinct in human nature, which if it were ever rooted out would lead to despair for mankind.[86]

Looking back at the results of our historical and systematic analysis we are now in a better position to judge the meaning and the influence of Carlyle's theory of hero worship. Perhaps no other philosophical theory has done so much to prepare the way for the modern ideals of political leadership. Had not Carlyle explicitly and emphatically declared that the hero as king, the commander over men, "is practically the summary for us of *all* the figures of heroism?" "Priest, Teacher, whatsoever of earthly or of spiritual dignity we can fancy to reside in a man, embodies itself here, to *command* over us, to furnish with constant practical teaching, to tell us for the day and hour what we are to do." [87] That was clear and plain spoken. The modern defenders of fascism did not fail to see their opportunity here and they could easily turn Carlyle's words into political weapons. But to charge Carlyle with all the consequences that have been drawn from his theory would be against all the rules of historical objectivity. In this regard I cannot accept the judgment that I find in recent literature on the subject.[88] What Carlyle meant by "heroism" or "leadership" was by no means the same as what we find in our modern theories of fascism. According to Carlyle there are two criteria by which we can easily distinguish the true hero from the sham hero: his "insight" and his "sincerity." Carlyle could never think or speak of lies as necessary or legitimate weapons in the great political struggles. If a man, like Napoleon in his later period, begins to lie, he immediately ceases to be a hero. " 'False as a bulletin' became a proverb in Napoleon's time. He makes what excuse he could for it: that it was necessary to mislead the enemy, to keep up his own men's courage, and so forth. On the whole, there are no excuses. . . . A lie is *no*-thing; you cannot of nothing make something; you make *nothing* at last, and lose your labour into the bargain." [89] When Carlyle spoke of his heroes it was always his first concern to convince us that they despised all manner of deception. There can be no greater mistake than to speak of men like Mahomet or Cromwell as liars. "From of old,

86. Cf. *Sartor Resartus*, Bk. I, chap. x, I, 54.
87. *On Heroes*, Lect. vi, p. 189. Centenary ed., V, 196.
88. See above, p. 190, n. 5.
89. *On Heroes*, Lect. vi, p. 230. Centenary ed., V. 238.

I will confess, this theory of Cromwell's falsity has been incredible to me. Nay I cannot believe the like, of any great man whatever." [90] "I will believe most things sooner than that. One would be entirely at a loss what to think of this world at all, if quackery so grew and were sanctioned here." [91]

There is still one other feature that distinguishes Carlyle's theory from the later types of hero worship. What he most admired in his heroes was not only the sincerity of feeling but also clearness of thought. Great energy of action and great will-power always imply an intellectual element. The strength of will and character would remain powerless without an equal power of thought. The equipoise between these two elements is the distinctive mark of the true hero. He is the man who lives among things, not among the shows of things. While others walk in formulas and hearsays, contented enough to dwell there, the hero is alone with his own soul and the reality of things.[92] Carlyle spoke as a mystic but his mysticism was no mere irrationalism. All his heroes—the prophets, the priests, the poets—are at the same time described as deep and genuine thinkers. In Carlyle's description even Odin, a mythical god, appears as a "thinker." "The first Norse 'man of genius,' as we should call him! Innumerable men had passed by, across this Universe, with a dumb vague wonder, such as the very animals may feel; or with a painful, fruitlessly inquiring wonder, such as men only feel;—till the great Thinker came, the *original* man, the Seer, whose shaped spoken thought awakes the slumbering capability of all into thought. It is ever the way with the thinker, the spiritual hero." [93] Thought, if it is deep, sincere, genuine, has the power to work wonders. In *Sartor Resartus* Carlyle speaks of "the grand thaumaturgic art of thought." "Thaumaturgic I name it; for hitherto all Miracles have been wrought thereby, and henceforth innumerable will be wrought." [94] Poetry, too, would be a very poor thing without this "thaumaturgic art of thought," for it is a very inadequate conception of poetry to see nothing in it except a play of imagination. Dante, Shakespeare, Milton and Goethe were great, deep, and genuine thinkers—and this was one of the most prolific sources of their poetical

90. *Idem*, Lect. VI, p. 203 f. Centenary ed., V, 211.
91. *Idem*, Lect. II, p. 43. Centenary ed., V, 44.
92. *Idem*, Lect. II, p. 53. Centenary ed., V, 55; Lect. IV, 125, Centenary ed., V, 128.
93. *Idem*, Lect. I, p. 21. Centenary ed., V, 21.
94. *Sartor Resartus*, Bk. II, chap. IV, I, 95 f.

imagination. Imagination without thought would be barren; it could produce nothing but mere shadows and illusions. "At bottom," says Carlyle, "it is the Poet's first gift, as it is all men's, that he have intellect enough." [95]

It is, therefore, the rare and happy union of all the productive and constructive forces in man that, on Carlyle's theory, constitutes the character of the hero. And among all these forces the *moral* force obtains the highest rank and plays the preponderant role. In his philosophy "morality" means the power of affirmation over against the power of denial and negation. What really matters is not so much the thing affirmed as the act of affirmation itself and the strength of this act.

Here too Carlyle could have appealed to Goethe who relates in his autobiography that, when, in his youth, his friends tried to convert him to a special credo, he constantly repelled their efforts.

In Faith, I said, every thing depends on the fact of believing; what is believed is perfectly indifferent. Faith is a profound sense of security in regard to both the present and the future; and this assurance springs from confidence in an immense, all-powerful, and inscrutable Being. The firmness of this confidence is the one great point; but what we think of this Being depends on our other faculties, or even on circumstances, and is wholly indifferent. Faith is a holy vessel into which every one stands ready to pour his feeling, his understanding, his imagination, as perfectly as he can. [96]

Here we have a striking expression of Carlyle's own religious feelings after he had abandoned his orthodox faith in the Calvinistic dogma. In his lectures on heroes he laid the whole stress not upon the kind but upon the intensity of religious feeling. The degree of it was to him the only standard. Hence he could speak with the same sympathy of Dante's catholicism and Luther's protestantism, of old Norse mythology and the Islam or Christian religion. What Carlyle admired most in Dante was that intensity. Dante, he said, does not come before us as a large catholic mind, rather as a narrow and even sectarian mind. He is world-great not because he is world-wide but because he is world-deep. "I know nothing so intense as Dante." [97]

95. *On Heroes,* Lect. III, p. 102. Centenary ed., V, 105.
96. Goethe, *Dichtung und Wahrheit,* Buch XIV. English trans. by John Oxenford (Boston, S. E. Cassino, 1882), II, 190.
97. *On Heroes,* Lect. III, p. 90. Centenary ed., V, 92.

Yet Carlyle was not always able to live up to this universal, all-embracing ideal of religion. There remained in him certain instinctive sympathies or antipathies that influenced his judgment. This becomes particularly clear in his attitude toward the eighteenth century. When Carlyle tried to describe the character of the historical process in a short formula he spoke of it as "the war of Belief against Unbelief." [98] "The special, sole and deepest theme of the World's and Man's history," Goethe had said in a note to his *West-Oestlicher Divan,*

whereto all other themes are subordinated, remains the conflict of unbelief and belief. All epochs wherein belief prevails, under what form it may, are splendid, heart-elevating, fruitful for contemporaries and posterity. All epochs, on the contrary, wherein unbelief, under what form soever, maintains its sorry victory, should they even for a moment glitter with a sham splendour, vanish from the eyes of posterity; because no one chooses to burden himself with study of the unfruitful. [99]

Carlyle quoted these words with whole-hearted assent at the end of his essay on Diderot. [100] But he did not understand them in the same sense as Goethe. His conception of "belief" or "unbelief" was very different. According to Goethe every productive period in human history is *ipso facto* to be regarded as a period of belief. The term has no theological not even a specific religious connotation but simply expresses the preponderance of the positive over the negative powers. Goethe could never speak of the eighteenth century, therefore, as a period of disbelief. He too had felt a strong personal aversion for the general tendency expressed in the Great Encyclopedia. "Whenever we heard the encyclopedists mentioned," he says in his autobiography,

or opened a volume of their immense work, we felt as if we were going between the innumerable moving spools and looms of a great factory, where, what with the mere creaking and rattling; what with all the mechanism, embarrassing both eyes and senses; what with the mere incomprehensibility of an arrangement, the parts of which work into each other in the most manifold way; what with the contemplation of

---

98. *Idem,* Lect. vi, p. 197. Centenary ed., V, 204.
99. Goethe, *Noten und Abhandlungen zu besserem Verständnis des West-Oestlichen Divan,* "Werke" (Weimar ed.), VII, 157.
100. *Essays,* III, 248.

all that is necessary to prepare a piece of cloth—we feel disgusted with the very coat which we wear upon our backs.[101]

Yet, in spite of this feeling, Goethe never thought or spoke of the period of the Enlightenment as an unproductive age. He criticized Voltaire severely; but he always professed a profound admiration for his work. Diderot was regarded by Goethe as a genius and he translated his *Neveu de Rameau* and edited and commented on his *Essai sur la peinture*.[102]

All this was inadmissible and even unintelligible to Carlyle. As a historian Carlyle was somewhat in a better position than Goethe. His interest in historical problems was much more intense; his knowledge of facts was more comprehensive. Yet, on the other hand, he could only understand history in terms of his own personal experience. His "Life-Philosophy" was the clue to his historical work. In the great crisis of his youth he had found the way that led him from denial and despair to affirmation and reconstruction—from the "Everlasting No" to the "Everlasting Yea." Henceforth he conceived and interpreted the whole history of the human race in the same way. In his imagination, the imagination of a puritan, history became a great religious drama—the perpetual conflict between the powers of good and evil. "Are not all true men that live, or that ever lived, soldiers of the same army, enlisted, under Heaven's captaincy, to do battle against the same enemy, the empire of Darkness and Wrong?"[103] So Carlyle never could simply "write" history. He had to canonize or anathematize; he must extol to the skies or damn. His historical portraits are very impressive. But we miss in them all those delicate shades that we admire in the works of other great historians. He always paints in black and white. And from his point of view the eighteenth century was doomed from the very beginning. Voltaire of whom Goethe spoke as this "universal source of light"[104] was and remained to Carlyle the spirit of darkness. If we believe Carlyle's description Voltaire lacked all power of

101. Goethe, *Dichtung und Wahrheit*, Bk. XI. English trans., *op. cit.*, II, 82.

102. "Werke" (Weimar ed.), XLV, 1–322. For further details see E. Cassirer, "Goethe und das achtzehnte Jahrhundert," *Goethe und die geschichtliche Welt* (Berlin, B. Cassirer, 1932).

103. *On Heroes*, Lect. IV, p. 117. Centenary ed., V, 120.

104. See Eckermann, *Conversations with Goethe*, December 16, 1828; English trans. by John Oxenford (see above, p. 208, n. 65), p. 286.

imagination and, therefore, all productivity. The whole eighteenth century invented nothing; not one of man's virtues, not one of man's powers is due to it. The "philosophers" could only criticize, quarrel, rend to pieces. The age of Louis XV was "an age without nobleness, without high virtue or high manifestations of talent; an age of shallow clearness, of polish, self conceit, scepticism and all forms of *persiflage*." [105]

In this judgment Carlyle simply followed the example of the romantic writers. But he spoke with an increasingly fanatic hatred. A man like Friedrich Schlegel would hardly have denied that the eighteenth century, with all its limitations, was an age of talents. Here Carlyle did not speak as a historian or literary critic but as a theological zealot. He described the work of the Encyclopedists as the "Acts and Epistles of the Parisian Church of Antichrist." [106] He completely failed to see the positive element in the cultural life of the Enlightenment. The most fearful disbelief is the disbelief in yourself. Can we charge the thinkers of the Enlightenment, the writers of the Great Encyclopedia with this disbelief? Indeed it would be much more correct to accuse them of the very opposite fault, of an overconfidence in their own powers and the power of human reason in general.

On the other hand it is hardly possible to see in Carlyle's aversion for the ideals of the French Revolution a definite political or social program. His interest always remained biographical rather than social, although he became more interested later in the social problems of his own age. His principal concern was the individual men not the forms of civil government or social life. The attempts made in recent literature to connect him with St.-Simonism or to read into his work a sociological conception of history are futile. [107] Ernest Seillière has tried to prove in his book *L'actualité de Carlyle* that Carlyle belongs to the long list of thinkers whom he formerly had studied in his great work on the philosophy of imperialism. [108] Other authors have described Car-

105. "Voltaire," *Essays*, I, 464 f.
106. "Diderot," *idem*, III, 177.
107. See the books of Mrs. L. Mervin Young, *Thomas Carlyle and the Art of History* (Philadelphia, University of Pennsylvania Press, 1939), and Hill Shine, *Carlyle and the Saint-Simonians* (Baltimore, The Johns Hopkins Press, 1941). For a criticism of these books see René Wellek, "Carlyle and the Philosophy of History," *Philological Quarterly*, XXIII, No. 1 (January, 1944).
108. See Ernest Seillière, *La philosophie de l'impérialisme* (Paris, Plon-Nourrit et Cie., 1903–6). 4 vols.

lyle as the "father of British Imperialism." [109] There is, however, a clear and unmistakable difference between Carlyle's views, even his views on colonial policy [110] and other forms of British imperialism. Even Carlyle's nationalism had its specific color. He saw the real greatness of a nation in the intensity and depth of its moral life and its intellectual achievements and not in its political aspirations. He spoke very bluntly and boldly. "Which Englishman we ever made, in this land of ours," he asked his aristocratic audience speaking of Shakespeare,

which million of Englishmen, would we not give up rather than the Stratford peasant? There is no regiment of highest dignitaries that we would sell him for. He is the grandest thing we have yet done. For our honour among foreign nations, as an ornament to our English Household, what item is there that we would not surrender rather than him? Consider now, if they asked us, Will you give up your Indian Empire or your Shakespeare, you English; never have had any Indian Empire, or never have had any Shakespeare? Really it were a grave question. Official persons would answer doubtless in official language; but we, for our part too, should not we be forced to answer: Indian Empire, or no Indian Empire; we cannot do without Shakespeare! Indian Empire will go, at any rate, some day; but this Shakespeare does not go, he lasts forever with us; we cannot give up our Shakespeare.[111]

That sounds vastly different from the imperialism and nationalism of the twentieth century. However we may object to Carlyle's theory of hero worship, a man who spoke thus ought never to be charged with being an advocate of contemporary National Socialistic ideas and ideals. It is true, that Carlyle did not refrain from saying that "might makes right." But he always understood the very term "might" in a moral rather than in a physical sense. Hero worship always meant to him the worship of a moral force. He seems often to have a deep distrust of human nature. But he is confident and optimistic enough to assume and assert that "man

109. See G. von Schulze-Gaevernitz, *Britischer Imperialismus und englischer Freihandel* (Leipzig, Duncker & Humblot, 1906); Gazeau, *L'impérialisme anglais.* That this description is incorrect has been shown by C. A. Bodelsen, *Studies in Mid-Victorian Imperialism* (Copenhagen and London, Gyldendalske Boghandel, 1924), pp. 22–32.
110. On this point see Bodelsen, *op. cit.*
111. *On Heroes,* Lect. III, p. 109 f. Centenary ed., V, 113.

never yields himself wholly to brute force, but always to moral greatness." [112] If we ignore this principle of his thought we destroy his whole conception of history, of culture, of political and social life.

112. "Characteristics," *Essays*, III, 12.

XVI

FROM HERO WORSHIP TO RACE WORSHIP

Gobineau's "Essai sur l'inégalité des races humaines"

IN THE political struggles of the past decades hero worship and race worship have been in such a close alliance that, in all their interests and tendencies, they seemed to be almost one and the same thing. It was by this alliance that the political myths evolved into their present form and strength. In a theoretical analysis, however, we should not allow ourselves to be deceived by this league between the two forces. They are by no means identical—neither genetically nor systematically. Their psychological motives, their historical origin, their meaning and purpose are not the same. To understand them we must separate them.

We can easily convince ourselves of this difference by studying the authors who, in the second half of the nineteenth century, became the chief representatives of the two trends of thought. There was scarcely anything that these authors had in common, for Carlyle's lectures on hero worship and Gobineau's *Essai sur l'inégalité des races humaines* are, in a sense, incommensurable. The two books are dissimilar in ideas and intellectual tendency and in style. Between the Scotch puritan and the French aristocrat there could be no real solidarity of interests. They stood for widely divergent moral, political, and social ideals. The fact that their ideas could be used later for a common end does not obliterate this discrepancy. It was a new step, and a step of the greatest consequence, when hero worship lost its original meaning and was blended with a race worship and when both of them became integral parts of the same political program.

In order to grasp the purport of Gobineau's book, too, we must not read into it these later political tendencies. They are quite alien to the meaning of the author. Gobineau did not intend to write a political pamphlet but rather a historical and philosophical treatise. He never thought of applying his principles to a reconstruction or revolution of the political and social order. His was not an active philosophy. His view of history was fatalistic. History follows a definite and inexorable law. We cannot hope to change the course of events; all we can do is to understand and accept it. Gobineau's book is filled with a strong *amor fati*. The destiny of the human race is predetermined from the very beginning. No effort of man can avert it. Man cannot change his fate. But, on the other hand, he cannot refrain from asking over and over again the same question. If he cannot master his destiny, he wants at least to know where he comes from and whither he goes. This desire is one of fundamental and ineradicable human instincts.

Gobineau was not only convinced that he had found a new approach to the problem but also that he was the first who had really succeeded in solving the old riddle. All the former religious and metaphysical answers are declared by him to be inadequate. For all of them missed the principal point, the essential factor in human history. Without an insight into this factor history remains a sealed book. But now the seal is broken and the mystery of human life and human civilization is revealed. For the *fact* of the moral and intellectual diversity of races is obvious. Nobody can deny or neglect it. But what has been entirely unknown is the significance and the vital importance of this fact. Until this importance is clearly understood all historians of human civilization are groping in the dark.

History is no science; it is only a conglomerate of subjective thoughts; a wishful thinking rather than a coherent and systematic theory. Gobineau boasted of having made an end to this state of affairs. "It is a question of making history join the family of the natural sciences, of giving it . . . all the precision of this kind of knowledge, finally of removing it from the biased jurisdiction whose arbitrariness the political factions impose upon it up to this day." [1] Gobineau did not speak as an advocate of a definite political program but as a scientist, and he thought his deductions were infallible. He was convinced that history, after innumerable vain efforts, had at last come to its maturity and virility in his work. He looked upon himself as a second Copernicus, the Copernicus of the historical world. Once we have found the true center of this world, everything is changed. We are no longer concerned with mere

1. Gobineau, *Essai sur l'inégalité des races humaines* (2d ed. Paris, Firmin-Didot), "Conclusion générale," II, 548. 2 vols.

opinions about things, we live and move in the things themselves; our eyes are able to see, our ears to hear, our hands to
touch.[2]

But no reader of Gobineau's work can help feeling deep disappointment when comparing this magnificent and gigantic plan
with its execution. In the history of science there is perhaps no
other example where so high a purpose was pursued with such
insufficient means. It is true that Gobineau had amassed vast
material taken from the most various sources. He spoke not only
as a historian but also as a linguist, anthropologist, and ethnolo-
gist. Yet when we begin to analyze his arguments we find them,
in most cases, extremely weak. A high and proud edifice is erected
upon a very small and fragile basis. The first French critics of
Gobineau's book immediately saw the fundamental defects of his
historical method.[3] Even Gobineau's partisans and followers had
frankly to admit the lacunae and the obvious fallacies in his pretended "scientific" demonstration. Houston Stewart Chamberlain
spoke of Gobineau's "childish omniscience." As a matter of fact
he does seem to know everything. To him history has no secret.
He knows not only its general course; he knows all its details, he
feels himself able to answer the most intricate questions. He pene-
trates into the remotest origin of things; and he sees everything
under its true conditions and in its right place. But as soon as it
comes to the crucial point, the empirical proofs of his thesis, the
weakness of Gobineau's *Essai* becomes palpable and unmistakable. He deals with the facts in the most arbitrary way. Everything
that seems to support his thesis is readily admitted. On the other
hand the negative instances are completely ignored or, at least,
minimized. He shows a complete lack of that critical method
which had been taught by the great historians of the nineteenth
century.

Let us take a few concrete examples of his way of arguing and
reasoning. One of his firmest convictions was that the white race
is the only one that had the will and power to build up a cultural
life. This principle became the cornerstone of his theory of the
radical diversity of human races. The black and yellow races have
no life, no will, no energy of their own. They are nothing but

2. *Idem*, II, 552.
3. See, for instance, Quatrefage's article, "Du croisement des races humaines,"
Revue des deux mondes, March 1, 1857.

dead stuff in the hands of their masters—the inert mass that has to be moved by the higher races. On the other hand Gobineau could not entirely overlook the fact that there are definite traces of human civilization in some regions of the world in which the influence of the white race is highly improbable. How did he overcome this obstacle? His answer is very simple. The dogma itself is firmly established. It admits of no doubt and no exception. If our evidence is too scanty to confirm the dogma, or if it seems to be in open contradiction to it, it is for the historian to complete and correct the evidence. He must stretch the facts to make them fit into the preconceived scheme.

Gobineau never feels the slightest scruples about filling in the lacks of our historical knowledge by the boldest assumptions. China, for instance, shows in very ancient times a highly developed cultural life. But since, on the other hand, it is quite certain that the two inferior varieties of the human race, the Negroes and the yellow race, are only the gross canvas, the cotton and wool, upon which the white race has spun their own delicate and silky threads,[4] the conclusion is unavoidable that Chinese culture was not the work of the Chinese people. We have to regard it as a product of foreign tribes which immigrated from India, of those Kschattryas who invaded and conquered China and laid the foundations for the central kingdom and the celestial empire.[5] The same holds for those traces of a very old culture that we find in the Western hemisphere. It is impossible to assume that the American aboriginal tribes could, by their own efforts, find the way to civilization. According to Gobineau the Indians of the American continent form no separate race. They are only an amalgam, a mixture of the black and yellow races. How should these poor bastards ever have been able to govern and organize themselves? No history and no development were possible as long as the black races only struggled among themselves and the yellow races moved in their own narrow circle. The results of these conflicts were entirely unproductive; they could leave no trace in human history. Such was the case in America, in the greatest part of Africa, and in a considerable part of Asia. But whenever and wherever we find history and culture we must be on the lookout for the white man. We are sure of finding him; for his

4. *Essai,* "Conclusion générale," II, 539.
5. *Idem,* Bk. III, chap. v, I, 462 ff.

presence and his activity may be inferred, by a mere process of deductive reasoning, from the first principle of Gobineau's theory: "History springs only from contact of the white races." [6]

Gobineau admits that there is no evidence of a contact between the white races and the aboriginal tribes of America before the discovery of the Western hemisphere. But the fact can be affirmed on the strength of general a priori principles.

Of the multitude of peoples which live or have lived on the earth, ten alone have arisen to the position of complete societies. The remainder have gravitated round these more or less independently, like planets round their suns. If there is any element of life in these ten civilizations that is not due to the impulse of the white races, any seed of death that does not come from the inferior stocks that mingled with them, then the whole theory on which this book rests is false. [7]

Gobineau was absolutely sure of his results. His self-confidence was unlimited. He declared that his proofs were "incorruptible as a diamond." The viperine tooth of the demagogic idea, he exclaimed, will never be able to bite upon these incontrovertible proofs. But it is easy to see the true character of these so-called adamantine and incontrovertible proofs. They are nothing but a *petitio principii*. If in a logical textbook we were in need of a striking example of this fallacy we could do no better than to choose the work of Gobineau. His facts are always in agreement with his principles; for, if the historical facts are missing, they are framed and forged according to his theories. And the same facts are used again for proving the truth of the theory. Assuredly Gobineau did not mean to deceive his readers, but he constantly deceived himself. He was quite sincere and quite naïve. He never was aware of the vicious circle, on which his whole theory depends. He spoke as a scholar and as a philosopher; but he never claimed to have found his principles by rational methods.

To him personal feelings were always better and more convincing than logical or historical arguments. And these feelings were very clear and outspoken. He belonged to an old aristocratic family and was filled with an immoderate pride, which was constantly humiliated. He, the member of a noble race, had to live under

6. *Idem*, Bk. IV, chap. I, I, 527.
7. *Idem*, Bk. I, chap. XVI, I, 220, quoted from the English trans. by A. Collins (London, William Heinemann; New York, G. P. Putnam's Sons, 1915), p. 210. Of the six books of Gobineau's work this translation contains only the first one.

the petty conditions of a bourgeois system for which he felt a deep disgust. To him it was not only natural, it was in a sense a moral duty to think in terms of his caste. The caste was to him a much higher and nobler reality than the nation or the individual man. In his book he praised the Aryan Brahmans for having first understood and firmly established the value and the paramount importance of the caste. Theirs was a real stroke of genius, a profound and original idea that showed an entirely new way for the progress of the human race. In order to prove the claims of the French nobility Gobineau went back to a doctrine that had been propounded and defended in the eighteenth century by Boulainvilliers and that had become the basis of the theory of French feudalism. In his analysis of Boulainvilliers' book Montesquieu described it as a "conspiracy against the third estate." Boulainvilliers had emphatically denied that France is a homogeneous whole. The nation is divided into two races that have at bottom nothing in common. They speak a common language; but they have neither common rights nor a common origin. The French nobility draws its origin from the Franks, the German invaders and conquerors; the mass of the people belongs to the subjugated, to the serfs who have lost every claim to an independent life. "The true French," wrote one of the advocates of this theory, "incarnated in our day in the nobility and its partisans, are the sons of free men; the former slaves and all races alike employed primarily in labor by their masters are the fathers of the Third Estate." [8]

All this was eagerly accepted by Gobineau. But he had set himself a greater and much more difficult task. He spoke of human civilization as a philosopher who could not confine himself within the narrow limit of French history. What we see in the French nation is only an example and a symptom of a much more general process. French history is, as it were, a portrait in miniature. It shows the image of the whole cultural process on a small and reduced scale. That conflict between patricians and plebeians, between the conquerors and the serfs, is the eternal theme of human history. He who understands the nature and the reasons of this conflict has found the clue to man's historical life.

8. For more details see A. Thierry, *Considérations sur l'histoire de France* (5th ed., Paris, 1851), chap. II, and Ernest Seillière in the introduction to his book *Le Comte de Gobineau et l'aryanisme historique* (Paris, Plon-Nourrit et Cie., 1903).

This starting point of Gobineau's theory shows at once the deep difference between hero worship and race worship. They express widely divergent and even opposite conceptions of human history. "Is not the whole purport of history," asked Carlyle, "biographic?" And he did not hesitate to answer this question in the affirmative. This interest in the individuals is entirely absent in Gobineau's work. His whole exposition was, indeed, given without even mentioning proper names. When reading Carlyle we have the impression that with every new great man, with every religious, philosophical, literary, political genius, there begins a new chapter in human history. The whole character of the religious world was completely changed, for example, by the appearance of Mahomet or Luther; the political world and the world of poetry were revolutionized by Cromwell or by Dante and Shakespeare. Every new hero is a new incarnation of one and the same great invisible power of the "Divine Idea." In Gobineau's description of the historical and cultural world this divine Idea has vanished. He too is a romantic and a mystic; but his mysticism is of a much more realistic type. The great men do not fall from the heavens. Their whole force originates in the earth; in the native soil in which they have their roots. The best qualities of the great men are the qualities of their races. By themselves they could do nothing; they are only the embodiments of the deepest powers of the race to which they belong.

In this sense Gobineau could have subscribed to Hegel's words that the individuals are only "the agents of the world-spirit." But when Gobineau wrote his book the times had changed. Gobineau and his generation no longer believed in lofty metaphysical principles. They were in need of something more palpable: of something that "our eyes are able to see, our ears to hear, our hands to touch." The new theory seemed to satisfy all these conditions.

Practically speaking this was a great and obvious advantage. Here was something that could fill a lack which, in the second half of the nineteenth century, was felt everywhere. Man is, after all, a metaphysical animal. His "metaphysical need" is ineradicable. But the great metaphysical systems of the nineteenth century were no longer able to give a clear and understandable answer to these questions. They had become so intricate and sophisticated that they were almost unintelligible. With Gobineau's book it was quite different. To be sure, his own theory of the race as the fundamental and predominant power in human history was still thoroughly metaphysical. But Gobineau's metaphysics claimed to be a natural science and seemed to be based upon an experience of the simplest kind. Not everyone is able to follow a long chain of metaphysical deductions; not everyone can study Hegel's *Phenomenology of Mind* or his *Philosophy of History*. But anybody understands the language of his race and his blood —or believes he understands it. Since its first beginnings metaphysics had sought for an undoubtable, unshakable, universal principle but was constantly frustrated in its hopes. According to Gobineau this was unavoidable as long as metaphysics persisted in its traditional intellectualistic attitude. The problem of the so-called "universals" and their reality has been discussed throughout the whole history of philosophy. But what philosophers never realized was the fact that the real "universals" are not to be sought in the thoughts of men but in these substantial forces that determine his destiny. Of all these forces the race is the strongest and the most unquestionable. Here we have a fact, not a mere idea.

Newton had found a fundamental fact of the physical world through which he was able to explain the whole material universe. He had discovered the law of gravitation. But in the human world the common center toward which all things gravitate was still unknown. Gobineau was convinced that he had found the solution of this problem. And he imposed the same feeling upon the minds of his readers. Here was a new type of theory that, from the outset, had a strong and strange fascination. It is foolish in a man to deny or to resist the power of his race, just as foolish as if a material particle should attempt to resist the force of gravitation.

The Theory of the "Totalitarian Race"

That race is an important factor in human history; that different races have built up different forms of culture; that these forms are not on the same level; that they vary both in their character and in their value—all this was a generally acknowledged fact. Since Montesquieu's *Esprit des Lois* even the physical conditions of these variations had been carefully studied. It was not, however, this well-known problem with which Gobineau was concerned. His was a much more general and difficult task. He had to prove that race is the *only* master and ruler of the historical world; that all the other forces are its underlings and satellites. Our modern idea of the totalitarian state was entirely unfamiliar to Gobineau. If he had known it he would have vehemently protested against it. Even patriotism was to him a mere idol and prejudice. Yet, however opposed to all nationalistic ideals, Gobineau belongs to those writers who, in an indirect way, have done most to prepare the ideology of the totalitarian state. It was the totalitarianism of race that marked the road to the later conceptions of the totalitarian state.

From the point of view of our present problem this is one of the most important and interesting features in Gobineau's theory. But, so far as I see, this point has not yet had its due in the literature on the subject. Gobineau's doctrine has been analyzed and criticized from every possible angle and philosophers, sociologists, politicians, historians, anthropologists have had their share in these discussions.[9] But to my mind it is not the glorification of the race as such that is the most important element in Gobineau's theory. To be proud of his ancestors, of his birth and descent, is a natural character of man. If it is a prejudice it is a very common prejudice. It need not necessarily endanger or undermine man's social and ethical life. But what we find in Gobineau is something quite different. It is *an attempt to destroy all other values.* The god of the race, as he was proclaimed by Gobineau, is a jealous god. He does not allow other gods to be adored beside himself. Race is everything; all the other forces are nothing. They have no independent meaning or value. If they have any power this power is not an autonomous one. It is only delegated to them by their superior and sovereign: the omnipotent race. This fact appears in all forms of cultural life, in religion, in morality, in philosophy and art, in the nation and in the state.

In proving this thesis Gobineau proceeded very methodically. The description of his doctrine is always clear and coherent. We need only compare Gobineau's work with that of Carlyle to be aware of the wide difference between the two authors. In Carlyle's *Sartor Resartus* everything is bizarre, burlesque, discon-

9. See, for instance, "Numéro consacré au Comte de Gobineau," *Revue Europe,* October 1, 1923, and "Numéro consacré à Gobineau et au gobinisme." *La nouvelle revue française,* February 1, 1934.

nected, and desultory. In Gobineau's *Essai* we find quite the contrary. Gobineau's style is imaginative and passionate, but it is not involved or incoherent. The influence of his French education was not lost. His exposition has all the merits of the French analytical mind. He progresses slowly and continuously. Gobineau could not force his way. He had to overcome great obstacles and to challenge many and great authorities. The way in which he tried to achieve his end proves a great skill, a dexterity, that shows he was not only conversant with the art of writing but also with the art of diplomacy.

Gobineau's most potent adversary was, of course, the religious conception of man's origin and destination. That his theory is entirely irreconcilable with it was clear from the very beginning. The first critics of his book immediately insisted upon this point. Tocqueville was a personal friend and had a high opinion of Gobineau's talents and personal character. But when he first read his book he vehemently reacted against Gobineau's theory. "I confess to you," he wrote to Gobineau, "that . . . I remain utterly opposed to these doctrines. I think them probably false and certainly pernicious." [10] To refute the arguments of Tocqueville was an extremely hard task. For on this point Gobineau not only had to combat his critic; he had to struggle against himself. He was a devout Catholic; he accepted the Christian dogma in its entirety and submitted himself to the authority of the Church. The Bible remained to him an inspired book, the literal truth of which was never denied. He could, therefore, not openly attack the biblical theory of the creation of the world and of the origin of man. But, on the other hand, it was impossible from this starting point to find an argument for his thesis as to the radical diversity between the human races. He could not even admit that the Negroes or the members of the yellow race belong to the same human family as the white races. What we find in those people is barbarism in its utter ugliness and egoism in its greatest ferocity.[11] Can we admit that these beings draw their origin from the same source as the white races? How can the Negroes who in some respects

10. Lettre du 17 novembre 1853, *Correspondance entre Alexis de Tocqueville et Arthur de Gobineau*, 1843–59, publ. par L. Schemann (Paris, Plon, 1908), p. 192. On the relation between Tocqueville and Gobineau see Romain Rolland, "Le conflit de deux générations: Tocqueville et Gobineau," *Revue Europe*, No. 9 (October 1, 1923), pp. 68–80.

11. *Essai*, Bk. II, chap. I, I, 227.

are far below the animals belong to the same class as the members of the Aryan family, these demigods? Gobineau made desperate efforts to escape from his dilemma; but at the end he seems to give up. He confesses that the knot was inextricable, not only to himself but to human reason in general.

Owing to my respect for a scientific authority which I cannot overthrow, and, still more, for a religious interpretation that I could not venture to attack, I must resign myself to leaving on one side the grave doubts that are always oppressing me as to the question of original unity. . . . As no one will venture to deny, there broods over this grave question a mysterious darkness, big with causes that are at the same time physical and supernatural. In the inmost recesses of the obscurity that shrouds the problem, reign the causes which have their ultimate home in the mind of God; the human spirit feels their presence without divining their nature, and shrinks back in awful reverence.[12]

• • • • •

It is better to let darkness gather round a point of scholarship, than to enter the lists against such an authority.[13]

This was, however, a merely formal submission which did not prevent Gobineau from developing his own theory in flagrant contradiction to the ethical ideals of the Christian religion. He tried to conceal these contradictions not only from the minds of his readers but also from himself by making a sharp distinction between the metaphysical truth and the cultural value of Christianity. The former is beyond all doubt; the latter is negligible. In fact the Christian religion never had the slightest influence on the development of human civilization. It neither created nor changed the capacity for civilization.

Christianity is a civilizing force in so far as it makes a man better minded and better mannered; yet it is only indirectly so, for it has no idea of applying this improvement in morals and intelligence to the perishable things of this world, and it is always content with the social conditions in which it finds its neophytes, however imperfect the conditions may be. . . . If their state can be improved as a direct consequence of their conversion, then Christianity will certainly do its best to bring such an improvement about; but it will not try to alter

12. *Idem*, Bk. I, chap. xi, I, 137 f. English trans., p. 134.
13. *Idem*, I, 120. English trans., p. 117.

a single custom, and certainly will not force any advance from one civilization to another, for it has not yet adopted one itself.[14]

. . . . .

Even as a matter of justice we must leave Christianity absolutely out of the present question. If all races are equally capable of receiving its benefits, it cannot have been sent to bring equality among men. Its kingdom, we may say, is in the most literal sense, "not of this world." [15]

That seemed to elevate Christianity to the highest place, but this glorification had to be bought dearly. If we accept Gobineau's interpretation, Christianity has neither the will nor the power to help man in his earthly struggles. It remains a great and mysterious force but a force that can do nothing to move our human world. In this conclusion the end of Gobineau was attained: in man's historical life Christianity abdicates all its rights and bows to the new god of race.

This was, however, only a first step. There was still another obstruction in Gobineau's way, the "humanitarian" and "equalitarian" ideas of the eighteenth century. These ideas were not based upon religion but upon a new type of philosophical ethics. They had found their clearest systematic description in the work of Kant, the cornerstone of which was the idea of freedom—and freedom meant "autonomy." It is the expression of the principle that the moral subject has to obey no rules other than those which he gives to himself. Man is not only a means that may be used for external ends; he is himself the "legislator in the realm of end." That constitutes his true dignity, his prerogative above all mere physical being.

In the realm of ends everything has either price or dignity. Whatever has price, is exchangeable by another thing; it can be replaced by something else. Whatever, on the other hand, is above all price, and therefore admits of no equivalent, has a dignity. . . . Thus morality and humanity, as capable of it, is that which alone has dignity.[16]

All this was not only entirely unintelligible to Gobineau, but simply intolerable. It was in flagrant contradiction to all his instincts and deepest feelings. Perhaps no other modern writer was so deeply penetrated with that feeling which Nietzsche described

14. *Idem*, Bk. I, chap. VII, I, 64. English trans., p. 65.
15. *Idem*, I, 69. English trans., p. 70.
16. Kant, *Grundlegung sur Metaphysik der Sitten*, Sec. II, "Werke," ed. E. Cassirer, IV, 293.

as *Pathos der Distanz* as Gobineau. Dignity means personal distinction, and we cannot be aware of this distinction without looking down upon others as inferior beings. In all great civilizations and all noble races this was a predominant feature: "everyone feeling proud of his lineage and descent refused to be mixed up with the vulgar." [17] To seek universal ethical standards and values is absurd. To Gobineau universality meant vulgarity. As a born aristocrat he could feel his value only by distinguishing himself from the plebeians and the vulgar. He projected this personal feeling from the individual sphere into ethnology and anthropology.

The superior races can only know what they are and what they are worth by comparing themselves with those other races that are crouching servilely at their feet. Their self-confidence cannot be complete without this element of contempt and disgust; the one implies and demands the other. From this point of view Kant's famous formula of the categorical imperative becomes a contradiction in terms. To act only on that maxim, whereby we can at the same time will that it should become a universal law, is impossible. How can there be a universal law since there is no universal man? An ethical maxim that claims to be valid for all cases is valid for no case; a rule that applies to anyone applies to no one. It is a mere abstract formula that has no equivalent in the human and historical world. In this regard, too, the instinct of the race proved itself to be highly superior to all our philosophical ideals and our metaphysical systems. Gobineau accepts an etymology of the term "Aryan" according to which this term originally meant nothing but "honorable." The members of the Aryan race knew very well that a man is not honorable by virtue of individual qualities but by the inheritance of his race. "Personal honor and dignity we possess only in fee of a higher liegelord, of the race as the true sovereign. The white people who gave themselves the title Aryans understood very well its haughty and pompous meaning. They clung to it forcibly." [18] A man is great, noble, virtuous not by his actions but by his blood. The only test that our personal work has to stand is the test of our ancestors. It is his birth certificate that gives to a man the certainty of his moral value. Virtue is not a thing to be acquired. It is a gift from

17. *Essai*, Bk. IV, chap. III, II, 21 f.
18. *Idem*, Bk. III, chap. I, I, 370.

heaven or, to speak more correctly, a gift from the earth, from the physical and mental qualities of the race. To speak of members of the lower races as "moral" or "rational" beings proves a very low sense of morality. "The beasts of prey," says Gobineau in his description of the black race, "would seem of too noble stuff to serve as a point of comparison with these hideous tribes. Monkeys would suffice to give an idea of them physically, and morally one feels obliged to evoke a resemblance to the spirits of darkness." [19]

When Gobineau spoke of the ethical and religious ideals of Christianity he spoke with great circumspection and reserve. Although he denied that these ideals had any practical meaning and influence, he did not fail to profess a deep reverence for them. His true opinion appears much more clearly when he is no longer checked by such traditional scruples. What was still praised and admired in the Christian religion is severely reprehended on the other hand in Buddhism, where he could speak frankly and bluntly. He saw in Buddhism one of the greatest perversities in human history. Here was a man endowed with the greatest physical and intellectual gifts, of noblest descent, a son of kings belonging to the highest caste, suddenly deciding to resign all these privileges to become the preacher of a new gospel of the poor, the miserable, the outcast. In Gobineau's eyes all this was an unpardonable sin, a sort of high treason. It was a crime against the majesty of the Aryan race that had created the caste system to protect itself from the danger of blood mixture.

But Buddhism was not only a moral but also a grave intellectual mistake to Gobineau's way of thinking. It was not only a perversity of feeling but of judgment. In opposition to all sound principles of the philosophy of history Buddhism tried to found ontology upon morality, whereas, in truth, morality is dependent on ontology. The development of Buddhism, its decay and degeneration is one of the best and most convincing examples of what we have to expect from a political and religious doctrine which claims to be entirely based upon morality and reason.[20]

As long as the race instinct was still in full vigor, as long as it followed its own way without being deflected by other forces, people were not liable to this mistake. This was the case with the

19. *Idem*, Bk. II, chap. i, I, 227.
20. *Idem*, Bk. III, chap. iii, I, 442.

German races. In German mythology a man was not saved by virtue of his moral actions. The paradise was open to the heroes, the warriors, the noblemen, regardless of their deeds. "The man of noble race, the true Aryan arrived at all honors of Valhalla by the sole force of his origin; whereas the poor, the captives, the serfs, in one word the mestizos, the half-castes of inferior birth indifferently fell into the icy darkness of Niflzheim." [21]

No great effort of thought is required to discover the logical fallacy in this argument. What we find here is the same *petitio principii* that is characteristic of Gobineau's method. The circular argument and reasoning is typical of his whole book. When comparing different races as to their moral qualities we need a certain standard of evaluation. Where can we find this standard? Since all so-called universal ethical principles have been declared to be null and void we must choose between particular systems. And obviously the higher races are alone able to give us the true and higher values. What they *call* noble, good and virtuous *becomes* virtuous by this token. So the thesis of the moral preeminence of the white races, especially the Aryan race, becomes a sheer tautology. It is an analytical judgment which follows from the very definition of these races. We do not have to judge their actions. These actions must be good because they are done by good men. Ontology precedes morality and remains the decisive factor in it. Not what a man *does* but what he *is* gives him his moral value. "One is not good for having acted well, but one acts well when one is good, that is to say well born." That sounds extremely simple, but at the same time it is amazingly naïve. Curiously enough it was precisely this naïveté that gave to Gobineau's theory its great practical force and influence. By this circular definition the theory became, in a sense, invulnerable. You cannot argue against an analytical judgment; you cannot refute it by rational or empirical proofs.

But besides the universal values of religion and morality there are others of a more particular kind. The state and the nation seem to be the greatest powers in human history, the strongest impulses of man's social life. But to think of them as independent forces, as things that have worth in themselves would be in contradiction to the first principles of Gobineau. He had to challenge the political ideals in the same way as the religious and moral

21. *Idem,* Bk. VI, chap. III, II, 370.

ones. To us it seems natural to connect racism and nationalism. We are even prone to identify them. But this is incorrect, both from a historical and a systematic point of view. They are sharply distinguished in their origin and in their purport and tendency.[22] This distinction becomes very clear if we study Gobineau's work. He was no nationalist nor was he a French patriot. He had accepted and renewed the thesis of Boulainvilliers, according to which France never had a real national unity. As we have seen, it is divided into the conquerors and the subjugated, the nobility and the plebs, who are not on the same level and who cannot share the same political and national life.[23] Gobineau applied this view to the whole of human history. What we call a nation is never a homogeneous whole. It is a product of blood mixture, the most dangerous thing in the world. To speak with awe and reverence of such a hybrid would violate the first principles of a sound theory of human history. Patriotism may be a virtue for democrats or demagogues; but it is no aristocratic virtue; and the race is the highest aristocrat. What is the idea of our "native country"? It is a mere word to which no physical or historical reality corresponds. The country, says Gobineau, does not speak, it cannot command in vivid voice. The experience of all centuries had shown that there is no worse tyranny than that which is exerted by mere fictions. They are, by their very nature, insensitive, pitiless and of an insupportable arrogance in their claims. According to Gobineau one of the greatest merits of the feudal system was that, under this system, men were not liable to bow to such idols. "In our feudal period the word *patrie* was scarcely used; it only really came back to us when the Gallo-Roman clans again raised their heads and played a role in politics. With their triumph patriotism began again to be a virtue." [24]

If we accept the methodological maxims of Gobineau's theory the simplest way to determine the real value of an idea is always the genetic way. We must know its origin to judge its worth. And what is the origin of the ideal of patriotism? That it is no Aryan ideal is proved by the fact that the Teutonic races, the best and noblest representatives of the Aryan family, never accepted it in

22. A very clear statement of the difference between "racism" and "nationalism" has recently been given in an article of Hannah Ahrendt, "Race-Thinking Before Racism," *The Review of Politics*, VI, No. 1 (January, 1944), 36–73.
23. See above, p. 229.
24. *Essai*, Bk. IV, chap. III, II, 29, n. 2.

its full strength. Patriotism is no German virtue. In the Germanic world the man was everything, whereas the nation meant very little. That makes a deep difference between the Germans and the other races—the Semitic mestizos of Hellenistic, Roman, Cimmerian extraction. "There one sees only multitudes; the individual counts for nothing, and as the confusion increases—the ethnic mixture to which he belongs becoming more complicated—he becomes further eclipsed." [25] In European civilization the Greeks, in their blind admiration for the polis, are responsible for the false ideal of patriotism. In Greece the individual was commanded by the law. The prejudice, the authority of public opinion compelled everyone to sacrifice to this abstraction all his inclinations, his ideas and customs, even his fortune and his most intimate personal and human relations. But the Greeks had not forged this ideal themselves; they had borrowed it from the Semites. When all is said patriotism is nothing but a "Canaan monstrosity." [26]

After this severe criticism of Greek culture there follows, in Gobineau's work, a criticism of Roman life and civilization. Here too he uses the same method. He tries to convince us that what usually is regarded as the highest mark of the Roman spirit, is, in fact, its inherent weakness. The Roman Empire had its firmest foundation in the Roman law. The law had become the only binding force in Roman life. It was collected, codified, commented on and analyzed. Finally Roman jurisprudence has survived the decline and fall of the Roman Empire. According to Gobineau the whole construction of the Roman law is exactly in the same predicament as the highly praised Greek polis. It is a lifeless abstraction. The Romans made a virtue of necessity. They had to create an artificial bond between the most disparate elements. That could only be done by legislation of compromise, the only one that was possible among a population that consisted of dregs of all races. [27] It is useless to glorify institutions, for they have only a secondary and subordinate value. They are derived from and depend on the ethnic state of the people. This state was never worse and more execrable than under the Roman law. In no field of human culture was Rome productive or original. It had nothing of its own—no religion, no art, no literature. Everything was borrowed from

25. *Idem*, Bk. VI, chap. III, II, 365.
26. *Idem*, Bk. IV, chap. III, II, 29 and 31.
27. *Idem*, Bk. V, chap. VII, II, 260 ff.

other peoples. Even the Augustan age was by no means great, beautiful, and praiseworthy in itself. The only thing that can be said in its favor is that, under the given historical conditions, in face of the mixed and most disparate populations of the Roman Empire, it offered the only possible solution. The defects of the Roman Empire were not the faults of its individual rulers but the faults of the confused mass that had to be controlled and to be brought under a certain discipline.[28] "I am far," says Gobineau, "from inclining before the majesty of the Roman name and applauding such a result." [29]

But the analysis of human culture has not yet come to its end. Besides religion, morality, politics, and law there remains the other great sphere of art. Can we apply to it the same principles? In his *Letters on the Esthetical Education of Man* Schiller had tried to prove not only that art is a particular quality in man but also that it constitutes his nature and essence. It is not the work of man but of his Creator. The atmosphere of humanity is created by art. If this be true a bond had been found that connected all races. For art is not the privilege of one race. It is like the sun that shines for the just and the unjust, for the lower races as well as for the higher. This fact Gobineau does not deny. On the contrary he admits and emphasizes it. And the inference that might be drawn against his theory must have had for him a particular strength. For he had not only a deep interest in art; it was one of the great passions of his life. He was a poet and a sculptor and had tried many fields of art. If his thesis failed him in this point of paramount importance, he could hardly maintain it.

His way of escape from the dilemma is, at first sight, very surprising. He frankly admits that art is not among the particular gifts of the Aryan race. Left to themselves the members of the Aryan family would in all probability never have developed great art. Art is a product of imagination; and imagination is not characteristic of a true Aryan. It is an alien drop of blood in his veins; for it comes from the Negroes. In the Negroes imagination is the predominant, the excessive and the exuberant force. Here is the true origin of art; it is an inheritance from the black races. To the readers of Gobineau this discovery must have come as a great shock. Had he not spoken of the Negroes with the greatest con-

28. *Idem*, Bk. V, chap. vii, II, 249 ff.
29. *Ibid.*

tempt and disgust? Had he not said that in their bodily constitution they are below the apes, that in their brute instincts they are worse than the beasts of prey; that morally they are on the same level as the evil spirits from hell? That these creatures should now be regarded as the first artists, and that all the other races are indebted to them as their heirs was, indeed, a great paradox. But Gobineau did not refrain from it.

The man of a noble race once aware of this origin must be on his guard against this dangerous inheritance. He should not accept it without serious scruples and he should not yield to its charm. Art always remains the great siren that tries to lure and lull asleep our best intellectual and moral gifts. We may listen to it, but the wise man will act like Odysseus who had taken his precautions against being captivated by the Sirens. Gobineau himself had always a certain mistrust of his own artistic instincts. He looked upon them with a sort of bad conscience. They did not fit into his image of the true Aryan. The Aryan cannot contract a legitimate marriage with art which always remains to him the great seducer or his courtesan not his wife.

There remains, however, one last question. Is there not, at least, a subjective bond uniting the different races? Gobineau had declared that, according to an inexorable natural law, the inferior races are forever condemned "to crawl before the feet of their masters." But should not these masters themselves have a certain understanding of this miserable condition? Gobineau would not have absolutely denied such an obligation. To be sure he always spoke with a great hauteur but as a born nobleman he knew very well that *noblesse oblige*. He denied all "humanitarian" ideals but on this point he was not too sure of himself. His actions were not always in strict agreement with his principles. We find a very characteristic proof of this tension in a letter addressed to the famous Hebrew scholar Adolf Frank. He relates that, during his sojourn in Persia, he had many occasions to protect the Jews of Teheran from injustice, suppression, and prosecution.[30] We cannot, therefore, charge Gobineau with a lack of human sympathy, gentleness, or benevolence. He was by no means secured against a relapse into all sorts of "humane" ideals. But his theory itself left

30. See A. Combris, *La philosophie des races du Comte de Gobineau* (Paris, F. Alcan, 1937), p. 232.

him no choice. His individual feelings had to be silenced; they had no place in the development of his general thesis.

In this regard, too, a comparison between Gobineau and Carlyle is highly instructive. At first sight their political tendencies seem to be very near akin. They are both sworn enemies of the political ideals of the eighteenth century: the ideals of liberty, equality, and fraternity. Carlyle saw no other escape from the subversive influence of these ideals than by the return to hero worship. He declared hero worship to be the only thing that can save us from decay, ruin, and complete anarchy. Nevertheless there is a fundamental difference between Carlyle's hero worship and Gobineau's race worship. The former tries to connect and unify; the latter divides and separates. All the heroes of Carlyle speak the same language and stand for the same cause—they are all "the inspired speaking and acting texts of that divine book of revelations whereof a chapter is completed from epoch to epoch, and by some named History." At bottom the great man as he comes from the hand of nature is ever the same kind of thing. "I hope to make it clear," said Carlyle, "that these are all originally of one stuff." But to Gobineau such an identity was unthinkable. To speak of the Nordic Odin and the Semite Mahomet as if they belonged to the same human family would have seemed to him blasphemous. And to speak of a universal justice, the same for all men, is more than a mistake, it is a mortal sin. "Justice, justice," exclaimed Carlyle, "woe betides us everywhere when, for this reason or for that, we fail to do justice! . . . There is but one thing needed for the world; but that one is indispensable. Justice, Justice, in the name of Heaven; give us Justice and we live; give us only counterfeits of it, or succedanea for it, and we die!" [31]

This personal feeling pervades Carlyle's social philosophy. While he never was a socialist and remained an English Tory, he had been used from his early youth to regard the cause of the poor as his own. We remember the scene in *Sartor Resartus* in which Professor Teufelsdröckh, sitting in his coffee-house, suddenly stands up, lifts his huge tumbler and proposes his toast: "Die Sache der Armen in Gottes und Teufels Namen." [32] But Gobineau spoke of the poor in a very different key. He gave his

31. *Latter-Day Pamphlets*, No. II, "Model Prisons." Centenary ed., XX, 68.
32. *Sartor Resartus*, Bk. I, chap. III, I, 11.

hearty assent to the old German system in which only the rich and the nobles were admitted to the glory of Valhalla.[33] Poverty is contemptible. The Aryan German conceived a very high idea of himself and his role in the world because he was by rights a feudal lord and landowner; a proprietor of a part of the world.[34] The man who could not claim such an original and hereditary title always remained an outcast. That was part and parcel of the old caste system introduced by the Aryan priests.[35]

The theory of Gobineau had apparently encompassed the whole circle of civilized life and attained its end. The new religion, the worship of the race, is firmly established. There is no longer fear of any adversary. The Christian religion ineffective and impotent, Buddhism a moral perversity, patriotism a Canaan monstrosity, law and justice mere abstractions, art a seducer and prostitute, compassion for the oppressed and pity for the poor sentimental illusions: the list is complete. This is the triumph of the new principle.

What was left after this systematic work of destruction? What remained for Gobineau himself, and what could he promise his followers and believers? We find the answer to the first question in Gobineau's last book. In 1879 he published his *Histoire d'Ottar-Jarl, pirate norvégien, conquérant du pays de Bray en Normandie, et de sa descendance.*[36] This book is perhaps one of the most curious in the whole history of literature. Here Gobineau is no longer concerned with the history of human civilization. His interest has shifted. All he wishes to know is his *own* descent and the descent of his family. He believes himself to be in possession of definite proofs that his family is directly descended from Ottar Jarl, a famous Norwegian pirate, a member of the royal race of the Ynglings who traced back their own origin to Odin, the highest god. And what a narrow-minded view of human life and human history we find in this book! If Gobineau, at the time of its publication, had not been a well-known author, the author of the *Essai* and the *Renaissance,* nobody would have taken it seriously. He had always spoken with an immoderate and extravagant aristocratic pride. But this time his pride became absurd and ridicu-

33. See above, p. 238.
34. *Essai,* Bk. VI, chap. III, II, 372.
35. *Idem,* Bk. III, chap. I, I, 388.
36. Paris, Didier-Perrin, 1879.

lous and bordered on megalomania. The philosopher of universal history has become the philosopher of the history of his own family. Instead of studying the genealogy of culture he is only engrossed in his own genealogy. That was a sad issue of so great an enterprise. Gobineau had begun with a great promise of making history an exact science and freeing us from all subjective illusions and preconceived opinions about its course.[37] But at the end of his literary career this horizon has dwindled away. His feelings and thoughts are fixed upon one point—his own pedigree! "Parturiunt montes, nascetur ridiculus mus."

All this reveals to us a general feature of Gobineau's thought. The impoverishment of his personal life and the narrowing of his mental horizon was in a sense the necessary outcome of his theory. His discovery of the excellence and the incomparable value of the Aryan race had filled him with the greatest enthusiasm. If he speaks of the moment in which this race made its first appearance in human history he can hardly find words that are strong enough to describe its vital importance. This was not only an earthly, but also a cosmic moment—a spectacle not only for men, but for the gods and the heavens.[38] This seemed to be an ecstatic view of human history, a beginning filled with the greatest expectations and promises. If the Aryan family, the noblest, the most intelligent and most energetic race, is the real actor in the great historical drama, what unlimited hopes can we not entertain for the progress of human civilization! Gobineau's work thus begins with a sort of intoxication, an intoxication of race worship and self worship.

But this first feeling is superseded by a deep disillusionment. By a sort of dialectic in reverse the first optimistic view suddenly turns into a deep and incurable pessimism. The higher races, in fulfilling their historical mission, necessarily and inevitably destroy themselves. They cannot rule and organize the world without being in close contact with the world. But to them contact is a dangerous thing, the permanent and eternal source of infection. The result could not be but disastrous for the higher races. Cooperation between different races means cohabitation, cohabitation means blood mixture, and blood mixture means decay and degeneration. It is always the beginning of the end. With the

37. *Essai*, "Conclusion générale," II, 548.
38. *Idem*, Bk. III, chap. I, I, 374 f.

passing of the purity of the race its strength goes and its organizing power. The higher races become the victims of their own work, the slaves of their slaves.

At the end of his book Gobineau drew the general conclusions from the principles of this theory. In his imagination he conjures the image of the last men who shall live on earth. At this time the degeneration of the nobler races will be complete and all race distinctions will be extinct. Then the vivifying principle in human history will have ceased to exist. To be sure people will live peacefully together. There will be no contest between them but, on the other hand, there will be no energy, no sense of enterprise, no will to power and conquest. The equalitarian ideals of our modern demagogues will be fulfilled. But human life will have lost everything that made it worth living. Men will live in a state of happiness like a flock of sheep or a herd of buffaloes. This period of great and content somnolence will be followed by a period of stupor, and, at last, of complete lethargy. Gobineau even undertook to estimate the length of these different periods. His verdict is that the period of strength, of real life, has long ago faded away. We are now living in a state of decrepitude and exhaustion. The human race can perhaps drag along its petty and miserable existence for some more hundred years; but its fate is sealed; its death is inevitable.

That is the last word of Gobineau's theory; and it is, indeed, the quintessence of his whole work. In the first sentences of his book he had already foreshadowed this end. Race worship was to Gobineau the highest form of worship, the worship of the highest god. But this god is by no means invincible and immortal. On the contrary he is extremely vulnerable. Even in the moments of highest exaltation Gobineau could never forget the coming fate: the fate of the "twilight of the gods." Les dieux s'en vont—the gods must die.

The fall of civilizations is the most striking, and, at the same time, the most obscure of all the phenomena of history. It is a calamity that strikes fear into the soul, and yet has always something so mysterious and so vast in reserve, that the thinker is never weary of looking at it, of studying it, of groping for its secrets . . . we are forced to affirm that every assemblage of men, however ingenious the network of social relations that protects it, acquires on the very day of its birth, hidden among the elements of its life, the seed of an inevitable death. But what is this seed, this principle of death? Is it uniform, as its results are, and do all civilizations perish from the same cause? [39]

Now we see the solution before our very eyes. The result is not only a deep pessimism but also a complete negativism and nihilism. Gobineau had made a clean sweep of all human values. He had decided to offer them to the new god, to the Moloch of the race. But this god was a dying god, and his death sealed the fate of human history and human civilization: it entangled them in his own ruin.

39. *Idem*, Bk. I, chap. I, I, 1 f. English trans., pp. 1 f.

XVII

HEGEL

*The Influence of Hegel's Philosophy upon the Development of
Modern Political Thought*

No other philosophical system has exerted such a strong and
enduring influence upon political life as the metaphysics
of Hegel. All the great philosophers before him had propounded theories of the state which had determined the general
course of political thought but played only a very modest role in
political life. They belonged to the world of "ideas" or "ideals,"
not to the "actual" political world. Philosophers have often complained of this fact. Kant wrote a special treatise in which he
tried to refute the slogan "That may be right in theory but it is
not applicable to practical life." Yet all such efforts were vain,
for the gulf between political thought and life remained insurmountable. Political theories were eagerly discussed; they were
attacked and defended, proved and refuted; but all this had little,
if any, effect upon the struggles of political life.

When studying the philosophy of Hegel we meet with an entirely different situation. His logics and metaphysics were at first
regarded as the strongest bulwarks of his system; yet it was precisely from this side that the system was open to the most violent
and dangerous attacks. And after a short struggle they seemed
to have been successful. Yet Hegelianism has had a rebirth not
in the field of logical or metaphysical thought, but in the field of
political thought. There has hardly been a single great political
system that has resisted its influence. All our modern political
ideologies show us the strength, the durability and permanence
of the principles that were first introduced and defended in Hegel's philosophy of right and in his philosophy of history.

It has however been a Pyrrhic victory. Hegelianism has had to
pay the penalty of its triumph. It has immensely extended its
sphere of action but its unity and inner harmony are lost. It is
no longer a clear, homogeneous, consistent system of political
thought. Different schools and parties all appeal to Hegel's au-

thority but, at the same time, they give entirely different and incompatible interpretations of his fundamental principles. These principles have become the scattered remains of a philosopher. To Hegel's political theory we may apply the saying of Schiller in his prologue to *Wallenstein,* "Confused by party hate and party favor his portraiture in history is varied." Bolshevism, Fascism, and National Socialism have disintegrated and cut into pieces the Hegelian system. They are incessantly quarreling with each other about the remnants of the booty. And this is no longer a mere theoretical dispute. It has tremendous political effects.

From the beginning Hegel's commentators were divided into two camps. The Hegelian "Right" and "Left" wings incessantly fought one another. This discussion was comparatively harmless as long as it was a mere contest between philosophical schools. In the last decades, however, the situation has completely changed. What is now at stake is something quite different from the previous controversies. It has become a mortal combat. A historian recently raised the question whether the struggle of the Russians and the invading Germans in 1943 was not, at bottom, a conflict between the Left and Right wings of Hegel's school.[1] That may seem to be an exaggerated statement of the problem but it contains a nucleus of truth.

For a study of the philosophy of Hegel we cannot proceed in the same way as in the case of other thinkers. We may hope to come to an insight into the character of Plato's theory of knowledge, of Aristotle's natural philosophy, or of Kant's ethical theory by simply describing the principal *results* of these philosophers. In a discussion of Hegel's system, however, such a description would be entirely insufficient. "Where could the inmost truth of a philosophical work be found better expressed than in its purposes and results?" asks Hegel in the preface to his *Phenomenology of Mind.*

And in what way could these be more definitely known than through their distinction from what is produced during the same period by others working in the same field? If, however, such procedure is to pass for more than the beginning of knowledge, if it is to pass for actually knowing what a philosophical system is, then we must, in point of fact, look on it as a device for avoiding the real business at

1. See Hajo Holborn, "The Science of History," *The Interpretation of History,* ed. Joseph R. Strayer (Princeton, University Press, 1943), p. 62.

issue. . . . For the real subject-matter is not exhausted in its purpose . . . nor is the mere result attained the concrete whole itself, but the result along with the process of arriving at it. . . . The naked result is the corpse of the system which has left its guiding tendency behind it. . . . Instead of laying hold of the matter itself, a procedure of that kind is all the while away from the subject altogether. . . . The easiest thing of all is to pass judgments on what has a solid substantial content; it is more difficult to grasp it, and most of all difficult to do both together and produce the systematic exposition of it.[2]

This difficulty accounts for the various and divergent interpretations of Hegel's philosophy. If we single out a particular feature, it is not only easy, it is even necessary, to find its very opposite. Hegel was not afraid of these contradictions; he saw in them the very life of speculative thought and philosophic truth. Over and over again he challenged the famous principle of identity and contradiction. This principle is not untrue; but it is merely formal and abstract and, therefore, a shallow principle. What we find in reality is always an identity of opposites.

Even in Hegel's political thought every thesis is followed by its antithesis. It is, therefore, impossible to define this political system by a special catchword. He always asserted himself to be a philosopher of *freedom*.

As the essence of matter is gravity, so, on the other hand, we may affirm that the substance, the essence of Spirit is Freedom. All will readily assent to the doctrine that Spirit, among other properties, is also endowed with Freedom; but philosophy teaches that all the qualities of Spirit exist only through Freedom. . . . It is a result of speculative philosophy that Freedom is the sole truth of Spirit.[3]

Hegel's opponents were convinced that this was a caricature rather than a true description of his doctrine. The philosopher Fries declared that Hegel's theory of the state had grown "not in the gardens of science but on the dunghill of servility." All the German liberals felt and spoke the same way. They saw in the Hegelian system the firmest stronghold of political reaction. In their judgment Hegel was the most dangerous enemy of all demo-

2. Hegel, *Phenomenology of Mind*, English trans. by J. B. Baillie (London S. Sonnenschein & Co.; New York, Macmillan, 1910, 2d ed. London, George Allen & Unwin; New York, Macmillan, 1931), I, 3 f. 2 vols.

3. *Lectures on the Philosophy of History*, English trans. by J. Sibree (London, Henry G. Bohn, 1857, p. 18; new ed. London, G. Bell & Sons, 1900).

cratic ideals. "So far as I can see," said Rudolf Haym in his book
Hegel und seine Zeit,

all that Hobbes or Filmer, Haller or Stahl have taught, is relatively
open-minded in comparison with the famous phrase regarding the
rationality of the real in the sense of Hegel's Preface (to his *Philosophy
of Right*). The theory of divine free grace and the theory of absolute
obedience are blameless and innocuous in comparison with the frightful doctrine which canonizes the subsisting as such.[4]

But here we have to face a great problem. How was it possible
that a philosophical system which canonized the "subsisting as
such" should become one of the greatest *revolutionary* forces in
modern political thought? How was it that, after Hegel's death,
his doctrine suddenly was seen from an entirely different angle
and used in a quite different way? The philosopher of the Prussian State became the teacher of Marx and Lenin—the champion
of "dialectic Marxism." Hegel himself is not responsible for this
development. He would surely have rejected most of the consequences drawn from the premises of his political theory. As regards his character and his personal temperament he was opposed to all radical solutions. He was a conservative who defended
the power of tradition. Custom (*Sitte*) was to him the basic element in political life. In his early writings Hegel had given a
description of the Greek polis and the Roman Republic, in which
he glorified this ideal. He always maintained and defended the
same view. He does not acknowledge any ethical order higher
than that which appears in custom.[5]

Here we grasp the fundamental difference between the "idealism" of Hegel and that of Plato. Plato spoke as a pupil of Socrates.
He appealed to the Socratic demand for individual responsibility.
Custom and habit were declared to be invalid. It is not in tradition or routine that we can find the principles of a true political
life. These principles are based not upon "right opinion" (*doxa*)
but upon knowledge (*epistēmē*), that new form of rationality

4. R. Haym, *Hegel und seine Zeit* (Berlin, R. Gaertner, 1857), p. 367. Cf.
Hugh A. Reyburn, *The Ethical Theory of Hegel; A Study of the Philosophy of
Right* (Oxford, Clarendon Press, 1921), p. 63.
5. *Rechtsphilosophie,* § 151. English trans., *The Ethics of Hegel; Translated
Selections from his "Rechtsphilosophie,"* by J. Macbride Sterrett (Boston, Ginn
& Co., 1893), p. 142. Complete English trans., *Hegel's Philosophy of Right,* trans.
by S. W. Dyde (London, G. Bell & Sons, 1896), p. 161.

and moral consciousness that had been discovered by Socrates. "Reason" for Hegel is not of this Platonic type.

In point of fact the notion of the realization of self-conscious reason . . . finds its actual fulfilment in the life of a nation. Reason appears here as the fluent universal substance . . . which at the same time breaks up into many entirely independent beings. . . . They are conscious within themselves of being these individual independent beings through the fact that they surrender and sacrifice their particular individuality, and that this universal substance is their soul and essence.[6]

Conservatism is, therefore, one of the most characteristic features in Hegel's ethical theory. Nevertheless it is not all. It is only a particular and one-sided aspect which we should not mistake for the whole. In Hegel's political theory and philosophy of history we find a strange mixture of two opposite tendencies. He tries to embrace the whole of the historical world. He speaks of Oriental culture, of China or India as well as of Greek, Roman, or German cultures. What he wants to reveal in his system is not the spirit of a particular nation but the universal spirit, the spirit of the world. "The *genii* of peoples as concrete *Ideas* have their truth and character in the *Absolute Idea*. They stand around the throne of the world-spirit as the executors of its realization, and as witnesses and ornaments of its glory. As world-spirit it is only its own need of coming to itself—to conscious knowledge of its own being and mission of freedom." [7]

Yet in his political system and practical politics Hegel was not equal to this all-comprehensive task. He himself always emphasized that the philosopher cannot avoid the limitations of his present world. And this "present world" of Hegel was a rather narrow one. It was tied down to Germany and Prussia. Hegel began as a German patriot. He was deeply concerned with the problems of his time and his own country. In one of his first political pamphlets, written in 1801, he deals with the constitution of Germany. He declares that Germany's political life is approaching a dangerous crisis, that it has lost its power and all its dignity. Later on, after the war of liberation, he was convinced that the crisis of Germany's political life had found its solution. Since Prussia had

6. *Phenomenology of Mind*. English trans., I, 341 f.
7. *Philosophy of Right*, § 352. Sterrett trans., pp. 210 f. Dyde trans., pp. 345 f.

played the leading role in this solution all his thoughts and hopes were henceforward concentrated upon the Prussian State. When dealing with all these actual political problems Hegel had more and more to restrict his philosophical universalism. He passed from that universalism not only to nationalism but also to a sort of particularism and provincialism. In the preface to his *Philosophy of Right* he even gave vent to his personal feelings, antipathies, and idiosyncrasies.

In this regard the form of the Hegelian system was greatly superior to its immediate content. Long after the death of Hegel and after the breakdown of his metaphysics it continued to work. It became one of the explosive forces in the development of political thought during the nineteenth century. Henceforth it was exempt from all those personal and temporary conditions that had influenced Hegel's political theory. It very often worked against Hegel himself. It contradicted and undermined some of his firmest and dearest political convictions. This process is, indeed, entirely in keeping with the general character of the dialectic method. Thought always shows such a double face. Like a statue of the god Janus it looks backward and forward. In the dialectic process every new step contains and preserves all the former ones. There is no abrupt change and no break in continuity. But on the other hand this act of preservation is, necessarily, an act of abrogation. Whatever comes into being by the dialectic process has its truth and its value only as *aufgehobenes Moment*. It is preserved as integral element; but its isolated reality is annulled. Every finite existence has to perish in order to give place to new and more perfect shapes.

Such a conception is, however, not consistent with any "canonization of the subsisting as such." When Hegel, in his last period, yielded more and more to this temptation he acted contrary to the spirit of his own system. In one of his early treatises, *Concerning the Scientific Modes of Treating Natural Right*, written in 1802, he had stressed the opposite attitude. Here he had described the history of the world as a great tragedy of ethical life which the Absolute is constantly performing with itself. It is the destiny of the absolute spirit incessantly to give birth to itself into objectivity, to submit to suffering and death and to rise from its ashes to new glory. The Divine in its shape and objectivity has a duplicate nature and its life is the absolute unity of these two natures.[8] Obviously this is no mere conservatism or traditionalism but the very opposite.

If we are to understand the true character of Hegel's political theory we must, therefore, project the problem upon a larger plane. It is not enough to study his own opinions about concrete political problems. These opinions have only an individual, not a philosophic interest. *"Die Meinung ist mein,"* said Hegel in one of his famous puns. What matters here is not the political credo but the new *orientation* of political thought that was introduced by his system. It is much more the new mode of *questioning* than the particular answers given by Hegel which proved to be of prime importance and had an enduring interest and influence. But in order to clarify this point and to do full justice to Hegel's political thought we must enlarge our horizon; we must go back to the first principles of Hegel's philosophy.

The Metaphysical Background of Hegel's Political Theory

The problem of religion and the problem of history are the two intellectual centers of Hegel's doctrine. From the beginning they were the great and most powerful concerns of his philosophic thought. When studying the first writings of Hegel we can scarcely draw a line between them.[9] They are fused into each other and form an inseparable unity. We may describe the fundamental tendency of Hegel's thought by saying that he spoke of religion in terms of history and of history in terms of religion.

Thereby one of the oldest and most difficult problems of religious thought suddenly assumed a new shape. Ancient and modern thinkers had approached the problem of theodicy from various angles. The Stoics, the Neo-Platonists, and Leibniz had given their vindication of divine providence with the existence of physical or moral evil in view. The period of the Enlightenment rejected most of these theological solutions. Nevertheless the question was still in the focus of the general philosophic interest. It became the bone of contention between Voltaire and Rousseau. Now all the arguments used in this contest were declared by

8. Hegel, *Schriften zur Politik und Rechtsphilosophie*, ed. Georg Lasson, "Sämtliche Werke," VII (Leipzig, Felix Meiner, 1913; 2d ed. 1923), 384 f.

9. Hegel, *Theologische Jugendschriften*, ed. H. Nohl (Tübingen, Mohr, 1907).

Hegel to be obsolete. We need not seek an "excuse," a justification of physical and moral evil. Evil is not a merely accidental fact. It follows rather from the fundamental character, from the very *definition* of reality. To separate the positive and the negative pole of reality is arbitrary and superficial.

Nevertheless the old problem of a theodicy is not forgotten. On the contrary, Hegel is convinced that he was the first to see this problem in its true light. According to him we have to redefine the question: we have to discover, behind its religious and theological meaning, a more profound philosophic significance. This was the task to be performed in his philosophy of history. In general history is the development of Spirit in Time, as Nature is the development of Idea in Space.

It was for a while the fashion to profess admiration for the wisdom of God, as displayed in animals, plants, and isolated occurrences. But, if it be allowed that Providence manifests itself in such objects and forms of existence, why not also in Universal History? This is deemed too great a matter to be thus regarded. But divine wisdom, i.e. Reason, is one and the same in the great as in the little; and we must not imagine God to be too weak to exercise his wisdom on the grand scale. . . . Our mode of treating the subject is, in this aspect, a Theodicaea—a justification of the ways of God—which Leibnitz attempted metaphysically, in his method, i.e. in indefinite abstract categories—so that the ill that is found in the world may be comprehended, and the thinking Spirit reconciled with the fact of the existence of evil. Indeed, nowhere is such a harmonizing view more pressingly demanded than in universal history; and it can be attained only by recognizing the *positive* existence, in which that negative element is a subordinate and vanquished nullity.[10]

Hegel's opponents always declared this harmonization of history to be a mere falsification. They saw in it nothing but a shallow optimism. Hegel's philosophic opposite, Schopenhauer, said that such an optimism is not only absurd but nefarious. This is, however, an obvious misconstruction of Hegel's view. Hegel never denied the evils, the miseries, the cruelties and crimes that are inherent in human history nor did he intend to minimize or exculpate these evils. In this regard he admitted all the arguments of pessimism. What we call happiness, he declares, belongs to the sphere of particular purposes. "He is happy who finds his condi-

10. *Lectures on the Philosophy of History*, p. 16.

tion suited to his special character, will, and fancy, and so enjoys himself in that condition. The history of the world is not the theatre of happiness. Periods of happiness are blank pages in it, for they are periods of harmony—periods when the antithesis is in abeyance." [11] Without this antithesis history becomes lifeless; it loses its meaning and its impulse. What we seek and what we enjoy in the history of mankind is not man's happiness, but his activity and energy.

The harmonization of the historical world that is promised is, therefore, quite different from all the previous attempts of a theodicy. It stresses rather than eliminates or removes the fact of physical and moral evil. It does not assert that the individual will, as such, can find its satisfaction in the objective world. Such a demand is declared to be an idle hope. Reality does not comply with our personal wishes or desires. It is made of a harder stuff, it follows its own inexorable law. If we seek the fulfilment of our own purposes in the real world the only consequence can be deep disappointment. We are then led to a complete estrangement between the subjective and the objective sphere. But the same estrangement appears, in a much more dangerous form, in another trend of thought. All the idealistic schools, from Plato up to Kant and Fichte, have given us the advice to flee from the real world to a higher and more sublime order. They have constructed a moral order which is in strict opposition to our empirical world. "Nothing can possibly be conceived in the world or even out of it," said Kant, "which can be called good, without qualification, except a Good Will." But what does this "good" or "moral" will mean? It is no longer a particular but a universal will. But its universality remains entirely abstract. What we oppose here to the actual world, the world of human experience, is a formal moral demand. We look at the world not as it is, but as it ought to be. That seems to be a high and sublime conception. For here we are no longer concerned with our personal interests. We are ready to offer all these interests on the altar of duty. But when applied to the real world this moral altruism leads to the same disillusionment as the egoism of our private wishes. The course of the world constantly and inevitably frustrates our moral demands. Our consciousness does not accept this frustration; but instead of accusing ourselves, we accuse reality. And this estrangement from re-

11. *Idem*, p. 28.

ality goes so far as to attack and destroy the actual order of things.

Hegel has described this destruction in a famous chapter of his *Phenomenology of Mind* entitled "The Law of the Heart and the Frenzy of Self-conceit." Obviously he is thinking here of the French Revolution that began with the highest moral ideals—of liberty, equality, and fraternity—and ended with the reign of terror. By the French Revolution the "law of the heart" was declared to be the supreme moral principle. But opposed to this principle stood a reality, a violent ordinance of the world which contradicted the law of the heart, and a humanity suffering under that ordinance. It became the first and principal task to attack this reality. "There is in consequence no longer here the frivolity of the former mode, which merely wanted some particular pleasure; it is the earnestness of a high purpose that seeks its pleasure in displaying the excellence of its own true nature, and in bringing about the welfare of mankind. . . . The individual, then, fulfils, carries out the law of his heart. This law becomes a universal ordinance." But if we begin to enforce this law upon the actual world, if we try to carry our point, we meet with the strongest and fiercest resistance. We cannot overcome this resistance without abrogating the whole historical order of things. Thus the "law of the heart" instead of being a constructive principle, a principle that confirms and corroborates the true ethical order, becomes a destructive and subversive principle. The French Revolution has glorified this destruction. "The realization of the immediate undisciplined nature passes for a display of excellence and for bringing about the well-being of mankind." "When it gives expression to this moment of conscious destruction, . . . the law of the heart shows itself to be this inner perversion of itself, to be consciousness gone crazy, its own essence being at once not essence, its reality directly unreality." [12]

The reconciliation which Hegel attempted in his philosophy of history is quite a different type of thought. He accepts the given order of things; he sees in it the true ethical substance. He does not attempt to do away with the evils, the miseries, and the crimes of the historical world. All this is taken for granted. Nevertheless he undertakes to justify this hard and cruel reality. From the point of view of speculative thought it no longer appears as an accidental fact or as a dire necessity. It is not only "reasonable";

12. *Phenomenology of Mind*, English trans., I, 359, 363.

it is the very incarnation and actualization of reason. But by "reason" we must no longer understand the "practical reason" of Kant. It is not a mere abstract and formal principle, a moral demand like the Kantian categorical imperative. It is reason that lives in the historical world and organizes it. "The insight to which . . . philosophy is to lead us, is, that the real world is as it ought to be—that the truly good—the universal divine reason —is not a mere abstraction, but a vital principle capable of realizing itself. . . . Philosophy wishes to discover the substantial purport, the real side of the divine idea, and to justify the so much despised reality of things." [13]

But how could Hegel say that all philosophic thinkers before him had underrated the "substantial power" of reason? Were not most of them, Plato, Aristotle, Leibniz, and Kant, determined rationalists? And how could he charge the great religious thinkers—St. Augustine, Thomas Aquinas, and Pascal—with not having understood what "divine providence" really means? All this is understandable only if we bear in mind the specific tendency of Hegel's philosophy of religion and of his philosophy of history.

It is the synthesis, the correlation and mutual penetration of these two elements, of the historical and the religious, that was the principal theme of his philosophy. And he was convinced that he was the first to see this interdependence in its true light. From Plato to Kant the whole history of metaphysics was marked by a fundamental distinction between the "sensible" and the "intelligible" world. Philosophers did not agree about the relation of human knowledge to these two worlds. Plato was convinced that truth and reality are only to be found in the world of pure ideas or forms. In the phenomenal world we cannot find the truth; what we find here are only fugitive shadows. But Kant took the opposite view. He confines human knowledge within the limits of the empirical world. "The fundamental principle ruling all my idealism is this: All cognition of things from mere pure Understanding and Reason is nothing but mere illusion and only in experience is there truth." [14] But what was generally agreed, and what is common to all previous forms of philosophic idealism is that there is a demarcation which separates the *mundus sensibilis* from the

13. *Philosophy of History*, p. 38.
14. Kant, *Prolegomena, Kant's Critical Philosophy for English Readers*, trans. John P. Mahaffy and John H. Bernard (3d ed., London, Macmillan, 1915), II, 147.

mundus intelligibilis. This dualism had been the very basis of metaphysical thought.

It is true that there are great metaphysical thinkers whose systems are usually described as "monistic." Spinoza spoke of God not as a *causa transiens* but as a *causa immanens.* God is not beyond or outside Nature; God and Nature are one and the same. But even here the fundamental dualism of metaphysical thought is by no means overcome but only appears in a new shape. What we find in this Spinozistic God is, according to Hegel, only a lifeless unity. It is the rigid and abstract One that admits of no differences, of no change or variety. There remains a chasm, an insurmountable gulf between two different orders: the order of time and the order of eternity. In Spinoza's system time has no true reality. Since philosophic thought deals with reality, time is no proper subject of philosophy. It is only a mode of "imagination," not of philosophic thought or intuition. The idea of time is an "inadequate" idea. In his history of philosophy Hegel says that it is a misconstruction of the Spinozistic system to speak of it as a system of "atheism." What we find here is the very opposite. Spinoza did not deny the reality of God, but the reality of the world: we should call him an "acosmist" rather than an atheist. The reality of nature evaporates, so to speak, in Spinoza's thought. Nature has no longer a self-dependent meaning. It is absorbed by the abstract unity of God—by the Spinozistic substance that is in itself and is to be conceived by itself. Time is unsubstantial and unreal and unworthy of philosophic thought, for it is the fundamental characteristic of this thought to look at things under the form of eternity.

Christian philosophy seems to be fundamentally opposed to this abrogation and annihilation of time. The Christian religion is based upon the fundamental dogma of incarnation. But the incarnation of Christ is not a metaphysical but a historical fact. It is an event in time; it makes a sharp incision; it makes a new beginning in the life and destiny of mankind. Time can no longer, therefore, be regarded as a merely accidental thing; it is essential. All the great Christian thinkers had to face this problem. St. Augustine accepted the Platonic distinction between the sensible and the supra-sensible, the phenomenal and noumenal world. But in contradistinction to Plato and all the other philosophers of antiquity he had to add a new feature. He had to develop a philosophy of history in his *City of God.* He determined the relation between the eternal order and the temporal or secular order. He opposed the *civitas terrena* to the *civitas divina;* the visible worldly city to the invisible divine city. But even in St. Augustine the gulf that separates these two orders remains insuperable. There is no possible reconciliation between time and eternity. As regards the value of human history, the medieval dualism of the Christian thinkers since the time of St. Augustine, judged in quite the same way as Plato. All secular life is corrupt in its very principle; its redemption can only be brought about by its radical destruction which is the climax of the great historical and religious process. The estrangement between the divine and the temporal order cannot be removed by Christian thought; it is simply inevitable and incurable. Philosophy has to accept this fact. As Pascal emphasized, the Christian God will always remain a stumbling block to all philosophers. He is impenetrable to philosophic thought; he is a hidden God wrapped in mystery.

Hegel undertook to reveal this mystery. What he presents in his philosophy of history is a paradox. It is a "Christian rationalism" and a "Christian optimism." Hegel was convinced that only by this attitude can the Christian religion be understood and interpreted in its positive instead of in its merely negative sense.

In the Christian religion God has revealed Himself—that is, he has given us to understand what He is; so that He is no longer a concealed or secret existence. And this possibility of knowing Him, thus afforded us, renders such knowledge a duty. . . . The time must eventually come for understanding that rich product of active Reason, which the History of the World offers to us.[15]

Now we understand the purport of Hegel's saying that what he intended to do in his philosophy of history was to justify the "despised reality." The Christian thinkers had made a sharp distinction between what they called the realm of nature and the realm of grace. Even Kant's political system starts from the opposition between the "realm of nature" and the "realm of ends." All this is rejected by Hegel. He does not accept this opposition. According to him, a true, a speculative view of history is enough to convince us of the artificiality of this division. In history the two factors of "time" and "eternity" are not separated the one from the other; they interpenetrate each other. Eternity does not transcend

15. *Philosophy of History,* pp. 15 f.

time; it is, on the contrary, to be found in time itself. Time is not only a scene of change; it contains a true substantiality. "It is the theme of philosophy to ascertain the substance which is immanent in the show of the temporal and transient, and the eternal which is present." [16] Unlike Plato Hegel does not seek the "Idea" in a supercelestial space. He finds it in the actuality of man's social life and of his political struggles.

While we are thus concerned exclusively with the Idea of Spirit and in the History of the World regard everything as only its manifestation, we have, in traversing the past—however extensive its periods—only to do with what is *present;* for philosophy, as occupying itself with the True, has to do with the *eternally present.* Nothing in the past is lost for it, for the Idea is ever present; Spirit is immortal; with it there is no past, no future, but an essential *now.*[17]

From the very beginning Hegel had been accused of pantheism. All his theologian opponents charged him with it. This charge is not altogether unfounded; but it calls for an explanation and restriction. If "pantheism" means that all things are brought to the same level, that there are no intrinsic differences of being or value, neither Spinoza nor Hegel can be called a pantheist. In Spinoza's system there is a sharp and clear-cut distinction between the substance and its modes; between eternal and temporal, necessary and accidental things. The same holds for Hegel. He never identified reality with empirical existence. When his identification of the Real and the Rational was interpreted in this sense he regarded the interpretation as a complete misconstruction of his fundamental thought.

We must presuppose intelligence enough to know . . . that existence is in part mere appearance, and only in part reality. In common life, any freak of fancy, any error, evil and everything of the nature of evil, as well as every degenerate and transitory existence whatever, gets in a casual way the name of reality. But even our ordinary feelings are enough to forbid a fortuitous existence getting the name of a real; for by fortuitous we mean an existence which has no greater value than that of something possible which may as well not be as be. As for the term reality, these critics would have done well to consider the sense in which I employ it. In a detailed logic I had treated amongst other things of reality, and accurately distinguished it not only from the for-

16. *Philosophy of Right,* Preface. Dyde trans., p. xxvii.
17. *Philosophy of History,* p. 82.

tuitous, which, after all, has existence; but even from the cognate categories of existence and other modifications of being.[18]

When speaking of Hegel's system we must, indeed, always bear in mind these logical distinctions. He distinguishes sharply between what he calls "reality" and what he calls *faule Existenz* (idle, worthless existence).[19] That marks the peculiar type of his "pantheism." Hegel was no Spinozist; he never accepted the identification of God with nature. In Hegel's system nature has no independent being. It is not the Absolute; it is the "Idea in its otherness"—*Die Idee in ihrem Anderssein.*

Nature . . . is not to be deified; nor are the sun, the moon, animals, plants to be regarded as works of God rather than human deeds and events. Nature in itself, in its idea, is divine; but in its existence it does not conform to its notion. . . . Nature has, therefore, been described as the defection of the Idea from itself—the idea being in this shape of externality inadequate to itself. . . . It gives way to accidentality and chance; it cannot in all its particular determination be penetrated by reason.[20]

The true life of the Idea, of the Divine, begins in history. In Hegel's philosophy the Spinozistic formula *Deus sive natura* was converted into the formula *Deus sive historia.*

But this apotheosis does not apply to particular historical events; it applies to the historical process taken as a whole. "That this 'Idea' or 'Reason' is the True, the Eternal, the absolutely *powerful* essence; that it reveals itself in the world, and that in that world nothing else is revealed but this and its honour and glory—is the thesis which has been proved in philosophy, and is here regarded as demonstrated." [21] Even previous philosophic or theological thinkers as for instance St. Augustine, Vico, or Herder had spoken of history as a divine revelation. But in the Hegelian system history is no mere appearance of God, but his reality: God not only "has" history, he *is* history.

18. *Encyclopedia of the Philosophical Sciences,* § 6.
19. *Philosophy of History,* p. 38.
20. *Encyclopedia,* § 248.
21. *Philosophy of History,* p. 10.

Hegel's Theory of the State

The conception of the state follows from that of history. To Hegel the state is not only a part, a special province, but the essence, the very core of historical life. It is the alpha and omega. Hegel denies that we can speak of historical life outside and before the state.

Nations may have passed a long life before arriving at this their destination, and during this period, they may have attained considerable culture in some directions. . . . But that apparently so extensive range of events lies beyond the pale of history. . . . But it is the State which first presents subject-matter that is not only *adapted* to the prose of history, but involves the production of such history in the very progress of its own being.[22]

If *reality* must be defined in terms of history rather than in terms of nature, and if the state is the prerequisite of history, it follows that we have to see in the state the supreme and most perfect reality. No political theory before Hegel ever proposed this. To Hegel the state is not only the representative but the very incarnation of the "spirit of the world." While St. Augustine regarded the *civitas terrena* as a distortion and disfigurement of the *civitas divina,* Hegel saw in this *civitas terrena* the "Divine Idea as it exists on earth." This is an entirely new type of absolutism.

In order to carry his point Hegel had, however, to remove the obstacles created by previous political theories. His fight against the Natural Right theories of the state began as early as 1802 in his treatise *Concerning the Scientific Modes of Treating Natural Right* and was continued in all his later works. Up to the beginning of the nineteenth century it was the current opinion that the state originates in a contract. That such a contract is bound to certain conditions, to legal or moral restrictions, seemed to be a foregone conclusion. In order to avoid this difficulty Hegel had to take a very bold step. He had to change the very idea of "morality" that had prevailed for many centuries. He declared that this idea was merely a "subjective" conception which cannot lay claim to a true objective validity.

22. *Idem,* p. 62 f.

"Morality" in the sense in which it was understood by the previous ethical systems, as for instance by the systems of Kant or Fichte, pretends to be a universal law. "There is but one categorical imperative," says Kant, "namely, this: Act only on that maxim whereby thou canst at the same time will that it should become a universal law." But this categorical imperative gives us only an abstract and formal law, a law that binds the individual will but is entirely powerless against the reality of things. In Kant's system the moral world, the realm of ends, is opposed to the natural world, the world of causes and effects. We can *postulate* a unity of these two worlds but we can never *prove* it—it remains a vain desire. *Fiat iustitia, pereat mundus*—is the maxim of this morality. In doing his duty the individual must negate the world and must destroy himself. For his moral nature is incompatible with his physical nature—his duty is in eternal conflict with his happiness.

The moral consciousness takes duty to be the essential reality. . . . But this moral consciousness, at the same time, finds before it the assumed freedom of nature: it learns by experience that nature is not concerned about giving consciousness a sense of the unity of its reality with that of nature, and hence discovers that nature may let it become happy, but perhaps also may not. . . . It therefore finds reason for bewailing a situation where there is no correspondence between itself and existence, and lamenting the injustice which confines it to having its object merely in the form of pure duty but refuses to let it see this object and itself actually realized.[23]

One of the principal aims of Hegel's theodicy is to do away with such idle lamentations. According to him they follow from a deep misunderstanding of what ethical reality is and means. We cannot find the true ethical order, the ethical "substance" in a mere formal law. It is expressed in a much higher sense, in actual and concrete reality, in the life of the state. "The State," says Hegel in his *System der Sittlichkeit*, in which he first introduces his sharp distinction between *Moralität* and *Sittlichkeit*,[24] "is the self-certain absolute mind which acknowledges no abstract rules of good and bad, shameful and mean, craft and deception."

23. *Phenomenology of Mind*, English trans., II, 611 f.
24. English translations have tried various ways to express this distinction. Usually *Moralität* is rendered by "morality"; *Sittlichkeit* by "ethicality." See, for instance, J. M. Sterrett, *The Ethics of Hegel* (see above, p. 251, n. 5), p. 60.

Here is, in a sense, a complete transvaluation of values, a reversal of all previous standards. According to this revaluation there is no longer any moral obligation for the state. Morality holds for the individual will, not for the universal will of the state. If there is any duty to the state it is the duty to preserve itself. "It is a generally acknowledged and well known principle," says Hegel in his treatise on the constitution of Germany,

> that the particular interest of the State is the most important consideration. The State is the spirit that dwells in the world and realizes itself in the world through *consciousness,* while in nature the spirit actualizes itself only as the other of itself, as dormant spirit. . . . It is the course of God through the world that constitutes the State . . . When conceiving the State, one must not think of particular states, not of particular institutions, but one must much rather contemplate the *Idea,* God as actual on earth, alone.[25]

In this respect Hegel's doctrine is not only in sharp contrast to all the previous theories of natural right but also to the romantic theories of the state. To be sure Hegel was deeply indebted to romanticism. He accepts some of its fundamental ideas. In his general conception of history and in his idea of the "national spirit" the influence of Herder and of the writers of early romanticism is obvious. But his politics is based upon entirely different principles. His connection with romantic thought is only a negative one. He rejects the "mechanical" theories, according to which the state is no more than an aggregate of individual wills, held together by the legal bonds of a social contract or a contract of submission. Like the romantic political writers Hegel insists that the state possesses an "organic" unity. In such an organism the whole is, according to the definition of Aristotle, "prior" to the parts. But as to the nature of this organic whole Hegel's view deviates from almost all the romantic writers. The very term "organic unity" cannot be used by him in the same sense as it was used by Schelling, the real philosopher of romanticism. Hegel's unity is a dialectic unity; a unity of contraries. It not only allows but even requires the strongest tensions and oppositions. From this point of view Hegel had to reject the esthetic ideals of Schelling or Novalis. Novalis had spoken of the state as a "beautiful individual." In his essay on *Christianity or Europe* he had dreamed of a unity of all Christian nations under

25. *Philosophy of Right,* § 258. Sterrett trans., p. 191; Dyde trans., pp. 244–247.

the guidance and authority of a universal, a really "catholic" church.[26] This ideal of political and religious peace was not the ideal of Hegel. According to him it is necessary to introduce into political thought what he calls "the seriousness, the suffering, the patience, and the labour of the negative." [27]

The negative role of political life is contained in the fact of war. To abolish or terminate war would be the death blow of political life. It is a mere utopianism to think that the conflicts between nations could ever be settled by legal means—by international courts of arbitration. There is no praetor who can judge of states, and the Kantian idea of an everlasting peace by a league of nations settling disputes and arranging discords by virtue of a power acknowledged by every single state would presuppose the unanimity of the states which always would rest upon particular independent wills and would, therefore, be highly contingent.[28] "Since states in their relation of self-subsistence are opposed to one another as particular wills and the validity of treaties depends on this, and since the content of the particular will of the state is its welfare, this particular welfare is the highest law in the relation of one state to another." [29]

From his early youth Hegel had rejected all "humanitarian" ideals. He declared the "universal love of mankind" to be nothing more than an "insipid invention." Such a love that has no real concrete object is shallow and unnatural.[30] Much better to accept all the inherent defects of real political life than to indulge in such vague generalities.

Every state, though it may be declared wretched according to somebody's principles, though this or that imperfection in it must be admitted—possesses always, if it belongs to the developed states of our times, the essential elements of its true existence. But since it is easier to discover faults than to understand positive characteristics, it is easy to fall into the error of overlooking the internal organism of the state itself in dwelling upon extrinsic phases of it. The state is no work of art; it exists in the world, and hence in the sphere of choice, accidence, and error. Hence the evil behavior of its members can disfigure it in many ways. But the most deformed human being, the criminal, the

26. See above, p. 185, n. 13.
27. *Phenomenology of Mind*, Preface, p. 17.
28. *Philosophy of Right*, § 333. Dyde trans., p. 338.
29. *Idem*, § 336. Dyde trans., p. 339.
30. Hegel, *Theologische Jugendschriften* (see above, p. 254, n. 9), pp. 295, 323.

invalid, and the cripple are still always living human beings: the
affirmative, life, remains in spite of all defects, and here we have to do
with this affirmative alone.[31]

Unlike Novalis, Hegel is not interested in the beauty of the state
but in its "truth." And according to him this truth is not a moral
one; it is rather "the truth which lies in power." "Men are as foolish as to forget . . . in their enthusiasm for liberty of conscience
and political freedom, the truth which lies in power." These words
written in 1801, about 150 years ago, contain the clearest and
most ruthless program of fascism that has ever been propounded
by any political or philosophic writer.

The same principle holds not only for the actions of nations
and states, but also for those exceptional individuals who determine the course of the political world and are the real makers
of history. They too are exempt from all moral demands. To
measure their deeds by our conventional standards would be
ridiculous. In Hegel's system the worship of the state is combined with hero worship. The greatness of a hero has nothing to
do with his so-called "virtues." Since greatness means power it
is obvious that vice is just as great as virtue. An abstract moral
view gives rise to that "psychological" interpretation of history
which seeks to belittle all great deeds and heroes by reducing
them to petty and mean psychological motives. "This is the view
of psychological valets to whom no men are heroes, not because
there are no heroes but because they themselves are only valets." [32] Of such an interpretation of history Hegel always speaks
with utter contempt.

To be sure he himself had no illusions about the motives of
most of the great political actions. He never makes an attempt
to "idealize" these motives. Here too he is far from a trivial optimism. He knows very well that personal ambitions not only have
their share in all great political actions but that, in most cases,
they are the real driving force. All this does not detract from
their value but rather increases it. He who speaks of human passions in a disparaging tone blindfolds himself against the true
character of the historical process. The power that puts all historical actions in operation and gives them determinate existence,
is the need, instinct, inclination, and passion of man. This is the

31. *Philosophy of Right,* § 258. Sterrett trans., pp. 191 f.; Dyde trans., p. 247.
32. *Idem,* § 124. Sterrett trans., p. 113; Dyde trans., p. 120.

absolute right of personal existence, to find *itself* satisfied in its activity and labor.

We assert then that nothing has been accomplished without interest on the part of the actors and if interest be called passion we may affirm absolutely that nothing in the world great has been accomplished without *passion*. Two elements, therefore, enter into the object of our investigation; the first, the Idea, the second, the complex of human passions; the one the warp, the other the woof of the vast arras-web of Universal History.

By abstract moralists passion is regarded as a thing of sinister aspect, as more or less immoral. But here too Hegel accepts Machiavelli's conception of *virtù*. "Virtue" means strength; and there is no stronger and more powerful motive in human life than the great passions. The Idea itself would not actualize itself without engaging all human passions.

The special interest of passion is thus inseparable from the active development of a general principle: for it is from the special and determinate and from its negation, that the Universal results. Particularity contends with its like, and some loss is involved in the issue. *It* is not the general idea that is implicated in opposition and combat, and that is exposed to danger. It remains in the background, untouched and uninjured. This may be called the *cunning of reason*—that it sets the passions to work for itself, while that which develops its existence through such impulsion pays the penalty, and suffers loss.[33]

On this view of universal history Hegel abolishes the common distinction between "altruistic" and "egoistic" acts. Nietzsche's "immoralism" was no new feature; it was already anticipated in Hegel's system.

The first glance at History convinces us that the actions of men proceed from their needs, their passions, their characters, and talents; and impresses us with the belief that such needs, passions, and interests are the sole springs of action—the efficient agents in the scene of activity. Among these may, perhaps, be found aims of a liberal or universal kind—benevolence it may be, or noble patriotism; but such virtues and general views are but insignificant as compared with the World and its doings. . . . Passions, private aims, and the satisfaction of selfish desires are, on the other hand, most effective springs of action. Their power lies in the fact that they respect none of the limitations

33. *Philosophy of History*, p. 34.

which justice and morality would impose on them; and that these natural impulses have a more direct influence over man than the artificial and tedious discipline that tends to order and self-restraint, law and morality.[34]

Hegel was not afraid of egoism; he was the first philosophic thinker who not only regarded it as an unavoidable evil but elevated it to the rank of an "ideal" principle. He introduced that concept of *sacro egoismo* which after him has played such a decisive and disastrous role in modern political life. It is true that after Hegel's times the emphasis was shifted. He himself regarded the individuals as marionettes in the great puppet show of universal history. According to him the author and the dramaturge of the historical drama is the "Idea": the individuals are nothing but the "agents of the world-spirit."[35] Later on, when Hegel's metaphysics had lost its influence and binding power, this conception was turned upside down: the "ideas" became the agents of the individuals who are the real "leaders."

Hegel's political theory is a watershed between two great streams of thought. It marks the turning point between two ages, two cultures, two ideologies. It stands on the border line between the eighteenth and nineteenth centuries. Hegel was firmly convinced that no individual thinker could go beyond his own time. "Philosophy is its time apprehended in thoughts. It is, therefore, just as foolish to fancy that any philosophy can transcend its present world, as that an individual could leap out of his time and jump over Rhodes." That is the most characteristic expression of the difference between the spirit of the Enlightenment and the new spirit of the nineteenth century. Neither the French Encyclopedists nor Kant were afraid to think *against* their own time. They had to combat the *ancien régime;* and they were convinced that in this struggle philosophy had its share as one of the most powerful weapons. But Hegel could no longer assign this role to philosophy. He had become the philosopher of *history*. History can be described and expressed but it cannot be created or transformed by philosophic thought. Hegel's "historism" is the necessary correlate of his rationalism. The two illustrate and interpret each other. That is one of the greatest merits, but at the same time it is one of the essential limitations of He-

34. *Idem,* p. 21.
35. *Idem,* p. 32.

gel's political theory. This theory seems to be the outcome and the culminating point of purely speculative thought. But amidst those speculations we always feel the pulse beat of actual political life. This gives to all the Hegelian concepts, notwithstanding their universality, their special color and aspect. Almost all the previous concepts undergo a profound change of meaning in his system. Every thinker of the eighteenth century could have subscribed to Hegel's definition of the history of the world as "progress in the consciousness of freedom." As a matter of fact it was not Hegel but Kant who had first given this definition.[36] But neither the term "freedom" nor the term "progress" nor even the term "consciousness" meant the same in the Kantian and in the Hegelian system.

What Hegel objected to in Kant and Fichte was that their idealism was only a "subjective" idealism. According to him such an idealism gives us a philosophy of reflection (*Reflexionsphilosophie*), not a philosophy of reality. Hegel's theory has been extolled and criticized as an outgrowth of "constructive" thought. But it was no longer constructive in the same sense as the systems of the eighteenth century. It was rather contemplative; it contented itself with an interpretation of the given historical reality. Kant had declared that the human understanding does not simply find the laws of nature, but that it is itself the source of the laws of nature; "the understanding does not draw its laws (a priori) from nature, but prescribes them to it." [37] The same principle holds for him in the field of ethical thought. Even here man does not simply submit to laws imposed upon him by the will of God or by any other authority. The will of every rational being is a "universally legislating will." A rational being obeys no law but that which he himself also gives.[38] With Fichte this autonomy of the will becomes also the highest metaphysical principle.

Hegel did not simply deny or abrogate the idealism of Kant and Fichte nor did he underrate the value of the political ideals of the French Revolution. In his youth he had been deeply impressed by them. When Hegel was still a student in the theological seminary in Tübingen and the first news of the French Rev-

36. See Kant's treatise *Ideen zu einer allgemeinen Geschichte in weltbürgerlicher Absicht* (1784), "Werke," ed. E. Cassirer, IV, 149 ff.

37. Kant, *Prolegomena*, § 36, cf. *Critique of Pure Reason* (1st ed.), p. 127.

38. See Kant, *Fundamental Principles of the Metaphysic of Morals*, English trans. T. K. Abbott (6th ed., London, Longmans, Green & Co., 1927), pp. 50 ff.

olution came to Germany, it was hailed with enthusiasm both by himself and by his friends Schelling and Hölderlin. Even later, when Hegel had become a sharp adversary of the Revolution, he never spoke of it as a professed enemy.

These general conceptions . . . —the Laws of Nature and the substance of what is right and good—have received the name of Reason. The recognition of the validity of these laws was designated by the term *Eclaircissement* (Aufklärung). From France it passed over into Germany, and created a new world of ideas. The absolute criterion— taking the place of all authority based on religious belief and positive laws of Right . . . —is the verdict passed by Spirit itself on the character of that which is to be believed or obeyed. . . . It may however be remarked that the same principle obtained speculative recognition in Germany, in the Kantian philosophy. . . . This is a vast discovery in regard to the profoundest depths of being and freedom. The consciousness of the Spiritual is now the essential basis of the political fabric, and Philosophy has thereby become dominant. It has been said that the French Revolution resulted from philosophy, and it is not without reason that Philosophy has been called "Weltweisheit" (World Wisdom); for it is not only truth in and for itself, as the pure essence of things, but also truth in its living form as exhibited in the affairs of the world. . . . The conception, the idea of Right asserted its authority *all at once,* and the old framework of injustice could offer no resistance to its onslaught. A constitution, therefore, was established in harmony with the conception of Right, and on this foundation all future legislation was to be based. Never since the sun had stood in the firmament and the planets revolved around him had it been perceived that man's existence centres in his head, i.e. in Thought, inspired by which he builds up the world of reality. . . . This was accordingly a glorious mental dawn. All thinking beings shared in the jubilation of this epoch. Emotions of a lofty character stirred men's minds at that time; a spiritual enthusiasm thrilled through the world, as if the reconciliation between the Divine and the Secular was now first accomplished.[39]

The man who could speak in this way was not simply a political reactionary. He had not only a deep insight into the true character of the French Revolution and of all the ideals of the Enlightenment but also a profound respect for them. Nevertheless he did not think these ideas to be an adequate means of organizing the social and political world.

39. *Philosophy of History,* pp. 460–466.

What he objected to in Kant, Fichte, and the French Revolution was that the idea of freedom, enthroned and proclaimed by them, remained "merely formal." What does this "formality" mean? It means that thought, in finding and asserting itself, had, at the same time, lost touch with the real world. The real world is a historical world, and all that the French Revolution could do was to negate and destroy the historical order of things. Such an estrangement can never be deemed to be a true reconciliation between the "real" and the "rational." To design an ideal picture of things, a mere "ought to be" over against the historical world cannot be the task of philosophy. Such an idealism would be vain and futile. Hegel professes an "objective" idealism, therefore, which does not look at ideas as if they were only haunting men's minds. He seeks them in reality, that is, in the course of historical events.[40]

In the field of actual and practical politics this principle led to conclusions which sometimes seem to be very objectionable. Hegel could reconcile himself to almost everything—supposing it had proved its right by its power. When Napoleon in 1806, after the battle of Jena in which he had defeated the Prussian Army visited Jena, Hegel spoke of this event with the greatest enthusiasm. "I saw the emperor, this soul of the world," he wrote in one of his letters, "riding through the streets." Later on he judged quite differently. Napoleon was defeated and exiled; Prussia had become the predominant power in Germany. "The soul of the world" had shifted to another part of the political body. From now on Hegel became "the philosopher of the Prussian State"; when appointed to his professorship in Berlin he declared that the Prussian State is "based on intelligence." [41]

It would, however, be unjust to charge Hegel with a sheer political opportunism. He was no mere time server who trimmed his sails to the wind of the stronger party. As we pointed out, he always made a sharp distinction between what is "real" and what has only an "idle existence." [42] But how can we apply this distinction to our political and historical life? How can we know

40. See *idem*, pp. 9 f.
41. See Hegel's Address to his audience at his inauguration in Berlin on October 22, 1818, in "Sämtliche Werke," VI, xxxv–xl, and in *Encyclopädie der philosophischen Wissenschaften*, ed. G. Lasson (2d ed. Leipzig, Felix Meiner, 1905), pp. lxxi–lxxvi.
42. See above, p. 262.

what is substantial or accidental, what is apparent and transitory or real and permanent in the human world? To this question the Hegelian system can only give one answer. The history of the world is the judgment of the world. There is no way left other than to apply to this highest tribunal, the judgment of which is infallible and irrevocable. Even the "national spirits" cannot escape this judgment.

The spirit of a nation is an existing individual, having in particularity its objective actuality and self-consciousness. Because of this particularity it is limited. The destinies and deeds of states in their connection with one another are the visible dialectic of the finite nature of these spirits. Out of this dialectic the universal spirit, the spirit of the world, the unlimited spirit produces itself. It has the highest right of all, and exercises its right upon the lower spirits in world-history. The history of the world is the world's court of judgment.[43]

If we study the influence of Hegel's philosophy upon the subsequent development of political thought we find here a complete reversal of one of his fundamental views. In this respect Hegelianism is one of the most paradoxical phenomena in modern cultural life. There is perhaps no better and more striking example of the dialectical character of history than the fate of Hegelianism itself. The principle defended by Hegel is suddenly converted into its opposite. Hegel's logic and philosophy seemed to be the triumph of the rational. The only thought which philosophy brings with it is the simple conception of Reason; that the history of the world presents us with a rational process. But it was the tragic fate of Hegel that he unconsciously unchained the most irrational powers that have ever appeared in man's social and political life. No other philosophical system has done so much for the preparation of fascism and imperialism as Hegel's doctrine of the state—this "divine Idea as it exists on earth." Even the idea that, in every epoch of history, there is *one* and only one nation that is the real representation of the world spirit and that this nation has the right to rule all the others was first expressed by Hegel.

The world-spirit, in its onward march, hands over to each people the task of working out its own peculiar vocation. Thus in universal history each nation in turn is for that epoch (and it can make such an

43. *Philosophy of Right*, § 340. Dyde trans., p. 341.

epoch only once) dominant. Against this absolute right to be the bearer of the present stage of the development of the world-spirit, the spirits of the other nations are absolutely without right, and they, as well as those whose epochs are passed, count no longer in universal history.[44]

Never before had a philosopher of the rank of Hegel spoken in this way. In the first decades of the nineteenth century we find the rise and ever-increasing influence of nationalistic ideals. It was, however, a new event in the history of political thought, an event pregnant with far-reaching and fearful consequences, when a system of *Ethics* and a philosophy of *Right* defended such a ruthless imperialistic nationalism, when Hegel declared the spirits of other nations to be "absolutely without right" against the nation which, at a given historical moment, is to be regarded as the only "agent of the world-spirit."

There is, however, one point in which the difference between Hegel's doctrine and modern theories of the totalitarian state becomes obvious. While it is true that Hegel exempted the state from all moral obligations and declared that the rules of morality lose their pretended universality when we proceed from the problems of private life and private conduct to the conduct of states, still there remain other bonds from which the state could not be released. In the Hegelian system the state belongs to the sphere of the "objective mind." But this sphere is only one element or moment in the self-actualization of the Idea. In the dialectic process it is transcended by that other sphere which, in Hegel's language, is called the realm of the "Absolute Idea." The Idea develops itself in three moments: Art, Religion, and Philosophy. It is clear that the state cannot treat these highest cultural goods as mere means for its own purposes. They are ends in themselves that have to be respected and furthered. It is true that they have no separate existence outside the state, for man cannot develop them without having organized his social life. Nevertheless these forms of cultural life have an independent meaning and value. They cannot be brought under a foreign jurisdiction. The state remains, as Hegel says, "on the territory of finitude."[45] Hegel could not subordinate art, religion, and philosophy to it.

There exists then a higher sphere that stands above the objec-

44. *Idem*, § 347. Sterrett trans., 209. Dyde trans., pp. 343 f.
45. *Encyclopedia*, § 483.

tive mind embodied in the state which is conceived as a spiritual and, therefore, as a generous power. It should never attempt to suppress the other spiritual energies but should recognize them and set them free. "The highest aim that the state can attain is that art and science are cultivated and come to a height corresponding to the spirit of the people. That is the principal end of the state—but an end that it must not bring about as an external work but that must arise from itself." [46]

Hegel spoke not only of the power of the state but also of its "truth," and he was a great admirer of "the truth that lies in power." Nevertheless he did not confuse this power with sheer physical force. He knew very well that a mere increase of material wealth and power is not to be regarded as a standard of the wealth and health of a state. In a passage of his *Greater Logic* he has emphasized this view. As he points out, the enlargement of the territory of a state may very often enfeeble or even dissolve its form and, therefore, become the beginning of its ruin.[47]

Even in his treatise on the *Constitution of Germany* Hegel had emphasized that the strength of a country lies neither in the multitude of its inhabitants and fighting men nor in its size. The guarantee of a constitution lies rather "in the indwelling spirit and the history of the nation by which constitutions have been made and are made." [48] To make this indwelling spirit subservient to the will of a political party or of an individual leader was impossible to Hegel. In this respect he would have rejected and abhorred the modern conceptions of the "totalitarian" state.

And there is still another reason why Hegel never could subscribe to these views. One of the principal aims and fundamental conditions of the totalitarian state is the principle of *Gleichschaltung*. In order to subsist it has to eliminate all other forms of social and cultural life and efface all distinctions. According to Hegel such an elimination can never lead to a true, organic unity. Its result would only be that "abstract" unity which he incessantly denounced. A real unity does not erase or obliterate the differences; it must protect and preserve them. Though Hegel was strongly opposed to the ideals of the French Revolution he was

46. *Vorlesungen über die Philosophie der Geschichte*, ed. Georg Lasson, "Sämtliche Werke," VIII–IX (Leipzig, F. Meiner, 1919–20), 628.

47. *Science of Logic*. English trans. by W. H. Johnston and L. G. Struthers (London, George Allen & Unwin, 1929), I, 354.

48. *Encyclopedia*, § 540.

convinced, nevertheless, that to abolish all distinctions in the social and political body, under the pretense of strengthening the power and unity of the state, would mean the very end of freedom. "The one essential canon to make liberty deep and real is to give every business belonging to the general interests of the state a separate organization wherever they are essentially distinct. Such real division must be: for liberty is only deep when it is differentiated in all its fullness and these differences manifested in existence." [49] Hegel could extol and glorify the state, he could even apotheosize it. There is, however, a clear and unmistakable difference between his idealization of the power of the state and that sort of idolization that is the characteristic of our modern totalitarian systems.

49. *Encyclopedia,* § 541.

XVIII

THE TECHNIQUE OF THE MODERN
POLITICAL MYTHS

IF WE try to resolve our contemporary political myths into their elements we find that they contain no entirely new feature. All the elements were already well known. Carlyle's theory of hero worship and Gobineau's thesis of the fundamental moral and intellectual diversity of races had been discussed over and over again. But all these discussions remained in a sense merely academic. To change the old ideas into strong and powerful political weapons something more was needed. They had to be accommodated to the understanding of a different audience. For this purpose a fresh instrument was required—not only an instrument of thought but also of action. A new technique had to be developed. This was the last and decisive factor. To put it into scientific terminology we may say that this technique had a catalytical effect. It accelerated all reactions and gave them their full effect. While the soil for the Myth of the Twentieth Century had been prepared long before, it could not have borne its fruit without the skilful use of the new technical tool.

The general conditions which favored this development and contributed to its final victory appeared in the period after the first World War. At this time all the nations which had been engaged in the war encountered the same fundamental difficulties. They began to realize that, even for the victorious nations, the war had, in no field, brought a real solution. On all sides new questions arose. The international, the social, and the human conflicts became more and more intense. They were felt everywhere. But in England, France, and North America there remained always some prospect of solving these conflicts by ordinary and normal means. In Germany, however, the case was different. From one day to the next the problem became more acute and more complicated. The leaders of the Weimar Republic had done their best to cope with these problems by diplomatic transactions or legislative measures. But all their efforts seemed to have been made in vain. In the times of inflation and unemployment

Germany's whole social and economic system was threatened with a complete collapse. The normal resources seemed to have been exhausted. This was the natural soil upon which the political myths could grow up and in which they found ample nourishment.

Even in primitive societies where myth pervades and governs the whole of man's social feeling and social life it is not always operative in the same way nor does it always appear with the same strength. It reaches its full force when man has to face an unusual and dangerous situation. Malinowski, who lived for many years among the natives of the Trobriand Islands and who has given us a searching analysis of their mythical conceptions and their magic rites, has repeatedly insisted upon this point. As he points out, even in primitive societies the use of magic is restricted to a special field of activities. In all those cases that can be dealt with by comparatively simple technical means man does not have recourse to magic. It appears only if man is confronted with a task that seems to be far beyond his natural powers. There remains, however, always a certain sphere which is not affected by magic or mythology, and which, therefore, may be described as the secular sphere. Here man relies on his own skill instead of the power of magic rites and formulae. "When the native has to produce an implement," says Malinowski in *The Foundations of Faith and Morals,*

he does not refer to magic. He is strictly empirical, that is, scientific, in the choice of his material, in the manner in which he strikes, cuts, and polishes the blade. He relies completely on his skill, on his reason and his endurance. There is no exaggeration in saying that in all matters where knowledge is sufficient the native relies on it exclusively. . . . The Central Australian possesses genuine science or knowledge, that is, tradition completely controlled by experience and reason, and completely unaffected by any mystical elements.

· · · · ·

There is a body of rules, handed from one generation to another, which refers to the manner in which people live in their little shelters, make their fire by friction, collect their food and cook it, make love to each other, and quarrel. . . . That this secular tradition is plastic, selective, and intelligent, and also well founded, can be seen from the fact that the native always adopts any new and suitable material.[1]

1. B. Malinowski, *The Foundations of Faith and Morals* (London, Oxford University Press, 1936), pp. 32 f.

In all those tasks that need no particular and exceptional efforts, no special courage or endurance, we find no magic and no mythology. But a highly developed magic and connected with it a mythology always occurs if a pursuit is dangerous and its issues uncertain.

This description of the role of magic and mythology in primitive society applies equally well to highly advanced stages of man's political life. In desperate situations man will always have recourse to desperate means—and our present-day political myths have been such desperate means. If reason has failed us, there remains always the *ultima ratio*, the power of the miraculous and mysterious. Primitive societies are not ruled by written laws, statutes, institutions or constitutions, bills of right or political charters. Nevertheless even the most primitive forms of social life show us a very clear and a very strict organization. The members of these societies are by no means living in a state of anarchy or confusion. Perhaps the most primitive societies we know of are those totemistic societies that we find among the American aboriginal tribes and among the native tribes of northern and central Australia, that have been carefully studied and described in the works of Spencer and Gillen. In these totemistic societies we find no complex and elaborate mythology, comparable to Greek, Indian, or Egyptian mythologies; we find no worship of personal gods and no personification of the great powers of nature. But they are held together by another, and even stronger, force; by a definite ritual based upon mythical conceptions—their beliefs in the animal ancestors. Every member of the group belongs to a special totemistic clan; and thereby he is bound in the chain of fixed tradition. He has to abstain from certain kinds of food; he has to observe very strict rules of exogamy or endogamy; and he has to perform, at certain times, in regular intervals and in a rigid and unchangeable order the same rituals which are a dramatic representation of the life of the totemistic ancestors. All this is imposed upon the members of the tribe not by force but by their fundamental and mythical conceptions, and the binding power of these conceptions is irresistible; it is never called into question.

Later on there appear other political and social forces. The mythical organization of society seems to be superseded by a rational organization. In quiet and peaceful times, in periods of relative stability and security, this rational organization is easily maintained. It seems to be safe against all attacks. But in politics the equipoise is never completely established. What we find here is a labile rather than a static equilibrium. In politics we are always living on volcanic soil. We must be prepared for abrupt convulsions and eruptions. In all critical moments of man's social life, the rational forces that resist the rise of the old mythical conceptions are no longer sure of themselves. In these moments the time for myth has come again. For myth has not been really vanquished and subjugated. It is always there, lurking in the dark and waiting for its hour and opportunity. This hour comes as soon as the other binding forces of man's social life, for one reason or another, lose their strength and are no longer able to combat the demonic mythical powers.

A French scholar, E. Doutté, has written a very interesting book *Magie et religion dans l'Afrique du Nord*. In this book he tries to give a concise and clear-cut definition of myth. According to Doutté the gods and demons that we find in primitive societies are nothing but the personifications of collective wishes. Myth, says Doutté, is "le désir collectif personifié"—the collective desire personified. This definition was given about thirty-five years ago. Of course the author did not know and did not think of our current political problems. He spoke as an anthropologist who was engaged in a study of the religious ceremonies and the magic rites of some savage tribes in North Africa. On the other hand this formula of Doutté could be used as the most laconic and trenchant expression of the modern idea of leadership or dictatorship. The call for leadership only appears when a collective desire has reached an overwhelming strength and when, on the other hand, all hopes of fulfilling this desire, in an ordinary and normal way, have failed. At these times the desire is not only keenly felt but also personified. It stands before the eyes of man in a concrete, plastic, and individual shape. The intensity of the collective wish is embodied in the leader. The former social bonds—law, justice, and constitutions—are declared to be without any value. What alone remains is the mystical power and authority of the leader and the leader's will is supreme law.

It is, however, clear that the personification of a collective wish cannot be satisfied in the same way by a great civilized nation as by a savage tribe. Civilized man is, of course, subject to the most violent passions, and when these passions reach their culminating point he is liable to yield to the most irrational impulses. Yet even in this case he cannot entirely forget or deny the demand of rationality. In order to believe he must find some "reasons" for his belief; he must form a "theory" to justify his creeds. And this theory, at least, is not primitive; it is, on the contrary, highly sophisticated.

We easily understand the assumption in savage life that all human powers and all natural powers can be condensed and concentrated in an individual man. The sorcerer, if he is the right man, if he knows the magic spells, and if he understands how to use them at the right time and in the right order, is the master of everything. He can avert all evils, he can defeat every enemy; he commands all natural forces. All this is so far removed from the modern mind that it seems to be quite unintelligible. Yet, if modern man no longer believes in a natural magic, he has by no means given up the belief in a sort of "social magic." If a collective wish is felt in its whole strength and intensity, people can easily be persuaded that it only needs the right man to satisfy it. At this point Carlyle's theory of hero worship made its influence felt. This theory promised a rational justification for certain conceptions that, in their origin and tendency, were anything but rational. Carlyle had emphasized that hero worship is a necessary element in human history. It cannot cease till man himself ceases. "In all epochs of the world's history, we shall find the Great Man to have been the indispensable saviour of his epoch; the lightning, without which the fuel never would have burnt." [2] The word of the great man is the wise healing word which all can believe in.

But Carlyle did not understand his theory as a definite political program. His was a romantic conception of heroism—far different from that of our modern political "realists." The modern politicians have had to use much more drastic means. They had to solve a problem that in many respects resembles squaring the circle. The historians of human civilization have told us that mankind in its development had to pass through two different phases. Man began as *homo magus;* but from the age of magic he passed to the age of technics. The homo magus of former times and of primitive civilization became a *homo faber,* a craftsman and artisan. If we admit such an historical distinction our modern po-

2. Carlyle, *On Heroes,* Lect. 1, pp. 13 ff. Centenary ed., V, 13.

litical myths appear indeed as a very strange and paradoxical thing. For what we find in them is the blending of two activities that seem to exclude each other. The modern politician has had to combine in himself two entirely different and even incompatible functions. He has to act, at the same time, as both a homo magus and a homo faber. He is the priest of a new, entirely irrational and mysterious religion. But when he has to defend and propagate this religion he proceeds very methodically. Nothing is left to chance; every step is well prepared and premeditated. It is this strange combination that is one of the most striking features of our political myths.

Myth has always been described as the result of an unconscious activity and as a free product of imagination. But here we find myth made according to plan. The new political myths do not grow up freely; they are not wild fruits of an exuberant imagination. They are artificial things fabricated by very skilful and cunning artisans. It has been reserved for the twentieth century, our own great technical age, to develop a new technique of myth. Henceforth myths can be manufactured in the same sense and according to the same methods as any other modern weapon—as machine guns or airplanes. That is a new thing—and a thing of crucial importance. It has changed the whole form of our social life. It was in 1933 that the political world began to worry somewhat about Germany's rearmament and its possible international repercussions. As a matter of fact this rearmament had begun many years before but had passed almost unnoticed. The real rearmament began with the origin and rise of the political myths. The later military rearmament was only an accessory after the fact. The fact was an accomplished fact long before; the military rearmament was only the necessary consequence of the mental rearmament brought about by the political myths.

The first step that had to be taken was a change in the function of language. If we study the development of human speech we find that in the history of civilization the word fulfils two entirely different functions. To put it briefly we may term these functions the semantic and the magical use of the word. Even among the so-called primitive languages the semantic function of the word is never missing; without it there could be no human speech. But in primitive societies the magic word has a predominant and overwhelming influence. It does not describe things or relations of things; it tries to produce effects and to change the course of nature. This cannot be done without an elaborate magical art. The magician, or sorcerer is alone able to govern the magic word. But in his hands it becomes a most powerful weapon. Nothing can resist its force. "Carmina vel coelo possunt deducere lunam," says the sorceress Medea in Ovid's *Metamorphoses*—by magic songs and incantations even the moon can be dragged down from the heavens.

Curiously enough all this recurs in our modern world. If we study our modern political myths and the use that has been made of them we find in them, to our great surprise, not only a transvaluation of all our ethical values but also a transformation of human speech. The magic word takes precedence of the semantic word. If nowadays I happen to read a German book, published in these last ten years, not a political but a theoretical book, a work dealing with philosophical, historical, or economic problems —I find to my amazement that I no longer understand the German language. New words have been coined; and even the old ones are used in a new sense; they have undergone a deep change of meaning. This change of meaning depends upon the fact that those words which formerly were used in a descriptive, logical, or semantic sense, are now used as magic words that are destined to produce certain effects and to stir up certain emotions. Our ordinary words are charged with meanings; but these new-fangled words are charged with feelings and violent passions.

Not long ago there was published a very interesting little book, *Nazi-Deutsch. A Glossary of Contemporary German Usage*. Its authors are Heinz Paechter, Bertha Hellman, Hedwig Paechter, and Karl O. Paetel. In this book all those new terms which were produced by the Nazi regime were carefully listed, and it is a tremendous list. There seem to be only a few words which have survived the general destruction. The authors made an attempt to translate the new terms into English, but in this regard they were, to my mind, unsuccessful. They were able to give only circumlocutions of the German words and phrases instead of real translations. For unfortunately, or perhaps fortunately, it was impossible to render these words adequately in English. What characterizes them is not so much their content and their objective meaning as the emotional atmosphere which surrounds and envelops them. This atmosphere must be felt; it cannot be translated nor can it be transferred from one climate of opinion to an entirely different one. To illustrate this point I content myself with one striking example chosen at random. I understand from the *Glossary* that in recent German usage there was a sharp difference between the two terms *Siegfriede* and *Siegerfriede*. Even for a German ear it will not be easy to grasp this difference. The two words sound exactly alike, and seem to denote the same thing. *Sieg* means victory, *Friede* means peace; how can the combination of the two words produce entirely different meanings? Nevertheless we are told that, in modern German usage, there is all the difference in the world between the two terms. For a Siegfriede is a peace through German victory; whereas a Siegerfriede means the very opposite; it is used to denote a peace which would be dictated by the allied conquerors. It is the same with other terms. The men who coined these terms were masters of their art of political propaganda. They attained their end, the stirring up of violent political passions, by the simplest means. A word, or even the change of a syllable in a word, was often good enough to serve this purpose. If we hear these new words we feel in them the whole gamut of human emotions—of hatred, anger, fury, haughtiness, contempt, arrogance, and disdain.

But the skilful use of the magic word is not all. If the word is to have its full effect it has to be supplemented by the introduction of new rites. In this respect, too, the political leaders proceeded very thoroughly, methodically, and successfully. Every political action has its special ritual. And since, in the totalitarian state, there is no private sphere, independent of political life, the whole life of man is suddenly inundated by a high tide of new rituals. They are as regular, as rigorous and inexorable as those rituals that we find in primitive societies. Every class, every sex, and every age has a rite of its own. No one could walk in the street, nobody could greet his neighbor or friend without performing a political ritual. And just as in primitive societies the neglect of one of the prescribed rites has meant misery and death. Even in young children this is not regarded as a mere sin of omission. It becomes a crime against the majesty of the leader and the totalitarian state.

The effect of these new rites is obvious. Nothing is more likely to lull asleep all our active forces, our power of judgment and critical discernment, and to take away our feeling of personality and individual responsibility than the steady, uniform, and monotonous performance of the same rites. As a matter of fact in all primitive societies ruled and governed by rites individual responsibility is an unknown thing. What we find here is only a collective responsibility. Not the individuals but the group is the real "moral subject." The clan, the family, and the whole tribe are responsible for the actions of all the members. If a crime is committed it is not imputed to an individual. By a sort of miasma or social contagion, the crime spreads over the whole group. Nobody can escape the infection. Revenge and punishment too are always directed to the group as a whole. In those societies in which the blood feud is one of the highest obligations it is by no means necessary to take revenge upon the murderer himself. It is enough to kill a member of his family or his tribe. In some cases, as for instance in New Guinea or among the African Somalis, it is the eldest brother rather than the offender himself who is killed.

In the last two hundred years our conceptions of the character of savage life, when compared to the life of civilized men, have completely changed. In the eighteenth century Rousseau gave his famous description of savage life and the state of nature. He saw in it a real paradise of simplicity, innocence, and happiness. The savage lived alone in the freshness of his native forest, following his instincts and satisfying his simple desires. He enjoyed the highest good, the good of absolute independence. Unfortunately the progress of anthropological research made during the nineteenth century has completely destroyed this philosophical idyll. Rousseau's description was turned into its very opposite. "The savage," says E. Sidney Hartland in his book, *Primitive Law,*

is far from being the free and unfettered creature of Rousseau's imagination. On the contrary, he is hemmed in on every side by the customs of his people; he is bound in the chains of immemorial tradition. . . . These fetters are accepted by him as a matter of course; he never seeks to break forth. . . . To the civilized man the same observations may very often apply; but the civilized man is too restless, too desirous of change, too eager to question his environment, to remain long in the attitude of acquiescence.[3]

These words were written twenty years ago; but in the meantime we have learned a new lesson, a lesson that is very humiliating

3. E. Sidney Hartland, *Primitive Law* (London, Methuen & Co., 1924), p. 138.

to our human pride. We have learned that modern man, in spite of his restlessness, and perhaps precisely because of his restlessness, has not really surmounted the condition of savage life. When exposed to the same forces, he can easily be thrown back to a state of complete acquiescence. He no longer questions his environment; he accepts it as a matter of course.

Of all the sad experiences of these last twelve years this is perhaps the most dreadful one. It may be compared to the experience of Odysseus on the island of Circe. But it is even worse. Circe had transformed the friends and companions of Odysseus into various animal shapes. But here are men, men of education and intelligence, honest and upright men who suddenly give up the highest human privilege. They have ceased to be free and personal agents. Performing the same prescribed rites they begin to feel, to think, and to speak in the same way. Their gestures are lively and violent; yet this is but an artificial, a sham life. In fact they are moved by an external force. They act like marionettes in a puppet show—and they do not even know that the strings of this show and of man's whole individual and social life, are henceforward pulled by the political leaders.

For the understanding of our problem this is a point of crucial importance. Methods of compulsion and suppression have ever been used in political life. But in most cases these methods aimed at material results. Even the most fearful systems of despotism contented themselves with forcing upon men certain laws of action. They were not concerned with the feelings, judgments, and thoughts of men. It is true that in the great religious struggles the most violent efforts were made not only to rule the actions of men but also their consciousness. But these attempts were bound to fail; they only strengthened the feeling for religious liberty. Now the modern political myths proceeded in quite a different manner. They did not begin with demanding or prohibiting certain actions. They undertook to change the men, in order to be able to regulate and control their deeds. The political myths acted in the same way as a serpent that tries to paralyze its victims before attacking them. Men fell victims to them without any serious resistance. They were vanquished and subdued before they had realized what actually happened.

The usual means of political oppression would not have sufficed to produce this effect. Even under the hardest political pressure nen have not ceased living their own lives. There has always remained a sphere of personal freedom resistant to this pressure. The classical ethical ideas of antiquity maintained and strengthened their force amidst the chaos and the political decay of the ancient world. Seneca lived in the times and at the court of Nero. But this did not prevent him from giving, in his treatises and moral letters, an epitome of the loftiest ideas of Stoic philosophy, ideas of the autonomy of the will and the independence of the wise man. Our modern political myths destroyed all these ideas and ideals before they begin their work. They do not have to fear any opposition from this quarter. In our analysis of Gobineau's book we have studied the methods by which this opposition was broken down. The myth of the race worked like a strong corrosive and succeeded in dissolving and disintegrating all other values.

To understand this process it is necessary to begin with an analysis of the term "freedom." Freedom is one of the most obscure and ambiguous terms not only of philosophical but also of political language. As soon as we begin to speculate about the freedom of the will we find ourselves involved into an inextricable labyrinth of metaphysical questions and antinomies. As to political freedom all of us know that it is one of the most used and abused slogans. All political parties have assured us that they are ever the true representatives and guardians of freedom. But they have always defined the term in their own sense and used it for their particular interests. Ethical freedom is, at bottom, a much simpler thing. It is free from those ambiguities that seem to be unavoidable both in metaphysics and in politics. Men act as free agents not because they possess a *liberum arbitrium indifferentiae*. It is not the absence of a motive but the character of the motives that marks a free action. In the ethical sense a man is a free agent if these motives depend upon his own judgment and own conviction of what moral duty is. According to Kant freedom is equivalent to autonomy. It does not mean "indeterminism," it rather means a special kind of determination. It means that the law which we obey in our actions is not imposed from without but that the moral subject gives this law to itself.

In the exposition of his own theory Kant always warns us against a fundamental misunderstanding. Ethical freedom, he declares, is not a fact but a postulate. It is not *gegeben* but *aufgege-*

ben; it is not a gift with which human nature is endowed; it is rather a task, and the most arduous task that man can set himself. It is no datum, but a demand; an ethical imperative. To fulfil this demand becomes especially hard in times of a severe and dangerous social crisis when the breakdown of the whole public life seems to be imminent. At these times the individual begins to feel a deep mistrust in his own powers. Freedom is not a natural inheritance of man. In order to possess it we have to create it. If man were simply to follow his natural instincts he would not strive for freedom; he would rather choose dependence. Obviously it is much easier to depend upon others than to think, to judge, and to decide for himself. That accounts for the fact that both in individual and in political life freedom is so often regarded much more as a burden than a privilege. Under extremely difficult conditions man tries to cast off this burden. Here the totalitarian state and the political myths step in. The new political parties promise, at least, an escape from the dilemma. They suppress and destroy the very sense of freedom; but, at the same time, they relieve men from all personal responsibility.[4]

That leads us to another aspect of our problem. In our description of the modern political myths one feature is still missing. As we pointed out, in the totalitarian states the political leaders have had to take charge of all those functions that, in primitive societies, were performed by the magician. They were the absolute rulers; they were the medicine men who promised to cure all social evils. But that was not enough. In a savage tribe the sorcerer has still another important task. The *homo magus* is, at the same time, the *homo divinans*. He reveals the will of the gods and foretells the future. The soothsayer has his firm place and his indispensable role in primitive social life. Even in highly developed stages of political culture he is still in full possession of his old rights and privileges. In Rome, for instance, no important political decision was ever made, no difficult enterprise was undertaken no battle was fought without the advice of the augurs and harus

4. "To a German grocer, not unwilling to explain things to an American visitor," relates Stephen Raushenbush, "I spoke of our feeling that something invaluable had been given up when freedom was surrendered. He replied: 'But you don't understand at all. Before this we had to worry about elections, and parties, and voting. We had responsibilities. But now we don't have any of that. Now we're free.'" See Stephen Raushenbush, *The March of Fascism* (New Haven, Yale University Press, 1939), p. 40.

ices. When a Roman army was sent out it was always accom-
anied by its haruspices; they were an integral part of the military
aff.

Even in this respect our modern political life has abruptly re-
irned to forms which seemed to have been entirely forgotten.
o be sure, we no longer have the primitive kind of sortilege, the
ivination by lot; we no longer observe the flight of birds nor do
e inspect the entrails of slain animals. We have developed a
iuch more refined and elaborate method of divination—a method
iat claims to be scientific and philosophical. But if our methods
ave changed the thing itself has by no means vanished. Our
iodern politicians know very well that great masses are much
iore easily moved by the force of imagination than by sheer
hysical force. And they have made ample use of this knowledge.
he politician becomes a sort of public fortuneteller. Prophecy
an essential element in the new technique of rulership. The
ost improbable or even impossible promises are made; the mil-
nnium is predicted over and over again.

Curiously enough this new art of divination first made its ap-
earance not in German politics but in German philosophy. In
)18 there appeared Oswald Spengler's *Decline of the West.* Per-
ips never before had a philosophical book such a sensational
iccess. It was translated into almost every language and read
y all sorts of readers—philosophers and scientists, historians and
oliticians, students and scholars, tradesmen and the man in the
reet. What was the reason for this unprecedented success, what
as the magic spell that this book exerted over its readers? It
ems to be a paradox; but to my mind the cause of Spengler's
iccess is to be sought rather in the title of his book than in its
ontents. The title *Der Untergang des Abendlandes* was an electric
iark that set the imagination of Spengler's readers aflame. The
ook was published in July, 1918, at the end of the first World
'ar. At this time many, if not most of us, had realized that some-
ing was rotten in the state of our highly praised Western civili-
ition. Spengler's book expressed, in a sharp and trenchant way,
iis general uneasiness. It was not at all a scientific book. Spengler
espised and openly challenged all methods of science. "Nature,"
e declared, "is to be handled scientifically, history poetically."
et even this is not the real meaning of Spengler's work. A poet
ves in the world of his imagination; and a great religious poet,

like Dante or Milton, also lives in a world of prophetic vision But he does not take these visions for realities; nor does he mak of them a philosophy of history. This, however, was precisely th case of Spengler. He boasted of having found a new method b which historical and cultural events could be predicted in th same way and with the same exactness as an astronomer predic an eclipse of the sun or the moon. "In this book is attempted f the first time the venture of predetermining history, of followin the still unraveled stages in the destiny of a culture, and specifi ally of the only culture of our times and our planet which is act ally in the phase of fulfilment—the West European-American."

These words give us a clue to Spengler's book and its enormo influence. If it be possible not only to relate the story of huma civilization but to predetermine its future course, a great step advance has, indeed, been made. Obviously the man who spol in this way was no mere scientist nor was he a historian or ph losopher. According to Spengler the rise, decline, and fall of civil zations do not depend upon the so-called laws of nature. The are determined by a higher power, the power of destiny. Destin not causality is the moving force in human history. The birth a cultural world, says Spengler, is always a mystical act, a decr of destiny. Such acts are entirely impenetrable to our poor, a stract, scientific, or philosophical concepts.

A culture is born in the moment when a great soul awakens out of th proto-spirituality of ever-childish humanity, and detaches itself, a for from the formless, a bounded and mortal thing from the boundless a enduring. . . . It dies when this soul has actualized the full sum of i possibilities, in the shape of peoples, languages, dogmas, arts, state sciences, and reverts into the proto-soul.[5]

Here, too, we find the rebirth of one of the oldest mythic motives. In almost all mythologies of the world we meet with th idea of an inevitable, inexorable, irrevocable destiny. Fatalis seems to be inseparable from mythical thought. In the Homer poems even the gods have to submit to Fate: Fate (Moira) ac independently of Zeus. In the tenth book of his *Republic* Pla gave his famous description of the "distaff of Necessity" on whic

5. Oswald Spengler, *Der Untergang des Abendlandes* (München, Beck. 1918 English trans. by Charles F. Atkinson, *The Decline of the West* (London, G. All & Unwin, 1926), p. 106. See the whole of chap. IV, "The Destiny-Idea and t Causality-Principle."

the revolutions of all the heavenly bodies turn. The spindle turns on the knees of Necessity while the Fates, daughters of Necessity, Lachesis, Clotho, and Atropos, sit on thrones, Lachesis singing of the past, Clotho of the present, Atropos of the future.[6] This is a Platonic myth, and Plato always makes a sharp distinction between mythical and philosophical thought. But in some of our modern philosophers this distinction seems to be completely effaced. They give us a metaphysics of history that shows all the characteristic features of myth. When I first read Spengler's *Untergang des Abendlandes* I happened to be engrossed in studies of the philosophy of the Italian Renaissance. What struck me most at this time was the close analogy between Spengler's book and some astrological treatises that I had quite recently read. Of course Spengler made no attempt to read the future of civilizations in the stars. But his prognostics are of exactly the same type as the astrological prognostics. The astrologers of the Renaissance did not content themselves with exploring the destiny of individual men. They applied their method also to the great historical and cultural phenomena. One of these astrologers was condemned by the Church and burnt at the stake because he had cast the horoscope of Christ and from Christ's nativity had predicted the near fall of Christian religion. Spengler's book was, as a matter of fact, an astrology of history—the work of a diviner who unfolded his somber apocalyptic visions.

But can we really connect the work of Spengler with the political prophecies of later times? Can we put the two phenomena on the same level? At first sight such a parallel seems to be highly questionable. Spengler was a prophet of evil; the new political leaders wished to rouse in their adherents the most extravagant hopes. Spengler spoke of the decline of the West; the others spoke of the conquest of the world by the German race. Obviously these are not the same things. Nor was Spengler personally an adherent of the Nazi movement. He was a conservative, an admirer and eulogist of the old Prussian ideals; but the program of the new men made no appeal to him. Nevertheless the work of Spengler became one of the pioneer works of National Socialism. For what was the conclusion that Spengler drew from his general thesis? He vehemently protested when his philosophy was termed a philosophy of pessimism. He declared himself to be no pessimist. It

6. Plato, *Republic*, 616 f.

is true that our Western civilization is doomed once for all. But it is no use lamenting this obvious and inevitable fact. If our culture is lost there still remain many other things to the present generation, and perhaps much better things.

Of great painting or great music there can no longer be, for Western people, any question. . . . Only *extensive* possibilities are left to them. Yet, for a sound and vigorous generation that is filled with unlimited hopes, I fail to see that it is any disadvantage to discover betimes that some of these hopes must come to nothing. . . . It is true that the issue may be a tragic one for some individuals who in their decisive years are overpowered by the conviction that in the spheres of architecture, drama, painting, there is nothing left for *them* to conquer. What matter if they do go under! . . . Now at last the work of centuries enables the West-European to view the disposition of his own life in relation to the general culture-scheme and to test his own powers and purposes. And I can only hope that men of the new generation may be moved by this book to devote themselves to technics instead of lyrics, the sea instead of the paint-brush, and politics instead of epistemology. Better they could not do.[7]

Technic instead of lyrics, politics instead of epistemology, this advice of a philosopher of human culture could easily be understood. The new men were convinced that they fulfilled Spengler's prophecy. They interpreted him in their own sense. If our culture—science, philosophy, poetry, and art—is dead, let us make a fresh start. Let us try our vast possibilities, let us create a new world and become the rulers of this world.

The same trend of thought appears in the work of a modern German philosopher who, at first sight, seems to have very little in common with Spengler and who developed his theories quite independently of him. In 1927 Martin Heidegger published the first volume of his book *Sein und Zeit*. Heidegger was a pupil of Husserl and was reckoned among the outstanding representatives of the German phenomenological school. His book appeared in Husserl's *Jahrbüchern für Philosophie und phänomenologische Forschung*.[8] But the attitude of the book was diametrically opposed to the spirit of Husserl's philosophy. Husserl had started from an analysis of the principles of logical thought. His whole philosophy depends on the results of this analysis. His highest aim

7. Spengler, *op. cit.*, pp. 40 f.
8. Vol. VIII (2d ed. Halle, Niemeyer, 1929).

was to make philosophy an "exact science," to found it upon unshakable facts and indubitable principles. Such a tendency is entirely alien to Heidegger. He does not admit that there is something like "eternal" truth, a Platonic "realm of ideas," or a strict logical method of philosophic thought. All this is declared to be elusive. In vain we try to build up a logical philosophy; we can only give an *Existenzialphilosophie*. Such an existential philosophy does not claim to give us an objective and universally valid truth. No thinker can give more than the truth of his own existence; and this existence has a historical character. It is bound up with the special conditions under which the individual lives. To change these conditions is impossible. In order to express his thought Heidegger had to coin a new term. He spoke of the *Geworfenheit* of man (the being-thrown). To be thrown into the stream of time is a fundamental and inalterable feature of our human situation. We cannot emerge from this stream and we cannot change its course. We have to accept the historical conditions of our existence. We can try to understand and to interpret them; but we cannot change them.

I do not mean to say that these philosophical doctrines had a direct bearing on the development of political ideas in Germany. Most of these ideas arose from quite different sources. They had a very "realistic" not a "speculative" purport. But the new philosophy did enfeeble and slowly undermine the forces that could have resisted the modern political myths. A philosophy of history that consists in somber predictions of the decline and the inevitable destruction of our civilization and a theory that sees in the Geworfenheit of man one of his principal characters have given up all hopes of an active share in the construction and reconstruction of man's cultural life. Such philosophy renounces its own fundamental theoretical and ethical ideals. It can be used, then, as a pliable instrument in the hands of the political leaders.

The return of fatalism in our modern world leads us to another general question. We are proud of our natural science; but we should not forget that natural science is a very late achievement of the human mind. Even in the seventeenth century, in the great century of Galileo and Kepler, of Descartes and Newton, it was by no means firmly established. It had still to struggle for its place in the sun. During the Renaissance the so-called occult sciences, magic, alchemy, and astrology, were still predominant, they even had a new flourishing period. Kepler was the first great empirical astronomer who was able to describe the movements of the planets in exact mathematical terms. Yet it was extremely difficult to take this decisive step. For Kepler not only had to struggle against his times but also against himself. Astronomy and astrology were still inseparable. Kepler himself was appointed as an astrologer at the Imperial Court of Prague, and at the end of his life he became the astrologer of Wallenstein. The way in which he finally freed himself is one of the most important and fascinating chapters in the history of modern science. He never broke away entirely from astrological conceptions. He declared astronomy to be the daughter of astrology and he said that it would not be becoming for the daughter to neglect or despise her mother. Prior to the seventeenth and eighteenth centuries of our modern era, it is impossible to draw a line between empirical and mystical thought. A scientific chemistry in the modern sense of this term did not exist until the time of Robert Boyle and Lavoisier.

How could this state of affairs be changed? How did natural science, after innumerable vain efforts, finally break the magic spell? The principle of this great intellectual revolution can best be described in the words of Bacon, one of the pioneers of modern empirical thought, "Natura non vincitur nisi parendo"—the victory over nature can only be won by obedience. Bacon's aim was to make man the master of nature. But his mastery must be understood in the right way. Man cannot subjugate or enslave nature. In order to rule her he must respect her; he must obey her fundamental rules. Man must begin by freeing himself; he must get rid of his fallacies and illusions, his human idiosyncrasies and fancies. In the first book of his *Novum organon* Bacon tried to give a systematic survey of these illusions. He described the different kinds of idols, the *idola tribus,* the *idola specus,* the *idola fori,* and the *idola theatri,* and he tried to show how to overcome them in order to clear the way that will lead to a true empirical science.

In politics we have not yet found this way. Of all human idols the political idols, the idola fori, are the most dangerous and enduring. Since the times of Plato all great thinkers have made the greatest efforts to find a rational theory of politics. The nineteenth century was convinced that it had at last found the right path. In 1830 Auguste Comte published the first volume of his *Cours de philosophie positive.* He began with analyzing the structure of natural science; he went from astronomy to physics, from physics to chemistry, from chemistry to biology. But according to Comte natural science is only a first step. His real aim and highest ambition was to become the founder of a new social science and to introduce into this science the same exact way of reasoning, the same inductive and deductive method as we find in physics or chemistry.

The sudden rise of the political myths in the twentieth century has shown us that these hopes of Comte and of his pupils and adherents were premature. Politics is still far from being a positive science, let alone an exact science. I have no doubt that later generations will look back at many of our political systems with the same feeling as a modern astronomer studies an astrological book or a modern chemist an alchemistic treatise. In politics we have not yet found firm and reliable ground. Here there seems to be no clearly established cosmic order; we are always threatened with a sudden relapse into the old chaos. We are building high and proud edifices; but we forget to make their foundations secure. The belief that man by the skilful use of magic formulae and rites can change the course of nature has prevailed for hundreds and thousands of years in human history. In spite of all the inevitable frustrations and disappointments mankind still clung stubbornly, forcibly, and desperately to this belief. It is, therefore, not to be wondered at that in our political actions and our political thoughts magic still holds its ground. Yet when small groups do try to enforce their wishes and their fantastic ideas upon great nations and the whole body politic, they may succeed for a short time, and they may even achieve great triumphs, but these must remain ephemeral. For there is, after all, a logic of the social world just as there is a logic of the physical world. There are certain laws that cannot be violated with impunity. Even in this sphere we have to follow Bacon's advice. We must learn how to obey the laws of the social world before we can undertake to rule it.

What can philosophy do to help us in this struggle against the political myths? Our modern philosophers seem long ago to have given up all hope of influencing the course of political and social events. Hegel had the highest opinion of the worth and dignity of philosophy. Nevertheless it was Hegel himself who declared that philosophy comes always too late for the reform of the world. It is therefore just as foolish to fancy that any philosophy can transcend its present time as that an individual can leap out of his own time. "When philosophy paints its grey in grey one form of life has become old and by means of grey it cannot be rejuvenated, but only known. The owl of Minerva takes its flight only when the shades of night are gathering." [9] If this dictum of Hegel were true, philosophy would be condemned to an absolute quietism; an entirely passive attitude toward man's historical life. It has simply to accept and to explain the given historical situation and to bow down before it. In this case philosophy would be nothing but a sort of speculative idleness. I think, however, that this is in contradiction both to the general character and to the history of philosophy. The classical example of Plato alone would be enough to refute this view. The great thinkers of the past were not only "their own times apprehended in thought." Very often they had to think beyond and against their times. Without this intellectual and moral courage, philosophy could not fulfil its task in man's cultural and social life.

It is beyond the power of philosophy to destroy the political myths. A myth is in a sense invulnerable. It is impervious to rational arguments; it cannot be refuted by syllogisms. But philosophy can do us another important service. It can make us understand the adversary. In order to fight an enemy you must know him. That is one of the first principles of a sound strategy. To know him means not only to know his defects and weaknesses; it means to know his strength. All of us have been liable to underrate this strength. When we first heard of the political myths we found them so absurd and incongruous, so fantastic and ludicrous that we could hardly be prevailed upon to take them seriously. By now it has become clear to all of us that this was a great mistake. We should not commit the same error a second time. We should carefully study the origin, the structure, the methods, and the technique of the political myths. We should see the adversary face to face in order to know how to combat him.

9. Hegel, *Philosophy of Right*. Dyde trans., Preface, p. xxx.

CONCLUSION

WHAT we have learned in the hard school of our modern political life is the fact that human culture is by no means the firmly established thing that we once supposed it to be. The great thinkers, the scientists, the poets, and artists who laid the foundations of our Western civilization were often convinced that they had built for eternity. When Thucydides discussed his new historical method that he opposed to the former mythical treatment of history he spoke of his work as a κτῆμα ἐς ἀεί—"an everlasting possession." Horace called his poems a "monumentum aere perennius"—a monument more enduring than bronze, which shall not be destroyed by the countless years and flight of ages. It seems, however, that we have to look upon the great master works of human culture in a much humbler way. They are not eternal nor unassailable. Our science, our poetry, our art, and our religion are only the upper layer of a much older stratum that reaches down to a great depth. We must always be prepared for violent concussions that may shake our cultural world and our social order to its very foundations.

To illustrate the relation between myth and the other great cultural powers we may perhaps use a simile that is borrowed from mythology itself. In Babylonian mythology we find a legend that describes the creation of the world. We are told that Marduk, the highest god, before he could begin his work had to fight a dreadful combat. He had to vanquish and subjugate the serpent Tiamat and the other dragons of darkness. He slew Tiamat and bound the dragons. Out of the limbs of the monster Tiamat he formed the world and gave to it its shape and its order. He made heaven and earth, the constellations and planets, and fixed their movements. His final work was the creation of man. In this way the cosmic order arose from the primeval chaos, and it will be preserved for all times. "The word of Marduk," says the Babylonian epic of creation, "is eternal; his command is unchangeable, no god can alter what proceeds from his mouth." [1]

The world of human culture may be described in the words of

1. See P. Jensen, *Die Kosmologie der Babylonier* (Strassburg, Trübner, 1890), pp. 279 ff.

this Babylonian legend. It could not arise until the darkness of myth was fought and overcome. But the mythical monsters were not entirely destroyed. They were used for the creation of a new universe, and they still survive in this universe. The powers of myth were checked and subdued by superior forces. As long as these forces, intellectual, ethical, and artistic, are in full strength, myth is tamed and subdued. But once they begin to lose their strength chaos is come again. Mythical thought then starts to rise anew and to pervade the whole of man's cultural and social life.

INDEX

Dita 3658